Carefully written and lucidly presented, Harper takes readers on a deep dive into the geopolitics of aid provision, making an irrefutable case for why everyone has a stake in human development outcomes.

Helen Clark, *Administrator of the United Nations Development Programme (2009–2017)*

A pathbreaking examination of how political economy in aid provision is obstructing progress towards a safer, more equal and socially cohesive world. Strongly recommended for practitioners, donors and policy makers alike.

Ertharin Cousin, *Executive Director of the United Nations World Food Programme (2012–2017)*

A major contribution to the scholarship on development effectiveness. Harper takes the frustration held by many and packages it in a solution-oriented account of how development cooperation can be transformed and strengthened in a pragmatic way but always keeping a people centered approach where their rights are respected, protected and promoted.

Najat Maalla M'jid, *Special Representative of the Secretary-General on Violence against Children*

In this highly readable exploration of development processes, Harper sets out a constructive argument for how better outcomes can be achieved by understanding the political economy of aid flows, making better use evidence and fostering innovation.

Gillian Triggs, *UN Assistant Secretary-General and Assistant High Commissioner for Protection with UNHCR*

THE LAST 10 PER CENT

Criticism that the development sector has not delivered in terms of eliminating extreme poverty, fast-tracking growth and preventing conflict, is neither new nor surprising. In fact, it may be the one thing that scholars, donors and practitioners agree on. While many of these concerns are valid, this book makes a case that the sector is closer to unlocking the gates to more effective and efficient development outcomes than is popularly believed. Specifically, it argues that by overturning a few myths, making better use of evidence and employing some different rules, practitioners, policy specialists and donors can foster the changes in the development architecture that are needed to reach the 10 percent of the world's population still living in extreme poverty.

Engaging, provocative and clear sighted, the book provides insight into interventions around democratic governance, refugee response, counterterrorism, gender mainstreaming, environmental protection and private sector engagement. It is instructive reading for professionals across the development sector, think tanks and NGOs.

Erica Harper is the Head of Research and Policy Studies at the Geneva Academy of International Humanitarian Law and Human Rights. She also serves as an affiliate researcher at the Van Vollenhoven Institute, Leiden University, Netherlands.

THE LAST 10 PER CENT

Why the World Needs a Leaner, More Innovative and Pragmatic Development Sector, Today

Erica Harper

Routledge
Taylor & Francis Group

LONDON AND NEW YORK

Designed cover image: Gettyimages

First published 2023
by Routledge
4 Park Square, Milton Park, Abingdon, Oxon OX14 4RN

and by Routledge
605 Third Avenue, New York, NY 10158

Routledge is an imprint of the Taylor & Francis Group, an informa business

© 2023 Erica Harper

British Library Cataloguing-in-Publication Data
A catalogue record for this book is available from the British Library

Library of Congress Cataloging-in-Publication Data
Names: Harper, Erica, author.
Title: The last 10 per cent : why the world needs a leaner, more innovative and pragmatic
    development sector, today / Erica Harper.
Other titles: Last ten per cent
Description: Abingdon, Oxon ; New York, NY : Routledge, 2023. | Includes bibliographical
    references and index. | Summary: "This book studies the role of the development sector in
    eliminating extreme poverty, fast-tracking growth, and preventing conflict in a post-pandemic
    world. It sets out 5 changes that are needed in the development architecture to reach that
    last 10 per cent of the world's population living in extreme poverty. Challenging traditional
    ideas of development programming, the book argues for a more evidence-based approach
    to designing engagement strategies and creating an enabling environment that will allow
    the sector to move towards innovation-centric development approaches. It also makes a
    case for securing small but firm wins by focusing on the development challenges that can be
    overcome easily and cost-effectively, and waging peace with the corporate sector to enable
    greater reach and synchronicities Engaging, provocative and clear-sighted, the volume draws
    on topical case studies in democratic governance, refugee response, counterterrorism, gender
    mainstreaming, environmental protection and private sector engagement. It will be essential
    for professionals in the development sector, thinktanks and NGOs"-- Provided by publisher.
Identifiers: LCCN 2022048528 (print) | LCCN 2022048529 (ebook) | ISBN 9781032152783
    (hardback) | ISBN 9781032152783 (paperback) | ISBN 9781003376996 (ebook)
Subjects: LCSH: Economic assistance--Developing countries. | Poverty--Developing countries. |
    Nonprofit organizations. | Development economics.
Classification: LCC HC60 .H323145 2023 (print) | LCC HC60 (ebook) | DDC
    338.91/1724--dc23/eng/20221013
LC record available at https://lccn.loc.gov/2022048528
LC ebook record available at https://lccn.loc.gov/2022048529

ISBN: 978-1-032-15278-3 (hbk)
ISBN: 978-1-032-45434-4 (pbk)
ISBN: 978-1-003-37699-6 (ebk)

DOI: 10.4324/9781003376996

Typeset in Sabon
by SPi Technologies India Pvt Ltd (Straive)

In memory of David Snider (1969–2020), exactly the brand of committed, curious and pragmatic humanitarian that the system needs but lost too soon.

CONTENTS

ACKNOWLEDGMENTS

Although writing a book is often a lonely process, it never takes place without the guidance, encouragement and support of many. I would first like to acknowledge the scholars who have most profoundly influenced my thinking on aid and development – Paul Collier, Alexander Betts, Steven Pinker, Mark Buntaine, Fareed Zakaria, Duncan Green, Daron Acemoglu, James Robinson and Paul Cairney. I am especially grateful to those of you who were generous enough to comment on this work or engage with my teaching on aid effectiveness at Leiden University, allowing me to understand your research more. Any misrepresentations of your works or opinions are solely my own.

I am likewise grateful to those within the donor, development and humanitarian communities of practice who volunteered their time to speak to me about their experiences, decision-making, aspirations and frustrations. Each did so without knowing exactly how this book would evolve, but trusted that the intention was to move the sector towards greater effectiveness and efficiency.

A few individuals took the time to read drafts of this work, either in full or in part and their comments greatly improved its content. I am especially grateful to Johanna Kruger, Skye Christensen, Gillian Triggs, Tessa Valk Mayerick and Benjamin Van Rooij. Equally important are the friends and colleagues who have shaped and deepened my thinking on development, perhaps without even knowing it – Helen Durham, Najat Maalla M'jid, Annette Lyth, Alison Hilliard, Amrita Kapur, Adel Sparr, Janine Ubink, Tanja Chopra, Hannah Derwent and Yann Colliou.

Robert Griffiths – my educator-in-Chief – invested much time and energy to extend my thinking, entertain unlikely solutions and save this book from many self-indulgences. His efforts to immerse himself in a world so far removed from his own sphere of expertise gave this book a human quality, relevance and humor.

Most importantly, I would like to thank Andrew Harper for crafting out a space in our hectic lives for me to write this book, and for the incredible journey he has taken me upon, without which the ideas expressed never would never have been born. And finally, to our children Isabella, Caitlin and Jessica, who each day provide the motivation and inspiration to make this world fit for generations to come.

INTRODUCTION

Is a little bit of sunlight the disinfectant the aid sector needs?

Whoever you are, and wherever you are from, there has never been a better time to be alive than 2021. On arguably every indicator of well-being, humans are advancing. If we fast forward a few generations, the likelihood is that our descendants will have continued down this path, and their lives will be better too. They will have more knowledge, live longer and healthier lives, enjoy greater safety, and have access to a wider range of technology.

This was the opening to a keynote address I delivered to a class of European law graduates last spring. The result was a riled up group of rowdy students. They were irate; there may have even been some booing.

What's interesting is not that this was a clumsy moment, but how *unsurprising* a moment this was. Indeed, the idea that life is on the improve is counterintuitive for many. And it's not only the young impassioned students, the farmer battling a fourth year of drought in the Sahel, or the Syrian teen marking their tenth year in a refugee camp. It's also the people reading this book, from the comfort of a secure home, following a day of paid labour, and reaping the benefits of heat, electricity and a full stomach. In fact, a vast majority view our world as sitting on a negative trajectory, and with few indicators of improvement.

These concerns supersede ideology. Whether you sit on the left or the right side of the political spectrum, there is agreement that civil conflict, environmental degradation and violent extremism are inexcusable tragedies of our time. The main difference is who we blame and what solution we favour. But the underlying message is stark and clear – the world is not fine, and unless radical changes are initiated, it may be too late to fix.

The evidence suggests that this kind of thinking – however newsworthy – is erroneous. Academics have been making this case, albeit relatively quietly, for decades. Paul Collier was among the first to report on the "outbreak of peacefulness" sweeping the modern world, and if anyone hasn't watched the late Hans Rosling's "200 Countries, 200 Years, 4 Minutes" they should

DOI: 10.4324/9781003376996-1

take a moment to do so. But it's perhaps Max Roser (whose web metrics on societal success have brought down countless university servers) who has come the furthest in calling out the elephant in the room called *progress*. These scholars each provide meticulous accounts that all measures of wellbeing – life expectancy, health, violence, safety, knowledge, governance and equality – are irrefutably pointing in a positive direction.

None claim that there is no more work to be done. One in ten people still live in extreme poverty; around 30 percent do not have access to safe drinking water, and more than 40 million are displaced within their own countries due to conflict and violence.

Even where trends are positive, change has been slow. Carbon intensity (carbon dioxide emissions per unit of GDP) at a global level has been declining for more than 50 years; deforestation and marine exploitation have likewise peaked and entered a phase of decline.[1] Still, this has not prevented a rise in severe weather events, and subsequent impacts on yields, food security and migration. There is also no guarantee that the amount of carbon being released into the atmosphere will abate before it reaches an irreversible level.

Declining inequality is another positive trend that must be monitored carefully. The same forces that have decreased income gaps at the global level have also – since around 1980 – been widening the gap between the rich and poor in Western countries. While development economists consider this an overall win, others are concerned. Historians through to conflict scholars know that a strong middle class is pivotal to innovation, growth and political stability. It is likely that some externalities are already being felt. In America, this disgruntled group was partly responsible for electing US President Donald Trump, and their message has been linked to the wave of populism and xenophobia currently sweeping across Europe. It is not clear how these trends will ultimately manifest; however, if history repeats and those countries currently catching up to the West inherit the burden of deeply unequal societies, the results are likely to be negative and intractable.

If we bring these stories together, while no one can claim that the world is perfectly on track, it cannot be denied that enormous progress has been made and continues to be made. As Steven Pinker aptly puts it, the only thing that's more incredible is that so few people know about it.[2]

This is indeed puzzling. Virtually everyone today is living an experience of betterment. I spent my childhood without the Internet, before there was a vaccine for cervical cancer, and when homosexuality was a criminal offense. For my parents and grandparents, the gains made are even more stark. My grandmother told stories of "real" air pollution, recalling when smog from coal fires killed more than 10,000 Londoners in the 1950s. This was before she was disabled by polio – another disease for which a lifesaving vaccine would be developed – and before her daughter had to buck social trends by continuing to work after giving birth to me.

What's perhaps even more puzzling is that development practitioners – the ones with the biggest stake in these findings – are not shouting about them. One might argue that this is because such gains spark reflection on development aid and its role in fighting global challenges. After all, if the world is getting so much better, the hundreds of thousands working in the development sector should perhaps start looking for new jobs. Such thinking may be true for some development practitioners, but certainly not all. Progress could equally be argued to demonstrate the efficacy of aid and justify its expansion.

More likely, development practitioners find it difficult to connect an ever-improving world with their lived reality. Their frustration is discernible; if these gains are so acute, they sure didn't happen on their watch. I greatly sympathise with this thinking. They have a front and center view of the rights abuses, corruption and mal-governance that keep that last 10 percent of humanity poor. They find this scandalous, and they should.

These practitioners are in good company. The idea that the aid system is broken is not new – it's perhaps the one thing development scholars agree on. Donors, taxpayers and the poor themselves have been questioning for decades why, given the sheer size of the sector, fundamentals such as clean water, sanitation, shelter and education are still not available universally. After all, overseas development assistance totaled more than USD165 billion last year – an amount roughly equal to the combined GDP of the world's poorest 70 countries. Said another way, if the development sector was a company, it would rank among the world's top 30 in terms of revenue – around the same size as Chevron, AT&T or Ford Motors. What disgruntled development practitioners do not see is how close the sector is to overcoming these hurdles. And that how, by overturning a few myths, making better use evidence and employing some different rules, that last 10 percent is within reach.

This is the problematic that I am interested in. Because in a world where we can fly from New York to London in less than 5 hours, chart our own DNA and use facial recognition to pay for groceries, a sector with that kind of breadth *should* be able get this right. But we haven't, for one quite simple reason. For those with the power to make it happen, it hasn't been important enough.

This book is not an exposé of an inefficient or corrupt aid sector. Nor is it a manifesto on how to reach zero poverty, achieve world peace or halt climate change. This book is about how – practically and feasibly – practitioners, policy specialists and donors can foster the types of changes needed in the development architecture to reach that last 10 percent. It describes a system that – by design – is not supposed to work very effectively. Poverty, poor governance and conflict serve too many, too well. This tension needs to be exposed, not so that blame can be doled out, or even so it can be fixed, but because understanding *why* the aid sector operates the way it does opens the door to more effective ways of working. Justice Brandeis was right when he noted that sunlight really is the best disinfectant.

This book then sets out five changes to "business as usual" that have the potential to bring about unprecedented gains in development impact. None of these are particularly complex. Indeed, the biggest challenge will be modifying how we think about aid, the norms we apply and the standards we set for ourselves.

A first change is to call out programmatic approaches where the evidence on impact is at best thin – and at worst undeniably lacking in reason. The easiest and most cost effective way to do this is to make better use of the enormous body of evidence produced by the academic community – political economists, eco-economists and conflict analysts. The aid sector needs to find a way to work with this group, by finding a common language and letting go of the belief that academics have few practical ideas to contribute. In my experience, the scholars worth listening to often spend more time in the field than many Geneva- or New York–based technical experts. If this is unpalatable, the alternative is for development agencies to start making serious investments in generating their own evidence base. No one particularly wants to embrace this; in fact, it flies in the face of the widely held belief that less talk and more action is the change that the development sector needs most. But making evidence the anchor of engagement strategies may be the difference between reaching the last 10 percent, containing climate change or avoiding a migration crisis during this generation, or not at all.

A second change concerns the operating cultures of development agencies around innovation. Indeed, access to evidence means very little if practitioners are not given the space to exploit it and an incentive to do so. Drawing on the above analogy, if the development sector was competing with other firms the size of Ford Motors, would it still be in business? Ford is a successful company because it is forced to innovate, respond to its clients' needs, and remain competitive. If it doesn't, this is reflected in their profits and managers are held to account. The development sector does not work like this. Its unique composition means that there is no naturally occurring or intrinsic feedback mechanism, and the accountability instruments designed to replace it are unreliable and regularly malfunction. To understand why you will need to read Chapter 4, but the upshot is that agencies need to actively absorb some private sector values – they literally need to become more like Development Inc. An operating environment where staff are encouraged to innovate, take calculated risks and be permitted to fail, but at the same time are held accountable for outcomes, does not sound remotely like the sector any of us are familiar with. Such a transition will be painful and is likely to be met with huge resistance. But it is possible – private sector organisations do it all the time – and we need to learn from them.

The third change is also norm related – where and how high the goalposts are set. It seems that the more scrutiny the development sector has come under, the more pressure there is to provide silver bullet–type solutions. In my work as an evaluator, I spend a lot of my time listening to managers lament the impossible task of designing projects that promise complete and sustainable fixes while still being cost effective, and that fit a donor's programming cycle. This situation is understandable, but it lacks logic. The way to turn around an underachieving racehorse is not to enter the Melbourne Cup. It is to secure small but firm wins, and for the owner accept smaller but regular profits. The same applies to development.

The good news is that with a better understanding of the inner workings of the development sector, it becomes much easier to home in on what is realistically achievable. The bad news is that when programming opportunities are analysed through a political lens, the scope for engagement shrinks significantly. Development practitioners have become highly fearful of anything that might translate into budget cuts or an exit strategy. Tools that help them identify new entry points and strategies for scale up are far more attractive. But for those who read on, there is a reward. While there may be fewer genuine opportunities, these represent fertile territory for impact. I'm talking about the occasions where development objectives naturally align with the interests of key stakeholders, whether they be a host government, local elite, or donors. These moments are rare, so practitioners need to know how to identify them. A fourth change is allowing development to be understood – at least in part – as a political process. If we can take this step, practitioners get handed a new toolbox of knowledge, methods and shortcuts. Not only have these techniques been finessed by lobbyists over decades, but this knowledge is there for the taking – no MoU required! While this doesn't sound like a theory of change agencies are likely to endorse, history tells us that this is how the big wins in gender equality and environmental protection have accrued. Again, this will not be an easy transition. Along with a license to try out more effective ways of achieving results, organisations will need to become more forward looking and agile. This is because moments of profound change are almost always preceded by a critical juncture, during which practitioners need to leap into action with resources, evidence and a strategy in hand. This can rarely be reconciled with a 3-year funding cycle, proven value for money or guaranteed sustainability.

A final change is to broaden the range of stakeholders that the development community engages with, and to deepen those relationships. The private sector and multinational development banks (MDBs) follow a different approach to development, and one that many in the aid community are ideologically opposed to. This is another example of where a dose of sunlight is needed to overturn myths that are obstructing new, potentially fruitful, development pathways. While corporate practice is far from perfect, the evidence is that globalisation is responsible for a large chunk of the decline in poverty these past 50 years. Moreover, if we are intent on bean counting, the reality is that the development sector's modus operandi is far less pure than is popularly believed. For those who remain skeptical, the enormity of the financial resources wielded – around 1.7 trillion in assets held by MDBs alone – must be acknowledged.[3] Indeed, if we were to add the likes of Corporate Social Responsibility (CSR), remittance transfers and *zakat* to official aid revenues, Development Inc. just became the world's largest company – around 70 percent bigger than Walmart. There needs to be greater effort directed towards channeling these non-traditional forms of development assistance towards coordinated goals, or at minimum avoiding projects working at cross purposes.

Together, these chapters develop an evidence base around some of the structural deficits in the development architecture, and a framework for understanding them more critically and constructively. It is not a "how to" manual, but instead a set of ideas to encourage new thinking across the development community. I define this community liberally, and in particular to include humanitarian actors. Indeed, while most of the examples concern what would generally be termed classical economic and political development, the chapters equally examine humanitarian response, including post-conflict recovery and the changing nature of refugee flows. This is in part to unpack the siloing of aid along development and humanitarian lines. Moreover, it is to acknowledge that the interlinkages between poverty, weak governance, conflict and disaster are both evidenced and palpable, and only by seeing them as a whole can each be truly understood.

This book is not for everyone. For many, the idea of "fighting the fights you can win" as opposed to the "fights that need to be fought" is the antithesis of what development stands for. Others will argue that applying lobbyist approaches to development objectives and viewing beneficiaries as customers that can be experimented upon is repugnant. Those left standing might ridicule the suggestion of diverting scarce resources into research, changing organisation culture or narrowing agency scope towards more modest wins as naïvely unrealistic.

I acknowledge that these ideas are likely to take development practitioners far outside of their comfort zone. But I disagree that borrowing from private sector norms or experimenting with lobbyist techniques devalues the poor or the notion of poverty reduction. Quite the opposite; these challenges are so important that the poor deserve solutions that work. If we have to go through some institutional growing pains and moral re-evaluation to get there, then this is our problem.

This book is directed at those who are willing to entertain the idea that a large part of the aid system is fixable. The only real prerequisite is that we regard the last 10 percent as important enough to make this happen. Choosing not to will be the scandal that my generation will need to live with, and I hope it is one that my children do not inherit.

Notes

1 S. Pinker *Enlightenment Now: The Case for Reason, Science, Humanism and Progress*, Allen Lane (2018) 121–156.
2 S. Pinker *Enlightenment Now: The Case for Reason, Science, Humanism and Progress*, Allen Lane (2018) 39–53.
3 A Prizzon "A Guide to Multilateral Development Banks", Overseas Development Institute Working Paper (2018).

1

HOW THE WEST GOT RICH, AND OTHER CURIOUS QUESTIONS AROUND HUMAN DEVELOPMENT

The premise of this book is that development assistance works, but not nearly as well as it could or should. The good news is that there is a lot we can do about it. With small changes in the way the sector conducts "business as usual", huge progress can be made in combatting poverty, fostering development and promoting shared rights.

A good place to start is with the theories that underpin what today we call, "human development". This term gained popularity relatively recently, superseding Gross Domestic Product and economic growth as the popularly accepted indicators of a country's progress. The human development concept recognises that a state's wealth is not necessarily a good proxy for individual betterment; other social goods, including economic rights, wealth distribution, health and access to justice also matter, for both individuals and societal advancement more generally.

But while there may be more agreement over what human development comprises, theories around how to get there remain highly contested. One result is that development strategies have periodically gone through sizeable shakeups – even complete turnarounds – in short periods of time. In large part, these contestations lie at the heart of development failures, making them highly instructive.

This chapter starts with an historical interrogation of how disparities in global wealth came to be. It then outlines some of the main theories on how human development takes place, and reciprocally, the forces that stymie human development in particular places, times and contexts. These include the role of geography, governance, conflict and natural resource endowments, as well as dealings of luck. It also discusses the relationship between these theories and how aid policies have been structured, which countries benefit from assistance and how it is rolled out.

The conclusion posited is that each of the competing development models have merit, but none is a magic bullet. Human development is a dynamic, messy and political process, within which aid may be part of the solution, but not a solution itself. What the sector needs to work towards – is not more or better theories of development – but an improved understanding of the elements that make them up, and sufficient depth of insight to

DOI: 10.4324/9781003376996-2

determine where and how they should be applied. The current system of aid administration does not facilitate this. And this is the part that requires reform.

To keep this chapter as light and digestible as possible, I condense complex historical events and change processes derived from decades of research. Inevitably, much detail has been omitted. I also skip over some pressing questions such as whether human development, at least at its initial stages, can take place in the absence of human rights good governance. Many of these questions will be revisited in later chapters. For now, I can only hope that the architects of the work presented are not too affronted. Let's begin.

1.1 12,000 years of progress: from the Neolithic to the Industrial Revolution

Environmental historians through to development economists have all posited theories on how Western states won their spot at the top of the global economic order. While individual elements of these theories are challenged, there is basic agreement that this was not simply a matter of a superior development blueprint. Instead, the West stumbled awkwardly to the finish line, through a combination of natural advantages, a bit of luck and hundreds of years of – often very violent – conflict.

Jared Diamond's research pins the start point to the Neolithic revolution. During this period, humans lived in small hunter-gatherer populations scattered across Europe, Asia, Africa and the Americas. Constantly in search of nourishment, safety and shelter, these groups lived on the move. As a result, they had little incentive to invent (anything new would have to carried) and children were fairly well spaced (they had to be carried too). These limits operated to keep human development static for a long period of time. Some groups, however, happened to be located in areas such as Eurasia that were uniquely endowed in terms of vegetation and fauna. This was the first hand of luck dealt. Although it is far from obvious today, the vast majority of plant life on earth is not edible, and only a narrow range of crop species are suitable for cultivation. Happening upon large animals that could be domesticated was also critical; without them to plough fields and generate fertilizer, food production could not have been up-scaled. Large animals also carried the first communicable diseases, endowing this group with a more robust immune system compared to others. So, it was here, and in this moment, that a new phase in human advancement was kick started. With a reliable food supply, formerly nomadic populations were able to settle and have children in rapid succession. Greater numbers, coupled with the tools of social organisation that evolved to control them, facilitated task specialisation, which then freed up time for innovation. Equipped with rudimentary weapons, means of transport and immunity, they were primed to take over other weaker population groups. Thus by the 14th century, those in the lead had a firm geographic reference point: Europe.[1]

9

All this should not be taken to imply that these developments took place ubiquitously and simultaneously. Chance discoveries and fortuitous circumstances gave some groups an unexpected advantage. In a recent book, Lewis Dartnell explains how the development of different civilisations was influenced by geographical and other factors. The availability of game, arable land, a reliable source of water, and natural barriers like mountain ranges and seacoasts kept people well-nourished and safe from invasion. The Americas were not populated until about 20,000 years ago and then only because an ice-age land bridge connected America to Eurasia. Another factor that gave some groups an advantage was the availability of building stones and minerals such as copper and iron, and the discovery that zinc and copper could be combined to make brass.

This is not where the story ends. If we scratch beneath the surface of these early societies, small differences can be identified. To explain this properly, we need to pass the baton to scholars Daron Acemoglu and James Robinson. Their research shows that although feudal relations were the norm across Europe, in England the peasant masses were slightly more powerful vis-à-vis the landholding elite. Within this difference lay opportunity. When the bubonic plague struck in 1348 and created a huge scarcity in labour, this group was able to demand change, including with respect to wage levels. This slight altering in power relations made way for the Peasants' Revolt in 1381, shaking the social order yet again. A catalytic process had commenced. Slowly (meaning every few hundred years), additional constraints were placed on the elite, and additional rights were won by everyone else. These small yet accumulating gains set the stage for the Glorious Revolution in 1688, which dismantled monopolies, further curtailed exploitation and, critically, bestowed equal access to property rights. This levelling of the playing field continued; the rise of factories, merchants and towns diverted resources away from agriculture, reducing rents and increasing wages, further chipping away the economic power of the elite. At the same time, secure in the knowledge that their intellectual property would be protected, technological advances ascended at an unprecedented rate. What happened next is no secret. In the mid-18th century, the Industrial Revolution unleashed a wave of unchecked urbanisation, productivity gains and technological advancement, propelling England into modernity. A social tipping point was also reached. Birth was no longer determinant; social mobility had become more of a reality and the masses embraced it euphorically.[2]

1.2 The rise of "cut and paste" development assistance

The Industrial Revolution has been credited as the most efficient and effective poverty reduction program in human history. But for development scholars, this moment is pivotal for another reason. It was only then that inequality between states began to climb. The world divided into those who followed the path of trade and development and the rest, who didn't.

Within a century or so, the differences between the "haves" and the "have nots" was so stark that ideas around how to redress the situation started to evolve. This is not to say that the interventions that followed were solely, or even largely, driven by moral concern. Indeed, the missionary movements, economic exchange, and empire building that dominated the 19th century were efforts of capitalist domination rather than examples of Christian charity. But there was certainly an evolving sense that where populations were suffering from poverty due to war, economic downturn or disaster, foreign assistance was justified, if not compelled.[3]

Importantly, underpinning these early experiments was an assumption that rich states possessed talent, capital and practices that could help so-called backward countries develop. This notion would be carried forward in variant iterations to shape foreign aid and technical assistance policies, all the way through to their current forms.[4]

The idea also explains some of foreign aid's most decisive failures. In the 1960s, Africa and Latin America became the first targets in a new era in Western development assistance – the Law and Development Movement. These projects aimed to accelerate economic growth via free market governance, legislative revision and court reform. Although the results were weak, such work was carried over to Eurasia in the 1980s and, a decade later, to the post-communist societies of Central and Eastern Europe. These latter interventions followed a tweaked collection of economic policies known as the Washington Consensus.[5] By the turn of the century, both movements were declared failures. It seemed that the importation of Western legal codes and fiscal rules was not sufficient to overcome longstanding legacies of market failure, incoherent policy and limited rights.[6] Adding insult to injury, around the same time, the Asian Tiger economies of Hong Kong, Singapore, South Korea and Taiwan had caught the tailwinds of globalisation and joined the club of the rich in record time and with little, if any, prescribed assistance.

Today, the notion of Western transplants speaks more to ethnocentric bias and political incorrectness. But it is important to remember that those proffering such assistance had a sound precedent. Exporting the rule of law and liberal democracy to the defeated axis powers following World War II had been enormously successful, and while hindsight makes it easier to identify the enormous differences between these contexts, at that time they were obscure. The Bretton Woods institutions provided resources, and on a huge scale. Few strings were attached, and countries were largely at liberty to rebuild their societies as their saw fit. Through the lens of modern aid practices, this is very curious. Context, however, was hugely important. The allied powers had nothing to prove – they had won the war and had a strong vested interest in a renewed world marketplace for trade. Moreover, confidence was high that the beneficiary countries would build institutions in the style and manner intended. And they did. Within a generation, national socialism and fascism no longer defined governance models, and social groups had started to recalibrate around principles of equal opportunity, liberalism and broad economic and social rights.

Against these successes, the results of the aid experiments undertaken in the 1960s–1980s were hugely perplexing to the nascent community of development practitioners. On the one hand, it appeared that the West's path to prosperity was not a blueprint that could be exported as a formula for poverty reduction. On the other, it didn't seem reasonable that poor countries should have to follow the same slow and precarious path in order to reap basic benefits that rich societies now took for granted. Some wondered whether the answer might lie in flipping the question: if how the West became rich was not the key to unlocking development pathways, perhaps the answer lay in a better understanding of why the poor had remained poor.

1.3 It's governance, stupid

To answer the question of why some countries appear to have been locked in poverty, we need to return to the work of Acemoglu and Robinson and their account of how England's poor harnessed a random event to exploit micro-differences in power relations, thus sparking a process of small but accumulating gains. They note that while most historians understand this to be the headline story, what was happening across the channel was equally, perhaps even more, interesting.

Feudal lords, who were quite content with the status quo, watched the English intently as mercantile advances redistributed wealth and power. And it was at that point, they reasoned, that their neighbours got themselves into trouble. The masses demanded rights previously known only to the upper class, and more of a say in how they were governed. This process continued to the point where elite power was given up almost completely. For these privileged observers, there was nothing attractive about this trajectory; innovation, progress and diversification were all very bad ideas.

So, as the Industrial Revolution swept through England, Europe's aristocratic classes were not strumming their fingers, impatiently waiting for the winds of change to reach their shores, unleash market energy and bring prosperity to all. They were battening down the hatches. Some failed; France had its own critical juncture (the French Revolution), and this created a wide enough appetite for reform that progress quickly spread to Belgium and the Netherlands. Colonies such as Australia also developed, again with their own complicated stories. But following suit was not the norm, it was the heavily contested exception.

This insight is pivotal. It suggests that asking why poor countries did not, or have not, climbed on board with modernity is wrongheaded. In reality, it is just not that easy when those in control are doing everything in their power to stop it.[7]

This is not as fanciful as it sounds. Throughout history, technological advancement has been looked on suspiciously, and often rejected, by powerholders. Elsewhere in their research, Acemoglu and Robinson retrace the perilous path of early inventors and the battles they waged to introduce their ideas into society. William Lee pioneered the first knitting machine in 1589 and had his patent request rejected by Elizabeth I, then the French, then James I – each of whom cited the ruinous consequences that such a tool would bestow on those who made their living knitting by hand. When French physicist Dionysius Papin – inventor of the first steamboat – tried to pilot test his craft in 1705, opposition by the guilds who controlled river traffic for profit was so intense that the State had little choice but to withhold permission. When he ignored their directive, the vessel was impounded, and then destroyed.[8] This pattern, where those in power actively ward off not the innovation itself, but the consequences that might follow in terms of wealth acquisition, power dispersal and destabilisation, can be traced over centuries, through until today.

The upshot is that there is no place for rose-coloured glasses when it comes to examining these particular moments in history. There is a reason that the Industrial Revolution was so-labelled – these transitions were contested, fraught and bloody. Moreover, the lesson – that economic advancement causes winners and losers – is highly instructive for understanding development processes. It somewhat explains why exporting Western institutional codes and structures in the 1960–1980s produced underwhelming results. What those well-intentioned development practitioners failed to see was that ignorance was playing no role in poor countries' failure to develop. Quite the contrary, it was that the powerholders in those countries had made a calculated decision to trade off potential prosperity for the privilege of retaining control.

1.4 Human Development 101: how modern development theories translate into aid strategies

The idea that poverty is the result of weak governance and elite-controlled institutions is central to many modern development theories. But just because extractive governance keeps a country poor, doesn't mean that good governance is enough – or the only thing – needed to pull it out of poverty and push it forward.

Let's consider the work of renowned development economist Jeffery Sachs.[9] Sachs agrees that small differences in growth over centuries largely explain the income gap between rich and poor countries today. But he posits a slightly different explanation. He's troubled that some previously poor countries – such as Asian Tigers – managed to hoist themselves to middle income status largely in the absence of good governance, while others – mainly in Africa – have not. Indeed, his research demonstrates that even after controlling for governance and corruption, Africa's growth is still slower than countries at the same income level. His theory is that poor countries are caught in one or more reinforcing traps that keep them in a cycle of low or negative growth. These traps concern not only governance, but also geography, fiscal revenues, geopolitics and innovation. In short, governance is certainly a problem, but not the only one, or even the most important in many cases.

Oxford University's Paul Collier supports the "trap" thesis; he just doesn't think there are as many. His research identifies four situations that characterise very poor countries: conflict affected, abundant natural resource endowments with poor governance, landlocked in a bad neighbourhood, and small with poor governance.[10] My feeling is that he would rank poor governance towards the top of the list of problems in terms of intractability, but he maintains that dealing with this in isolation is not a solution.

Alongside Sachs and Collier sit numerous other scholars, whose theories have all pushed development thinking forward in important ways. Hernando de Soto has rallied the importance of property rights, arguing that poor countries' inability (or unwillingness) to unlock embedded capital is preventing their advancement[11]; while Armyta Sen's work illustrates how restrictions on freedom – in health, political participation and markets – operate to inhibit development both structurally and for individuals.[12]

These theories propose different models of development assistance, each trying to answer the questions "does aid work?" and "what kind of aid works?" This is where it gets messy, and political. After all, which theory rises to the top has a large influence on how those billions in development aid get apportioned.

Sachs' thesis renders him a huge aid proponent. When translated into development speak, his argument is that because poor countries are caught in one or more development traps, they cannot climb onto, let alone ascend, the global economic ladder. They need aid – usually a lot of it – to make this jump, after which economic growth will build on itself. Moreover, because underdevelopment is a multidimensional phenomenon, this aid should be disbursed in a comprehensive, diagnostic manner. It should come as no surprise that Sachs' theories are incredibly popular within UN and INGOs circles, and indeed, modern approaches to aid are largely structured around his ideas.[13]

Those who reject Sachs' approach criticise it as akin to "throwing money at everything and hoping for the best". At the front of the line is New York University's Bill Easterly. He argues that while poor countries may be held back by deficits around health, technology and governance, plugging these gaps is no panacea – the lines of causation are too opaque. In fact, structuring aid delivery around these priorities may be doing more harm than good insofar as this distorts market incentives.[14] Aid policies have to be reformed to set in place enabling conditions for good governance, including by stimulating those factors of production that have more evidential links to growth, and weaving them into global economic cycles. Readers will understand why the aid sector prefers Sachs' theories over Easterly's, and indeed, he concedes how unappealing they are, but maintains that this doesn't prove them incorrect.

Acemoglu and Robinson appreciate where Easterly is coming from. They agree that poor countries need better institutions, and aid – the way it is currently administered – does little to fix this. Development assistance should be principally directed into this type of development, especially supporting future leaders, and empowering broad sections of the population. This is because the opportunities for countries to set themselves on a positive development trajectory are scant; they will depend on the positioning and outlook of its economic and political institutions at moments of critical juncture. To the extent that these institutions are not inclined to take advantage of those moments, aid will be plundered and the status quo reinforced. Moreover, by not making institutional reform the locus of development assistance, struggling populations are denied the opportunity to capitalise on critical junctures as they arise.[15]

Collier also has much to say on the effectiveness of aid in contexts of bad governance, but his approach is more nuanced. For him, it is not a question of whether aid works or not. It does, but the form it should take is highly context specific. He also emphasises that these gains are only ever modest. Aid speeds growth up, on average by about 1 percent for 30 years, but it operates on the basis of diminishing returns. Once aid reaches around 16 percent of a country's GDP, it becomes less advantageous. It follows that unchecked giving is not a viable strategy. Assistance needs to be tailored to a country's specific development challenges, and unfortunately the current system does not do this well.[16] Oftentimes, this is because the type of aid that will be most effective runs contrary to widely held development norms, political correctness and donor interests. We will return to this argument in Chapter 3.

A side note on China

This discussion would not be complete without a side note on how these development theories reconcile with, or explain, the burgeoning economic prowess of China. This emerging superpower – and indeed all the Asian Tiger economies – call into question the idea that good governance, property rights and democratic freedoms are precursors to development. Of those scholars who have attempted to weave China's trajectory into the mainstream development theory, Acemoglu and Robinson perhaps offer the most complete explanation. They argue that countries ruled by autocrats can grow – both fast and significantly. China did this through a limited liberalisation of economic institutions, while retaining tight control over political, social and civic freedoms. This allowed the elite to allocate resources to high productivity activities, taking advantage of the country's low debt levels, coastline, remittance income and low-cost, voluminous

---

workforce. While the result was extraordinary and sustained rates of growth, Acemoglu and Robinson caution that this is largely "catch up", hollow growth. It will be inherently limited because it is not driven by the "creative destruction" that comes with secure property rights, equality in opportunity and the other protections that facilitate innovation. Moreover, China will soon face a choice. It might continue to liberalise and allow inclusive political institutions to evolve – in the same manner that South Korea and Taiwan evolved into vibrant, robust democracies – or it could cap change and reassert the power of the regime.[17]

Of course, this is not the only theory. Sachs links Asia's rise to its population density coupled with slightly better social conditions around literacy that allowed it to develop an advantage in food productivity relative to similarly struggling states.[18] Easterly, on the other hand, argues that China's growth started much earlier – even before Mao's death in 1976. He highlights that the population had already moved towards more efficient production practices, but kept these hidden from authorities. Following Mao's death, expanded freedoms allowed these informal practices to be formalised, allowing gains to be consolidated. The point for this discussion is not to overplay what has taken place in the Asian Tiger economies. Just because these economic "miracles" occurred under the watch of a benevolent autocrat, doesn't mean that benevolent autocracy is a strategy for growth.[19]

1.5 What can development scholars agree on?

The differences in these theories of development, and corresponding models of aid distribution, have important implications for discussions on aid effectiveness and development policy reform. Not all these scholars can be right, and if policy is informed – even to a small extent – by an incorrect hypothesis, the results range from wasteful to ineffective, and even counterproductive. Indeed, the theories that have had the most impact on the design of aid policies are probably the most contested within the academic community.

This leaves us in a quandary. No one is in favour of allocating money to situations where governance is so weak that it will be ineffective, plundered or used to reinforce the status quo. At the same time, directing aid solely towards governance reform sounds painfully colonial and, moreover, the development sector is yet to work out an unambiguously successful way of doing this. A third option – prioritising countries where aid is likely to have the best returns – effectively means sidelining the populations most ravaged

by poverty and predatory governance. In many of these places, foreign aid –
even if the vast majority of it never reaches the poor – is a lifeline and sometimes the only thing holding off humanitarian disaster.[20] The question is, are
we happy with this? Or in an age of driverless cars and artificial intelligence,
can we expect a more robust theory on how to take the worst edges off
extreme poverty?

The perspectives on development summarised above have been judi-
ciously pieced together over decades by globally recognised scholars. I have
no intention of trying to dissect them, to put one forward as superior to the
others, or to present my own. Instead, I will default to logic and suggest that
none is a magic bullet. Instead, as with most complicated and contested
phenomena, the truth probably lies somewhere in the middle. It is likely
that there is such a thing as a development trap, but not just one. Likewise,
it's improbable that governance is all that matters, although better policy
will undoubtedly play a role in poverty alleviation.

This is not to suggest that any of these scholars' insights are redundant.
They are critical to our understanding of poverty and how to address it. The
point is that in working out the role of foreign aid, we must avoid overplay-
ing or underplaying the importance of any of them. We may also need to
accept the idea of a messy, incremental and unchartered process to poverty
elimination.

If we re-examine the above development theories through this lens, some
common and important themes can be identified.

One thing all development theorists seem to agree on is that humanity
started out on a fairly even playing field. Europe got a head start because of
natural resource advantages and a lot of luck. This initial advantage was
compounded through higher rates of growth, decade after decade, leaving
the poor further and further behind. The upshot is that the West's riches
have nothing to do with any form of superiority, differences in culture, colonialism or any other act of wealth expropriation. It follows that poor countries are not poor due to some form of ignorance. For readers who view this
comment as trite, or even abhorrent, it's important not to forget that "modernization theory" once dominated development policy, and for quite a long
time. Moreover, while transplant approaches ultimately did fail (even if
scholars can't agree whether this was because leaders prioritised power over
poverty reduction, or because there is something uniquely challenging about
kick-starting growth in these countries), the underlying ideas continue to
influence how aid is structured today.[21]

A second point of agreement is that underdevelopment is resilient, but
not an impossible legacy from which to break free. Poverty is "sticky"
within countries, because those in the best position to change things usually
do not want to; in fact, they create institutions that ward off innovation and
the destabilising processes that can follow.[22] But poverty is also sticky
between countries. This is because the wider the gap between the rich and

poor, the more difficult technological diffusion – the tool for catch up – is. During the rise of the Asian Tiger economies, students studied abroad, en masse. Back at home, new technology was imported, dismantled, techniques perfected and advances tinkered with. Within a decade or so, these countries had become the high-tech capitals of the world. Malawi and Haiti simply cannot do this. If students are lucky enough and have the riches to travel abroad to study, they have little incentive to return. In the absence of base level capacity, industrialisation, an export market and incentives, there is nothing to advance, and thus nothing to return to.

But while the path to prosperity is precarious and slow, history is not destiny.[23] Japan, Botswana and South Korea are each living examples of this. Moreover, when a step forward is made, these outcomes are also sticky. Once the rule of law, socio-economic rights and institutional restraint take root and power is disbursed, these norms tend to reinforce over time.

Third, innovation plays a critical role in how to take countries from poverty to prosperity. Key to closing the innovation gap is democratic capital – the idea that members of society are motivated to invest their intellect and resources to innovate in ways that will benefit whole groups, safe in the knowledge that a powerholder will not frustrate their efforts, dispossess them or throw them in jail. This was true for the early inventors, and it is true today.[24]

Finally, all scholars of development – from political scientists to development economists – agree that the current system for delivering development aid needs fundamental reform. This is both the message to take away from this chapter and the start point for the remainder of this book.

The idea to carry forward is that there is no one theory underpinning human development. There is also much in the legacies of poverty that we cannot change – we cannot modify natural resource endowments, rewrite history or manufacture critical junctures. What we do have is a set of solid and well-reasoned ideas that will apply, in different measures, to certain places, at particular moments. The development community of practice needs to understand these insights in sufficient depth to be able to leverage them prudently, objectively and nimbly. Unfortunately, the modern development architecture is not set up to do this. So rather than searching for a better or different "development solution", we must instead look inside the system – the one in which development assistance is strategised and administered – to see where and how seeds of change might be planted.

Notes

1 J. Diamond *Guns, Germs and Steel: A Short History of Everybody for the Last 13,000 Years*, Vintage (2005) 88–92, 103, 195–205, 401–408.
2 D. Acemoglu and J. Robinson *Why Nations Fail: The Origins of Power, Prosperity and Poverty*, Random House (2012) 84–85, 98–104, 300–301; see

also J. Sachs *The End of Poverty: Economic Possibilities for Our Time*, Penguin Press (2005) 33–37.

3 As Picad and Buss highlight, the idea of one state extending assistance to another is an historical one; records of inter-state grants, loans and subsidies date back to 650 BC. As a tool of state policy, however, intervention commenced in the 1800s with missionaries and tithing, followed by technical assistance by powerful states to gain a foothold in markets in Asian, African, Caribbean and Latin American markets. L. Picard and T. Buss *A Fragile Balance: Re-examining the History of Foreign Aid, Security, and Diplomacy*, Lynne Rienner Publishers (2009) 14–16, 24–29.

4 L. Picard and T. Buss *A Fragile Balance: Re-examining the History of Foreign Aid, Security, and Diplomacy*, Lynne Rienner Publishers (2009) 8, 25–29.

5 J.C. Reitz "Export of the Rule of Law" *Transnational L and Contemporary Problems* 13 (2003) 433, 449–452, 482.

6 S Chesterman *You, The People: The United Nations, Transitional Administration, and State Building*, Oxford University Press (2004) 213.

7 D. Acemoglu and J. Robinson *Why Nations Fail: The Origins of Power, Prosperity and Poverty*, Random House (2012) 122–123.

8 D. Acemoglu and J. Robinson *Why Nations Fail: The Origins of Power, Prosperity and Poverty*, Random House (2012) 84–85, 182–183, 202–203.

9 J. Sachs *The End of Poverty: Economic Possibilities for Our Time*, Penguin Press (2005) 19, 30–31, 191, 226, 312–314. Sachs also highlights that post–WWII, the socialist world remained largely cut out of international trade due to low competitiveness; he contrasts this to countries in Asia and Africa which also could not benefit from globalisation trends due to underdevelopment; J. Sachs *The End of Poverty: Economic Possibilities for Our Time*, Penguin Press (2005) 46–48.

10 P. Collier *The Bottom Billion: Why the Poorest Countries Are Failing and What Can Be Done About It*, Oxford University Press (2007) 17–64.

11 H. de Soto *The Mystery of Capital: Why Capitalism Triumphs in the West and Fails Everywhere Else*, Basic Books (2003).

12 See generally A. Sen *Development as Freedom*, Anchor Books (1999).

13 J. Sachs *The End of Poverty: Economic Possibilities for Our Time*, Penguin Press (2005) 83–88, 246–250.

14 W. Easterly *The White Man's Burden: Why the West's Efforts to Aid the Rest Have Done So Much Harm and So Little Good*, Penguin Press (2006) 45–50; W. Easterly *The Tyranny of Experts: Economists, Dictators and the Forgotten Rights of the Poor*, Basic Books (2013) 216–218.

15 D. Acemoglu and J. Robinson *Why Nations Fail: The Origins of Power, Prosperity and Poverty*, Random House (2012) 431–436, 454–455.

16 P. Collier *The Bottom Billion: Why the Poorest Countries Are Failing and What Can Be Done About It*, Oxford University Press (2007) 100.

17 D. Acemoglu and J. Robinson *Why Nations Fail: The Origins of Power, Prosperity and Poverty*, Random House (2012) 420–443, 71, 93–94.

18 J. Sachs *The End of Poverty: Economic Possibilities for Our Time*, Penguin Press (2005) 69–71, 155–167; See also J. Sachs *The Price of Civilization: Economics and Ethics After the Fall*, Random House (2011) 18.

19 W. Easterly *The Tyranny of Experts: Economists, Dictators and the Forgotten Rights of the Poor*, Basic Books (2013) 311–320.

20 D. Acemoglu and J. Robinson *Why Nations Fail: The Origins of Power, Prosperity and Poverty*, Random House (2012) 452–454.

21 J. Sachs *The End of Poverty: Economic Possibilities for Our Time*, Penguin Press (2005) 43, 50, 81–82; D. Acemoglu and J. Robinson *Why Nations Fail: The Origins of Power, Prosperity and Poverty*, Random House (2012) 64–68.

22 D. Acemoglu and J. Robinson *Why Nations Fail: The Origins of Power, Prosperity and Poverty*, Random House (2012) 81–82.
23 D. Acemoglu and J. Robinson *Why Nations Fail: The Origins of Power, Prosperity and Poverty*, Random House (2012) 364–365, 426–427.
24 J. Sachs *The End of Poverty: Economic Possibilities for Our Time*, Penguin Press (2005) 61–63.

2

BROKEN, BY DESIGN

In 2004, the documentary "Super Size Me" starring Michael Moore sparked a wave of debate around how modern eating habits were giving way to grave externalities, including obesity, heart disease and diabetes. However, it wasn't until 2015, when "That Sugar Film" exposed how brazenly food giants were profiting at the expense of our health, that a tipping point was reached. Parents around the globe were incensed to discover that industry practices such as "bliss point" science – the amount of sugar needed to make foods optimally desirable – were behind the making of children's breakfast cereals. The results were swift and impressive. In the documentary's country of origin, Australia, the National Heart Foundation was forced to retire its lucrative "Tick of Approval" program; elsewhere in the world, a swath of governments introduced sugar taxes, sending manufacturers scurrying to rethink both their recipes and marketing.

These events can tell us a lot about how the aid industry works, and doesn't work. As in food manufacturing, the aid sector is composed of principals, agents and consumers – labelled donors, implementing agencies, and beneficiaries respectively. The interconnections that make the private sector responsive and efficient, however, do not work as effectively. While consumers could express their outrage through their purchasing power, sending a clear and direct message to Kellogg, Nestle and Danone that all was not right, the beneficiaries of aid programs have no comparable axe to wield. Moreover, to the extent that they can assert dissatisfaction, the accountability relationship runs between the agencies running projects and their donors, largely bypassing the recipients of aid. For scholars such as Bill Easterly, this absence of a meaningful feedback loop is the single largest obstacle to better development practices.

The analogy also demonstrates that when there are deficits in accountability, there is a risk that defective products will enter the market. For almost a decade, consumers were misled into believing that products labelled "Heart Foundation Approved" or "fat free" were healthy. Had they known that the removal of trans-fats made for a highly unpalatable product – something that was masked by adding high amounts of sugar – they may have made a different choice. When it comes to development, we are also

DOI: 10.4324/9781003376996-3

prone to making assumptions. We have a tendency to believe that aid – because it is aid – must somehow be doing good.

In fact, aid flows are highly complicated. Ostensibly, assistance is provided for the purposes of governance, social or economic development, but it is also a tool – along with diplomacy, military force and cultural exchange – used by donor states to achieve foreign policy objectives. This is not to suggest that aid never produces positive outcomes, simply that when development outcomes are assessed, we must remember that just because something looks good and feels good, doesn't mean it does good. To make aid work more effectively, practitioners need to be able to identify these associations and learn to work with them.

Finally, we can glean some insight into how these challenges might be overcome. The aid sector doesn't have a Michael Moore or a Damon Gameau to start a more evidence-based discussion around aid ineffectiveness, and even if it did this might not be the answer. In the current populist climate, the effect might be to exacerbate scepticism in the efficacy of poverty-reduction efforts to date. Instead, those within the system need tools to better diagnose the various motivations that underpin aid flows, anticipate the consequences that might follow, and from there identify where the best development opportunities lie. In other words, we don't want to get the product off the shelf, but we need to learn to read the label in order to know what we're getting and how to use it most effectively.

This chapter discusses the evolution of modern development aid, defined as the transfer of resources, provision of goods and services or technical assistance (including military assistance) either bilaterally – from donor States to beneficiary States, or multilaterally – from one or more governments to one or more intermediaries.[1] For readability, the terms foreign aid/assistance and development aid/assistance will be used interchangeably. Likewise, I refer, in broad terms, to the "development sector" which, for the purposes of this chapter denotes development and humanitarian assistance agencies, international non-governmental organisations and civil society.

2.1 Myth 1: development aid is provided strictly for altruistic reasons

> Foreign aid is a method by which the US maintains a position of influence and control around the world and sustains a good many countries which would definitely collapse or pass into the communist soviet bloc.
>
> US President Kennedy (1961)

In the introduction to this book, it was posited that a number of myths were preventing development aid from being used as effectively as it might be. A first myth is that when donors allocate aid, the intention is to fight underdevelopment and its manifestations. The evidence – and it is very robust – is that aid is allocated, principally, to achieve foreign policy objectives, whether these be economic, security or diplomacy related. This is not to say that aid agendas necessarily exclude beneficial development outcomes, nor that aid allocations never produce them. However such gains are more likely to be a sub-outcome, a means to a parallel end, or otherwise tied to a broader objective that may or may not be related to the aid subject.

This disconnect between the goals of statecraft and development are observable throughout the history of modern aid programming. The Marshall Plan – which is often held up as the blueprint of development assistance – outlined a USD12 billion package (USD129 billion in today's terms) of financial and in-kind support provided by the United States (US) to the countries in Western Europe devastated by World War II. This endeavour was so successful that it is easy to forget how it was also the driving force behind a second wave of industrialisation and a shuffling in the ranks of global power holders. By expanding free market institutions and tying aid to the purchase of domestically produced goods and technical capacity, the US granted itself both an expanded product line to trade and a set of high-growth markets to trade with. Perhaps most importantly, as architect and benefactor of the Plan, the US cemented its image as an emerging geopolitical superpower.

Moving into the Cold War, the US unabashedly marketed foreign aid as the vehicle by which poor States would be transformed to protect against the spread of communism.[2] As indicated in President Nixon's 1968 statement "Let us remember that the main purpose of aid is not to help other nations but to help ourselves", none of this was particularly controversial. In universities, measuring how effectively aid disbursements were at realising benefactor policy goals was an "in vogue" area of research.[3]

Much has changed. We no longer use terms like "uncivilised populations" and "Western tutelage". Likewise, donors reassure constituencies that their tax dollars are used to fight worthy causes while academics study aid effectiveness, and when aid money is grossly misappropriated, it is headline news.

But the goal posts haven't shifted, which begs a question about the need for this smokescreen. Part of the explanation is sensibility; we all like the idea that rich countries are reallocating some of their wealth to fight global challenges. It also reflects an increased complexity in how the development sector thinks about poverty. It is understood, for example, that chronic marginalisation stokes extremism, and that strong health measures are imperative in preventing infectious diseases from becoming global pandemics. Sometimes these connections are obscure, which can make it difficult to identify where donor goals end and development goals begin. But rest assured, Ethiopia being the donor community's flavour of the month is not solely due to the humanitarian crisis evolving in Tigray. The country was already on the radar due to its manufacturing potential, the risk it poses for unregulated migration, and its geopolitical significance as a Christian bulwark against a geographic arc of Islam in northern Africa.

These points are not made to attribute blame or expose donors as self-serving or deceptive. Indeed, there is nothing particularly malign about donors allocating funds towards purposes that benefit them, directly or indirectly. And to reiterate, it is not that there is never an alignment between the strategic goal of aid and poverty reduction or other positive ends. It may be that an aid package is broadly designed to bolster security or trade cooperation but is composed of products that are undeniably beneficial for the recipient population generally like education or health. But we should not be confused. The evidence is very strong: strategic relationships predict aid flows, not development goals nor development needs.[4]

This is a critical distinction, and not discussing it has consolidated a perception that aid is, or should be, allocated in furtherance of human development goals. In turn, this is detracting from how effective it can be. It is clear that aid is most impactful when certain institutional characteristics and policy conditions are in place in the recipient country. If aid is allocated irrespective of the prerequisites that determine impact, the logical consequence is that at least some of this aid will be wasted. Moreover, there may be opportunities where aid has the potential for high impact that are being overlooked. It's akin to the marketing firms duping customers into buying sugar-laden dairy products by labelling them "fat free"; if we want to eat healthier, the lesson is to know how to read the fine print.

2.2 Myth 2: recipient states always channel aid into poverty reduction

Having read Chapter 1, the second myth – that governments benefiting from aid use it strictly for development purposes – should be easier digest. It's a crude analogy, but using aid money to combat poverty has limited utility. If poverty ends, then the aid flows are likely to dry up. Recipient governments are also savvy. If donors are giving aid for strategic ends, then development outcomes will not be their principal reference point. This means that they are unlikely to enforce conditions or withdraw aid if goals are not met.[5] Sceptics need only look to the failed experiments with aid conditionality to see that there is some truth to this.

This creates challenges for well-intentioned recipient governments, and opportunities for predatory ones. Without a robust system to guarantee donors value for money, even the most committed recipient states will struggle to turn aid money into development outcomes. As we established in Chapter 1, it's just not that easy.

For the rest, with few incentives to use aid monies properly, far more interesting purposes rise to the surface. Haiti did not fall to communism, but the USD1.27 billion provided in foreign aid during the Duvalier reign certainly did not do much to benefit the people. By the time then-President Jean-Claude Duvalier left on a US Air Force transport plane to exile in France in 1986, it was estimated that he had expropriated wealth valued in the hundreds of millions. Much the same can be said for the USD9.3 billion the international community channelled to Zaire (now the Democratic Republic of Congo) between 1975 and 1997, or the aid provided to Zimbabwe which, under Mugabe's rule, went from resource-rich agricultural producer to a failed state battling mass unemployment, uncontrollable inflation and food insecurity.[6]

2.3 Myth 1 + myth 2 = a principal-agent problem

So far, the case for foreign aid is not looking good. Beyond wasted funds and missed opportunities, aid may even play a more insidious role by helping authoritarian leaders profit and stay in power.[7] But we have overlooked one critical player: the world body mandated to oversee development outcomes. In 1945, 50 nations signed the Charter of the United Nations (UN) to further international peace and security, cooperate to solve economic and humanitarian challenges, and promote human rights and fundamental freedoms. The context leading up to this was immensely important. After six years of war and 60 million deaths, people from all socio-economic ranks were united in a shared sense of loss, camaraderie and confidence that right had won out over fascism. Against this backdrop, the egalitarian values that the war was ultimately fought over sat at the fore, allowing power holders to embrace the idea that all countries – irrespective of wealth or military prowess – had an equal stake, and thus deserved an equal say, in matters of global governance.

Today membership stands at 193 States, making it the world's largest international organisation. Wherever one sits on the political spectrum (and believes about what aid can or cannot achieve), the UN's existence and longevity is undeniably one of humanity's best wins of the last century.

The UN is made up of individual agencies mandated to promote certain goals, from economic development to human rights and gender equality. They work alongside international non-government organisations (INGOs) – which in many cases are larger and more powerful than individual UN agencies – and national organisations, which will be referred to as Community Service Organisations (CSOs).

These organisations play a critical role in the development sector by acting as the agents of donors. Remember, donors are also governments and they have their own countries to run. Not only is it more efficient to enlist specialists to administer aid monies, but the legacies of colonialism make direct implementation less politically palatable.

In theory, these agents *should* be able to overcome some of the problems that stem from myth 1 and myth 2. The idea behind the one country–one vote rule was precisely that decision-making would not be swayed by individual governments or vested interests. But life is not that kind. Together, these myths create what is known in economics as a principal-agent misallocation problem.

For a moment, let's think of the world as a huge private sector market-place. In free market relations, there is a seller (a company), consumers (you and me) and principals (company shareholders). The seller needs to offer consumers a sound product. If they don't – the product is overpriced, defective or lacks utility – this is quickly reflected in decreased sales. This sends a signal to the principals, who call for quick action. Sellers react purposefully and efficiently because the principals control their remuneration and job security.

The development sector is composed of a similar set of players. Think of donors as the principals. They contract UN agencies, INGOs and CSOs to "sell" their products (poverty reduction programs) to consumers – poor populations in beneficiary countries. Readers should have picked up why the aid sector does not work with the self-regulating efficiency of private markets. There are two flaws, and they are fatally wedded to each other.

First, remember that donors are not actually selling poverty reduction. They are after a different reward, whether this is trade links, military cooperation or diplomacy. Second, the beneficiary recipients aren't actually buying it. This makes sense as they can't pay for it anyway, but it also means that they cannot signal back to the principal, or even the seller, if the product they are receiving does not meet their needs. Recipient populations cannot fire an implementing agency, nor can they take their business elsewhere. This puts an ironic spin on calls for reducing duplication in service provision; indeed, it might be argued that greater competition – which implies more players rather than less – is actually what is needed.

How these flaws are connected is the jackpot. Even if beneficiary populations could route their views back to sellers, "feedback works only if some-one listens".[8] In this case, the principals are not listening – at least not in the way that they need to be. This absence of an effective accountability loop is arguably the principal factor driving aid ineffectiveness. And while each of these market failures could be dealt with in isolation, the way they reinforce each other makes the situation a whole lot more complicated.

Admittedly, this all sounds quite preposterous. How could the aid sector be stuck in such a quagmire, and still have grown into a billion-dollar industry? During the research for this book, I tried putting this hypothesis to a range of development stakeholders – mainly senior UN retirees. It was by no means a scientific process, but their responses were insightful, and worth discussing. They fitted neatly into two categories. Most pointed out that the sector has a safeguarding system for exactly this purpose: laborious, highly developed rules for project approval, monitoring and evaluation that govern funds allocation, disbursement and reporting. Others pointed to what can best be described as a system of internal checks and balances – an unwritten code of practice based on accumulated institutional knowledge. Let's play devil's advocate and examine the evidence around both of these arguments.

2.4 Check and balance 1: rules for project selection, monitoring and evaluation

The aid sector isn't the first to encounter the feedback loop problem. It is studied in public sector management, as a trade-off in tenured academic positions, as well as a structural deficit in rent-based economies. The broad conclusion is that when there is no market mechanism to signal how well sellers are doing their job, a proxy needs to be set in place, coupled with incentives to encourage the uptake of this information.

Some of the most insightful research into how these mechanisms work comes from Mark Buntaine. He has investigated the extent to which evaluations encourage programmatic selectivity (in layman's terms, better decision-making) in institutions such as the World Bank. His conclusion is that they don't. When devising new programmes, managers tend to draw upon their own experiences and rarely look to observable data or other lessons generated from evaluations. Where they do, internalisation is limited and geared towards lessons that can be easily reconciled with their current trajectory.[9]

When presented with this evidence, managers explain that this is usually because evaluations are backwards looking and there is a disconnect between lessons learned and current decision-making. There is little doubt that this is genuine, but there may be something more to the story. Behavioural psychologists think that it may be part of our hardwiring. Aligning retrospective analysis with forward-looking problem solving requires disproportionate brain effort vis-à-vis the anticipated reward. We don't need to understand the fine mechanics of this. In a nutshell, what it means is that it is quite difficult for humans to voluntarily absorb new learning that may send them down a different pathway than the one they are already on, or are inclined towards. We will internalise just enough to sustain or reinforce our beliefs; anything more than this and incentives are required.[10]

The literature has much to say about the trade-offs between positive incentives – career, financial or leisure rewards, and negative incentives – oversight, approvals processes and sanctions. These insights have important lessons for institutional reform, which we will return to later, but for now the takeaway is that non-profit sectors, which are more risk adverse, tend to favour negative incentives. Examples include approval processes that require managers to demonstrate how and where the results of past evaluations are integrated into new programming decisions. While these types of controls tend to be costly and detract from innovation, they do minimise the risk of large-scale errors in programming. But there are two problems with this approach to quality control that aid organisations are yet to completely overcome. First, incentives (positive or negative) are only as strong as their weakest link, and second, weak incentives tend to get crowded out by stronger ones.

2.4.1 *The weakest link problem*

An important flaw in the UN organisational architecture is that the one country–one vote principle doesn't reflect how most agencies operate and make decisions. The funding modalities set out in article 17–18 of the Charter of the United Nations (1945) require that countries contribute funds based on their capacity to pay, a modality referred to as "assessed contributions". The theory is that this allows the organisation to do its work, but without giving any country an advantage in terms of influence. This distinguishes UN organisations from International Financial Institutions (IFIs), such as the World Bank and the International Monetary Fund, which give greater control to the countries that contribute the most to operational costs. Assessed contributions, however, only fund the original organs established by the Charter – the General Assembly, Security Council, Economic and Social Council, International Court of Justice, Trusteeship Council and the Secretariat. Agencies such as UNHCR, UNDP, UNICEF and WFP receive a small amount of assessed contributions to cover administrative expenses, but the vast majority of their budgets come from voluntary contributions made by individual donors. These agencies are highly reliant on the hands that feed them, and this gives donors a great deal of influence over their operations. One convention is that a senior executive position is reserved for a national of a key donor: UNHCR's Deputy High Commissioner is always American, while the head of OCHA is traditionally granted to a Briton. It is no different with large INGOs; their management structure reflects the make-up and strategic objectives of key donors.

It is not to say that the donors contributing to these agencies do not care about effectiveness, and they certainly do not want to see wastage. But they definitely drive the types of interventions they care about and discourage the ones they don't. A widely cited example is how agencies reliant on US funding find it difficult to run projects around family planning that promote condom use, despite the evidence that this is impactful in reducing unwanted pregnancy and sexual disease transmission, including HIV/AIDs. Agencies have learned to play by these rules. Indeed, large donors can and do disrupt operations by withholding funds.[11]

Buntaine provides an insightful example from the World Bank. Since the 1990s, governments have come under increasing pressure – from their con-stituencies as well as geopolitically – to take actions that demonstrate their commitment to environmental protection. At the Bank, one result was donors encouraging an increase in environment-improving projects, with a particular preference for projects generating global public goods, such as emission reductions. For donors, this was strategic. Financing a clean energy project in Senegal, for example, might be a more efficient means of placat-ing voters or meeting international obligations compared to domestic regu-latory reform, which might increase taxpayer energy costs or generate other "messy" political externalities.[12]

A challenge in garnering support for such projects was that borrowing countries, unsurprisingly, preferred initiatives more aligned with their interests. Bank staff thus needed to do some convincing by structuring loans around different products – some of which met the needs of donors and some of the borrower. What happened next needs little spelling out. Where local benefits are low, borrowing countries are less invested, they have less incentive to implement projects well, and the outcomes are poor. This is not just an anecdotal or observational conclusion; Buntaine found that these loans performed badly compared to other portfolio products.

The most interesting finding though is that bad performance doesn't seem to matter. Because donors like these projects, they had limited interest in negative evaluation data. Even when they did receive it, they tended not to act. Buntaine found no correlation between continuity in lending and environmental performance. In short, because donors weren't solely concerned about outcomes, staff had reduced incentive to take into account information on performance. With nothing to interrupt the cycle, lessons were not fed up the information chain, projects were refinanced and mistakes were repeated. His conclusion is damning: because the system is geared away from promoting selectivity, it is not a sound model for facilitating environmental global public goods in a cost-effective manner.[13]

For readers who are skeptical to carry over findings from IFIs to the development sector, let's try another example. Food aid has played a longstanding and powerful role in development, as a tool to prevent large-scale casualties in times of famine or disaster, through to fighting child malnutrition and, indirectly, non-communicable disease. Up until the turn of the century, almost all food aid was provided in-kind, and principally from the US, Canada and Europe. This worked well for these donors; they were able to dispose of excess food and pay their "aid bill" at the same time. Other times, food would be sold, but at discounted rates.

Evidence that food aid – particularly the "dumping" of highly subsidised food products onto local markets – was negatively impacting local agricultural productivity and exacerbating longer-term food insecurity started to circulate as early as the 1950s. It took until the 2000s, however, for these messages to impact practice. Europe, in particular, has shifted away from in-kind food aid, preferring to purchase locally or augment domestic production. This said, 75 percent of the World Food Programme's support still runs through traditional mechanisms. Moreover, to the extent that practices are changing, this is less donor enlightenment than it is because donors' countries found a more astute means to dispose of surplus grain – the production of biofuels.[14] We return to this curiosity in Chapter 5.

2.4.2 The crowding-out problem

In addition to the weakest link problem, a further issue with incentives is that there are many of them flying around, and not all in the same direction.

In practice, even when oversight requirements and approvals processes feed lessons back into programming, they may be weakened or cancelled out by counter-incentives. Prestige, career advancement and norms around budget replenishment all operate to dissuade against finding (and thus perhaps having to report) negative outcomes about performance.

The IFI sector provides another powerful example. Alongside donor pressure to program in certain areas sits the "approval imperative" – a term used to denote how staff are evaluated and promoted based on the number and size of loans they issue (as opposed to their success in managing these loans). These same dynamics – disbursements acting as a proxy for outcomes – have been observed in donor agencies and (albeit to a lesser extent) in multilateral development agencies.[15] Certainly, few could deny that expending one's budget before the end of the accounting period is one of the tools used to ensure funding continuity.

The upshot is that while incentives are effective for overcoming what is a general aversion to upwards learning, the ones that development agencies have set in place are weak, which allows them to be crowded out by other, more potent, incentives. This can morph into organisational norms that – implicitly or explicitly – devalue information uptake and learning. The lynchpin seems to be leadership. Indeed, where rigorous evaluation has the potential to challenge a manager's preferred mode of action, or compromise their reputation, career prospects or ambit of responsibility, they will under-invest in it and/or undermine its worthiness to the extent that institutional culture will allow. Over time, these norms become entrenched and operate in a self-reinforcing manner that dissuades self-learning. The outcome: projects are driven less by evidence and more by "best practices", which are transplanted between projects as a tool to quickly mobilise resources, while poor impact may be explained as a capacity issue that can only be addressed through bigger budgets and broader programs.[16]

2.5 Check and balance 2: organisational culture

The second idea my interviewees offered to explain how development agencies overcome the principal-agent conundrum was a form of accountability embedded within institutional culture. They were referring to a documented perception that exists within parts of the sector that development work gets something akin to a "free pass" – that fewer controls or incentives are needed because of something to do with who they are or what their work represents.

The difficulty is that altruism is not a particularly good descriptive when applied to the development and humanitarian sectors as a whole. This is not intended to make practitioners bristle, and I appreciate that many enter the sector for philanthropic reasons and make enormous sacrifices. I know many such people, and they fight the good fights. But this is not everyone. Working in the development sector is appealing for a range of reasons, and this means that it attracts a variety of people. For those not interested in the demands and culture of the private sector, the packages offered have many advantages in terms of salary and benefits. For adrenalin junkies, they get a front seat as pages of history are written. And for those who find rewards in travel, culture and diversity, work can seem more like a privilege than an obligation. I see parts of myself and my friends in each of these archetypes.

The altruism explanation is also incompatible with how most individuals end up working in the sector. The national diversity that currently exists within UN agencies and INGOs (although far from sufficient) has been an accumulative process. Retired staff interviewed for this book – many now in their 80s – recalled when this was not case, and how difficult it was to get work done without local language skills, knowledge of cultural or political norms, or a way to get the ear of local powerholders. The answer was local recruitment. But this wasn't based on development expertise or commitment to UN values. It was, and to an extent still is, about an individual's ability to get that very important component of the job done; this meant a solid command of English (or French or Spanish depending on where you are) and political connections. Commitment to humanist values may have been considered an advantage, they posited, but it would not have been determinative. Over time, those locally recruited staff who performed well have made their way up through the ranks. This is by no means a complete explanation of the sector's current staffing composition, but it is an important one.

There is also nothing malign about this. Agencies should hire, promote and retain staff according to their ability to do the job. In fact, the idea that staff will self-regulate without incentives or accountability controls because they are morally committed to a cause is wrong-headed. Few would hire a hedge fund manager based on their personal feelings about wealth accumulation in the very rich, and then not even check in to see if they were performing well. Even in health care, a profession that is strongly and effectively regulated by its Hippocratic Oath, external controls are considered essential – society has learned that ideals are just not enough.

These are uncomfortable ideas. That aid workers represent the moral centre of development is a long-standing norm that has become embedded in institutional culture and staff self-identity.[17] But the idea needs to be challenged, because like the other myths, this one is preventing organisations from doing better. Human development is too important to be giving out free passes and hoping that staff dedication can cut through the significant, practical barriers outlined in this chapter.

2.6 Assembling the pieces: how political economy limits the utility of aid

The takeaway from this chapter is that if human development wasn't hard enough already, the inner workings of the aid sector are making the job even harder. The political imperatives underpinning donor strategies mean that there is no easy or predictable relationship between the ostensible goals of foreign aid, and the outcomes that result. Donors, agencies and beneficiaries are connected through a web of complex relationships determined by incentives that do not always align, and sometimes work at cross-purposes. As a consequence, the evaluation and monitoring systems set in place to ensure impact and efficiency do not work as robustly as they should. In the worst case, together these dynamics operate to mask programmatic failure, prevent upwards learning, discourage innovation, and create opportunities for elite capture.

This is not to say that all programs of foreign aid fail. Where interests align – fully or even partially – important gains can accrue. One need only look to the advances made in communicable disease prevention, agricultural productivity and girls' access to education. But it is important to push back on the assumption that aid, simply because it is aid, or because it is being given by a rich country to a poor country, must be doing good. It is these types of correlations that have prevented the critical interrogation needed for the aid sector to course correct.

From a practitioner's vantage point, these connections are often obscure and thus remain undiscussed. As one field worker interviewed for this book observed, "How would I know if the donor has some complicated higher strategy in play? And to the extent that I have the money I need to run my project, what does this matter?"[18] She makes a fair point, so let's bring together the key points raised in this chapter, and summarise where and how the politics behind aid flows can limit its utility as a tool in human development.

First are the outcomes that are less damaging than they are distasteful. For example, where aid is tied to the purchase of donor-produced goods and services, routing much of the benefit back to the country of origin. Certainly, the practice of multilateral aid-tying is on the decline (from around 85 percent in the 1970s to 15 percent today), thanks largely to the efforts of the OECD. Bilateral aid, however, has not followed such trends. Some empirical studies suggest that 10–20 percent of aid reaches its target.[19] Of course not all of this is due to aid-tying; another tranche gets lost in multiple layers of subcontracting, and in the worst cases aid monies are expropriated by corrupt officials.[20]

Political objectives also lead to missed opportunities. Buntaine provided insightful examples of how donors' penchant for climate-enhancing activities have resulted in poorly performing projects being continued, and even up-scaled. This kind of preference is exercised quite regularly. Many practitioners will have had experience with a donor that is inclined to channel money to their program, so long as it is spent in a certain way, for example to contribute to climate or gender goals. The result might be that UNHCR makes better use of solar lighting in refugee camps, or UNICEF builds more toilets in schools. No one is going to say that these works are not beneficial; lighting makes the routine activities of vulnerable groups safer, and in a more energy-efficient manner, while toilets greatly impact the number of girls who remain in education following menstruation. But donor money buying "good stuff" is very different from the execution of a carefully crafted, sequentially executed development strategy.

A more relatable example is perhaps the large packages of development assistance provided to refugee host states at the height of the so-called European migration crisis in 2016–2017. Turkey did particularly well: it secured €6 billion in grants and loans, access to Schengen visas for its citizens and moved one step closer to EU membership. There is no doubt that Turkey was facing complex development challenges, and that these were exacerbated by its hosting of 3.6 million refugees. But it is equally clear that this aid package had neither the country's development nor refugee welfare at its centre; it was a deal made to curtail the flow of unauthorised arrivals in Europe. This is not foreign aid facilitating human development solutions – it is the tail wagging the dog.

The worst outcomes tend to result when aid is a response to geopolitical events or public opinion. Retrospective inquiries into the efficacy of the humanitarian community's handling of the Ebola epidemic in 2013 indicate that experts foresaw the disease's potential human cost and raised the alarm relatively early. But a comprehensive response was delayed, meaning that the window to control the spread of the virus quickly closed, leaving a much larger problem to be dealt with. It seems that donors pushed back on these early warnings as alarmist; it was only when images of bodies reached Western screens that resources began to flow, attention became focused and evasive action commenced. Criticism of the COVID-19 pandemic response suggests that donors' tendency to act based on visual cues or existential threats remain an obstacle to more timely and efficient responses. Unfortunately, the missteps did not end here. Then–US President Donald Trump's de-funding of the World Health Organization in an effort to deflect attention away from a bungled early response shows that there is little to prevent political ambition giving way to actions that damage not only developing countries but the entire international community. These types of events have caused many to question whether aid (as long as it remains a political tool used to profit, insure, reward and punish) can ever do good.

2.7 Conclusion: the Tsunami of forces driving aid ineffectiveness approaches a crossroads

While the foreign policy aspects of aid provision clearly do undermine its potency as a tool for human development, hoisting all the blame onto "politics" is neither constructive nor completely fair. The programmatic agencies that make up the development sector also play a role. Criticisms that the sector is overly large, often inefficient and – at times – corrupt, are not unjustified. As Bill Easterly explains, an excessive number of actors sharing responsibility for broad development goals allow wins to be claimed by everyone and used as justification for more aid, while failures are easily blamed on insufficient resources, local incapacity or the complex cause-and-effect relationships underpinning development processes.[21]

But the system's Achilles heel – as we have learned in this chapter – is that it is not set up to self-learn. With few incentives to innovate or make use of evidence, plus the absence of a feedback loop connecting delivery to outcomes, it is very hard to know if programs are delivering as they should or how they could be better. In short, the sector is treading water rather than moving forward, and even for the most dedicated and well-intentioned staff, they are swimming upstream.[22]

Moreover, what the system needs to do to course correct, it cannot. This is not just because the tools are not available, but because self-learning involves risk, experimentation, and transparent discussions about failure. In a context of increased scrutiny, this is not something that agencies – which are already dependent on donors and competing fervently for funds – can do well. The risk of disaster far outweighs the potential for a development breakthrough. Instead, agencies have become increasingly risk adverse and chameleon, creating a vicious cycle of over-promising and under-delivering. To draw on the work of Nasim Taleb, the development sector is strong, but fragile. It is strong insofar as it is large, heavily resourced and – despite the criticism – no one believes it will be replaced any time soon. But it is fragile insofar as it lacks the type of robust, self-sustaining raison d'etre that can only come from repeated experiences of failure, learning and corrective adjustment.

Over the course of modern aid, this problem has built upon itself to a point where it is too obvious to be ignored, sparking a growing debate around aid effectiveness. A high-water mark was reached in 2000, when a World Bank Report issued a bold statement that captured something many had suspected for decades: "Despite the billions of dollars spent on development assistance each year, there is still very little known about the actual impact of projects on the poor".[23] These sentiments echoed around the sector, getting more critical over time. The following excerpt from a report into aid effectiveness commissioned by the Netherlands sums this up well:

> It can be stated with confidence that the rate of change in improving the quality of concepts and policies ... has significantly outpaced the rate of change in improving the quality of programming in these environments. For example, a series of conversations with over 6000 people on the receiving end of aid across a range of (largely) fragile states echoed – as recently as 2012 – many of the deficiencies in international development practice that have been known for years. In other words, the hard won insights into the operating realities of fragility are much better reflected in international policy than they are in international programming. The is partially the result of the vested interests and routine behaviours/procedures of

existing development actors (bilateral and multilateral): policy changes are relatively easy to realise while administrative and behavioural changes are much more difficult to accomplish.[24]

In an effort to right the situation, in 2005 more than 100 developed and developing countries signed the Paris Declaration on Aid Effectiveness. Comprising five principles and 56 partnership commitments, the Declaration focused on promoting local ownership (developing countries setting their own development agendas and donor states aligning their support with such strategies); heightening efficiency through a more coordinated and results-focused approach; and improving accountability for development outcomes on the part of both donor and recipient countries.

Needless to say, for all the reasons discussed in this chapter, the Paris Declaration has had limited impact. It offered nothing to counterbalance the political ends driving aid allocations, overcome the principal-agent conundrum or mandate a learning culture.

It may be that the scholars from Chapter 1 were right, and that the big change that needs to happen is a fundamental reform of the aid sector itself. And perhaps a crossroads has been reached. Donors, academics, civil society and staff from within the sector are all beginning to demand change. Some States are beginning to act.

In 2006, then–Secretary of State Condoleezza Rice announced that a gradual process of integrating the US development agency – USAID – into the State Department had commenced with a view to a better linking of foreign policy and foreign aid with defense priorities. These ideas were quickly operationalised. In 2007, a unified combatant command named AFRICOM was launched. Headed by a military leader and with a deputy appointed by the Department of State, its goal was to promote stabilisation in fragile collapsed states through transformational development strategy and humanitarian assistance. According to Picard and Buss, this shift sent a clear message: "[T]hat anti-poverty funds were ineffective and should be replaced by funding that promotes strategic and political interests".[25]

This triangulation of diplomacy, security and foreign aid soon spread to other lead donor states. On 17 June 2020, Prime Minister Boris Johnson announced that DFID would merge with a new Foreign, Commonwealth and Development Office, following in the footsteps of Australia, Canada, Denmark and Norway. This changed climate spells new challenges for the aid sector. It is likely that the coming decades will see more military involvement in humanitarian and development programming, a greater focus on governance and security issues, and a decline in programming around economic and social development.

The message for the development community of practice is that if change is going to happen, it needs to happen now. Business as usual will lead to a consolidation of aid into foreign policy and security goals, making progress towards inclusive human development even harder.

Key to any strategy will be a better understanding of the system we have and what can be done with it. To be clear, if donor states were serious about making development aid work, they would have done so. There is a very easy fix. They would allocate aid based on good performance and take it away for bad performance, and they would repair the principal agent problem by enforcing evaluation and fixing the incentive system.[26] But they haven't, and this is not going to change anytime soon. Instead of ignoring it, pretending it's not true, or apportioning blame, it's time to learn to dance with the system.

While it may sound counter intuitive, the idea that development outcomes play second fiddle to donor strategic goals needs to become part of the strategy for realising human development goals. You see, it's not that donors do not care about development outcomes, they just care about *other things more*. And this is where the answer lies.

The next chapter sets out a framework for how to navigate the development system to more easily identify the moments and spaces where positive outcomes can accrue. One change is to better capitalise on situations where the interests of donors and recipient states align with development imperatives. Another is for actors within the sector – particularly middle managers – to exploit system dynamics to encourage innovation, competition and synergies. None of this should imply lifting a lid on the messy inner workings of development sector practices – at the present time this would likely do more harm than good. But we do need to learn from the Mike Moore and Damon Gameaus of the world. Only with a better reading of "development aid labels" can we know what's really inside, and the potential it actually holds.

Notes

1 L. Picard and T. Buss *A Fragile Balance: Re-examining the History of Foreign Aid, Security, and Diplomacy*, Lynne Rienner Publishers (2009) 5–6.

2 L. Picard and T. Buss *A Fragile Balance: Re-examining the History of Foreign Aid, Security, and Diplomacy*, Lynne Rienner Publishers (2009) 75–76, 84–85; W. Easterly *The White Man's Burden: Why the West's Efforts to Aid the Rest Have Done So Much Harm and So Little Good*, Penguin Press (2006) 25–25.

3 M. Buntaine *Giving Aid Effectively: The Politics of Environmental Performance and Selectivity at Multilateral Development Banks*, Oxford University Press (2016) 25–30.

4 M. Buntaine *Giving Aid Effectively: The Politics of Environmental Performance and Selectivity at Multilateral Development Banks*, Oxford University Press (2016) 29–30.

5 A. Alesina and D. Dollar "Who Gives Foreign Aid to Whom and Why?" *Journal of Economic Growth* 5 (2000) 33–63.

6 T. Buss *Haiti in the Balance: Why Foreign Aid has Failed and What We Can Do About It* Brookings Institution Press (2008); L. Picard and T. Buss *A Fragile Balance: Re-examining the History of Foreign Aid, Security, and Diplomacy*, Lynne Rienner Publishers (2009) 238.

7 M. Buntaine *Giving Aid Effectively: The Politics of Environmental Performance and Selectivity at Multilateral Development Banks*, Oxford University Press

(2016) 215; W. Easterly *The White Man's Burden: Why the West's Efforts to Aid the Rest Have Done So Much Harm and So Little Good*, Penguin Press (2006) 132–133.

8   W. Easterly *The White Man's Burden: Why the West's Efforts to Aid the Rest Have Done So Much Harm and So Little Good*, Penguin Press (2006) 15–16, 167–171.

9   M. Buntaine *Giving Aid Effectively: The Politics of Environmental Performance and Selectivity at Multilateral Development Banks*, Oxford University Press (2016) 5, 36–41, 110–114, 177–178.

10 M. Buntaine *Giving Aid Effectively: The Politics of Environmental Performance and Selectivity at Multilateral Development Banks*, Oxford University Press (2016) 36, 66.

11 M. Buntaine *Giving Aid Effectively: The Politics of Environmental Performance and Selectivity at Multilateral Development Banks*, Oxford University Press (2016) 151–155, 64.

12 M. Buntaine *Giving Aid Effectively: The Politics of Environmental Performance and Selectivity at Multilateral Development Banks*, Oxford University Press (2016) 224, 145–146.

13 M. Buntaine *Giving Aid Effectively: The Politics of Environmental Performance and Selectivity at Multilateral Development Banks*, Oxford University Press (2016) 20–22, 147–160,179–181, 205–207.

14 F Mousseau "Food Aid or Food Sovereignty? Ending World Hunger in Our Time" The Oakland Institute (2005).

15 M. Buntaine *Giving Aid Effectively: The Politics of Environmental Performance and Selectivity at Multilateral Development Banks*, Oxford University Press (2016) 77, 156; L. Picard and T. Buss *A Fragile Balance: Re- examining the History of Foreign Aid, Security, and Diplomacy*, Lynne Rienner Publishers (2009) 198.

16 M. Buntaine *Giving Aid Effectively: The Politics of Environmental Performance and Selectivity at Multilateral Development Banks*, Oxford University Press (2016) 20, 46, 63, 142, 179.

17 G Hancock *Lords of Poverty*, Mandarin (1989) 79–82.

18 Interview dated 9 December 2020, notes on file with author.

19 D. Acemoglu and J. Robinson *Why Nations Fail: The Origins of Power, Prosperity and Poverty*, Random House (2012) 451–452. The positive trends in aid-tying are significant. According to Picard and Buss, from the 1970s through to the 1990s, 85 cents in each dollar of foreign aid allocated remained in the US either as a result of requirements due to technical assistance or purchase of US–produced aid supplies; in the early 90s 75 percent was going to US profit and non-profits, by the late 90s USAID was awarded 85 percent of contracts and grants to US organisations. By 2006, the OECD estimated that 41.7 percent of Official Development Assistance was untied; by 2017 this had risen to 83 percent.

20 M. Buntaine *Giving Aid Effectively: The Politics of Environmental Performance and Selectivity at Multilateral Development Banks*, Oxford University Press (2016) 52

21 W. Easterly *The White Man's Burden: Why the West's Efforts to Aid the Rest Have Done So Much Harm and So Little Good*, Penguin Press (2006) 171–172.

22 W. Easterly *The White Man's Burden: Why the West's Efforts to Aid the Rest Have Done So Much Harm and So Little Good*, Penguin Press (2006) 199.

23 J. Baker *Evaluating the Impact of Development Project's on Poverty: Handbook for Practitioner's, Directions in Development*, World Bank (2000); see further L. Picard and T. Buss *A Fragile Balance: Re-examining the History of Foreign Aid, Security, and Diplomacy*, Lynne Rienner Publishers (2009) 97–98, 131, 230.

24 *A Crisis of Confidence Competence and Capacity: Programming Advice for Strengthening Mali's Penal Chain*, IDLO and the Clingendael Institute (2015) 37.

25 L. Picard and T. Buss *A Fragile Balance: Re-examining the History of Foreign Aid, Security, and Diplomacy*, Lynne Rienner Publishers (2009) 269–271, 181.

26 M. Buntaine *Giving Aid Effectively: The Politics of Environmental Performance and Selectivity at Multilateral Development Banks*, Oxford University Press (2016) 26–27; W. Easterly *The White Man's Burden: Why the West's Efforts to Aid the Rest Have Done So Much Harm and So Little Good*, Penguin Press (2006) 369–370.

3

TOWARDS THE AID SECTOR
WE NEED

The previous chapter, admittedly, made for tough reading. It made a case that because aid flows along geopolitical lines, development opportunities principally benefit strategic partners as opposed to the governments that most need them, or intend to do good with them. One consequence is that the controls meant to ensure that development projects are devised and administered efficiently work imperfectly, at best. This has knock-on effects. Without strong incentives to build evidence, innovate or self-correct, the sector might be described as one that is fumbling through, as opposed to perfecting its course. This has not gone unnoticed by donors, academics and practitioners, who have grown increasingly sceptical about the efficacy of development programming.

There is nothing to suggest that the countries funding aid programs are likely to divert from their current approach. If anything, populism and an increasingly insular approach to development will further consolidate strategies that place national interests at the fore of their decision-making. Instead, it will be up to the development sector to find ways to work around these constraints and identify pockets of opportunity where positive development gains might accrue.

To this end, this chapter describes – not just the aid sector we need – but the steps needed to get there. But first let's hear from someone else. When I started teaching, I could only do so armed with a comprehensive set of lecture notes and visual aids. This caused a problem if my materials were forgotten or accidentally deleted. On one such occasion, as I frantically rebooted my laptop, I asked the class to come up with their own ideas on what an enabling policy environment for aid delivery might look like. One group submitted a quirky but beautifully insightful description of what they called "Aid Effectiveness-Land". Although quite a few in the group had worked in the foreign service and development sectors, I don't think any realised just how close their ideas hit the mark. I've reproduced a portion of their work below, with only a few tweaks and occasional ideas of my own.

Aid Effectiveness-Land is built around a working culture where thinking and knowledge are highly valued commodities. Managers

DOI: 10.4324/9781003376996-4

are not just given the time and space to read – it's an integral part of their job description. To support this, agencies have large, well-resourced research departments that – like the IMF and World Bank – publish in peer-reviewed academic journals. These departments are considered leaders within their organizations – not the underdogs. As a result, their findings quickly work their way into programming, and staff never find themselves alone in the cafeteria because someone is always looking to chew their ear.

Because delivering the best outcomes is a principal responsibility, agencies embrace innovation and the risk of failure that comes with it. Some have even adopted the Google model of allowing 20 percent of staff time to be allocated to staff-led "ideas" projects. To encourage this, managers tweaked incentive structures – heeding the lesson of the Industrial Revolution that innovation takes place only when inventors know they will be protected and rewarded. Of course, in development institutions, staff can't "own" their inventions, so they are compensated instead with prestige and career progression. Another lesson embraced was that the best inventions do not come pre-packaged. Ideas are generated, tinkered with, trialed – often shelved for a period – taken up by someone else, experimented with again, before finally, one rises to the top and is rolled out.

Managers particularly love ideas and innovation because they are non-rival goods and great multipliers of production. There are no turf battles over programming or beneficiaries, so when new ideas are stumbled upon, fellow agencies, INGOs and even CSOs freely try them out, sharing their wins and mistakes to feed into the making of a better product.

In Aid Effectiveness-Land, innovation, research and evaluation are comfortable bedfellows. Evaluations are scientifically rigorous; agencies regularly partner with academics, periodically engage independent evaluators for a fresh perspective, and raw data is made publicly available so that it can be further critiqued. Stapled to a corkboard someone has pinned a quote from the authors of the best seller "Freakonomics": "there is nothing like the sheer power of numbers to scrub away layers of confusion and contradiction". Every manager knows what a regression analysis is and someone on the team can run one and share the results in simple and accessible language.

Arguments around the ethics of randomised control trials are long resolved; a tough utilitarian approach is taken because learning sits at the top of everyone's agenda. Evaluation findings are brutally honest, so it's easy to see what works and what doesn't. But managers are smart – one bad experience doesn't preclude staff from acting on an idea again with a different iteration. Likewise, when something does work, it doesn't automatically become a "best practice". Negative evaluations are seen as highly contextu-alised, learning experiences. They are used to start conversations with donors, who don't see them as an excuse to cut funding, but to negotiate nuanced modifications in programming.

Through the culture of self-learning, agencies negotiated the tools and framework needed to do better work. Programming takes place under longer timeframes – around 10–15 years – because the evidence indicates that this is how long sustainable outcomes take to accrue. This was an easy sell after donors saw the evidence that carving up programming cycles was inhibiting long-term impact; after all, no one was asking for more money, just more security.

Along with longer time frames managers were also granted flex-ibility; the ability to pause, reflect, and change trajectory when needed. Over time, they became comfortable with "messiness", and this allowed them to better anticipate and exploit critical junctures. They also became more iterative, by investing more resources into understanding the nuances of the operating environment. It's fine that this knowledge doesn't fit easily into a log frame; everyone knows that over the long term there will be a payoff, even if it is not during the current programming cycle.

Because staff are more expert, they're better at designing sophis-ticated programs. Although mildly suspicious of "best practices", managers are constantly on the lookout for whether wins seen elsewhere might apply to their project, in some adapted form. But even with these advances, it is accepted that positive change will be incremental. Theories of change and log frames are from a bygone era; staff now use tools like power-systems analysis and differen-tial diagnoses to understand the complex and interlaced nature of development settings. Of course, they still have theories, but these are regularly challenged and updated; they are used more like a compass and map to find pathways through rough and unpredict-able terrain.

Finally, agencies have adopted a radically different definition of Value for Money. They still attach importance to quantifiable results, but knowledge outcomes and other non-visible outputs are equally prized. Staff enthusiastically engage in empowerment projects, for example, even though the results are harder to photo-graph and quantify on a spreadsheet. This was tough for donors, who now enjoy fewer marketing opportunities, and for some prac-titioners, as they were forced to give up sexy projects in lieu of more strategic ones. In short, we give out fewer branded school bags (sorry UNICEF) and build more roads.

All this was possible because we reset the goals posts for a more realistic view of what development aid can achieve. We know that aid alone cannot eliminate poverty. Only societies can do this, but aid can act as a force, along with free markets, to help push the process along. No longer under pressure to "fix", the sector is able to focus on more realistic goals like ending the most extreme forms of poverty, and bringing preventable disease under control.[1]

The workplace described above is not the workplace we have. Disruptors are not rewarded nor celebrated for their intellectual curiosity. Pressure to deliver tangible outcomes squeezes out any time for reading research or scholarly literature – this would likely be seen as self-indulgent and, if we are honest, a bit odd. At best, we catch snippets of learning from twitter, news feeds and opinion pieces. And we cringe at expressions like "embrace failure as a learning experience". Such ways of working are not realistic – it would be considered irresponsible to give donors any reason to cut scarce and highly sought-after funds.[2]

So how do we move from a culture where practitioners are too busy getting on with the job, to one where everyone is a "professor" of aid, committed to getting the right answers and armed with the tools to do so.

The idea that a changed aid landscape is long overdue has been proposed by many. As noted in Chapter 1, perhaps the one thing that Collier, Sachs, Easterly and the other great development minds agree on, is that the goals of development programming and how agencies' view their role, requires a fundamental rethink.[3] Where we are stuck seems to be how to make the transition. Most of the discussion about reform has focused on closing deficits in existing control systems and modifying institutional processes. Examples include tying project approval to proof that past information on outcomes has been integrated; altering rotation policies to promote accountability; or building local ownership over developing planning and execution. Although none of these recommendations are invalid, they are limited insofar as they overlook the wider political economy issues in play.

Other, more technical suggestions, are unlikely to yield impact of the magnitude required. There is evidence, for example, that managers are more likely to integrate lessons from past evaluations if that information is presented during the strategic planning and programme-design phases – the moments when managers are most open to changing their thinking. Modifying the format of evaluations and what content is emphasised, may also be impactful. Specifically, broad lessons gleaned from large (programme-level) operations have better uptake; likewise, having a small number of senior staff read a one-page executive summary as opposed to many junior staff reviewing an entire evaluation report. Even changing superficial details such as the name of the project that is the subject of an evaluation report so that it has more relevance to the reader's current decision-making or interests, makes a difference in how managers absorb and retain information.[4] All of this is important, but it makes for small gains.

In terms of what might spark change that is both realistic and sufficiently broad, the strongest clue comes from Buntaine, who readers will remember from Chapter 2. In the 1980s–1990s, the World Bank and the Asian Development Bank introduced units mandated to undertake environmental impact evaluation. These units were required to sign off on all projects before they could be rolled out. Risky projects were bogged down in approvals processes, which was costly (as project managers could not meet their lending targets) and reputationally damaging. To avoid this, staff started taking into account information generated about the past projects, and the number of "dirty projects" reduced quickly and dramatically.[5]

Buntaine's conclusion is fairly simple – better performance outcomes can be promoted by generating information on past performance *and* then integrating processes that make such information costly or prohibitive to ignore.[6] He's right of course. But I think he stumbled on something even more interesting. He notes that what sparked the creation of these environmental impact units was the Rio Summit, which took place in the wake of a series of projects that had ended in environmental calamity. The media reporting was savage, creating a storm of concern in donors and mounting political pressure. Suddenly, avoiding dirty projects became important to the principals, and because this mattered to them, controls were integrated into Bank processes and connected to their incentive systems. It worked like magic. But only because it mattered; after that the process took care of itself.

So perhaps the question is, in what circumstances do aid outcomes matter to donors, or can they be made to matter? And does it have to be donors, or could aid outcomes be made to matter to other stakeholders? Let's consider each of these possibilities in turn.

3.1 What matters to donors?

If the key to promoting better development outcomes is making them matter to donors, then a logical place to start is with what *already* matters: votes, avoiding crises, and (sometimes) geopolitical leadership.

Governments of all persuasions have an interest in the views and priorities of their constituencies. In democracies, it's how they get elected and stay in power. In non-democracies, leaders may be able to retain control irrespective, but keeping citizens placated is an integral part of the social contract.

It follows that if constituencies want their governments to resolve global problems, then this will figure among their priorities. Sweden's advances on gender equality have become part of citizens' identity and a symbol of national pride; this has carried over into the country's development strategies which prioritize women's empowerment and related goals. Norway doesn't particularly want to resettle refugees, but values its reputation as a generous and participatory international citizen, so it compensates through significant and liberal aid disbursements consistent with its size. And Canada may not be the largest of donors, but it enjoys a legacy of moral leadership that it exercises consistently and constructively.

This ethic is not unique to these select countries. The evidence is that a majority of voters in key donor states do care about global problems, but they lack in-depth understanding on the cause-and-effect relationships in play. Moreover, because they have few tools to gauge how effective their government's aid policies are, voters generally substitute volume as a proxy for success.[7] An added challenge is that voters – particularly those in large donor states – generally believe that their governments give far more than they actually do.[8] It is no wonder then, that when they hear about yet another aid scandals or displacement crisis, they signal back their frustration.

Together, this combination of weak insight and misinformation can drive donors to make unhelpful aid allocation decisions. The following chapter, for example, discusses how popular distaste for peacekeeping is not only misplaced, but that scale-backs are doing more to exacerbate inter-state conflict than contain it. Similarly, in Chapter 5, it is shown that burgeoning nationalism coupled with a misinterpretation of what drives violent extremism has perpetuated national policies that make us less safe in the long term.

Arguably, this could be turned around. Voters should care about development outcomes, if for no other reason than instability, conflict, rights abuses and poverty drive international crime, global disease and terrorism. Better insight into these correlations might encourage voters to demand better results. It follows that public sensitisation should be as much a part of development fundraising strategy as direct advocacy with donors.

At other times, it will be in a government's interest to play this liaison role, for example when an informed aid policy and requisite resource allocations are key to avoiding a domestic level crisis. When the Ebola and COVID-19 emergencies broke, it was not difficult to see that strengthening health infrastructure and capacity in affected countries and developing a vaccine that could bring the epidemic under control locally was in everyone's interests. Climate change and uncontrolled migration are equally areas where addressing problems in situ will be key to limiting the externalities that spill over to the developed world. Where these connections are obscure, the development sector might again play a role, by building evidence that governments can use to craft policy and communicate its logic to citizens.

A third thing that donors care about is global leadership. Every chief – even those in dysfunctional and draconian states – wants to look good in front of their peers and be offered a seat at the "popular kids" table. Such leadership will be key to solving collective action problems like food security and biodiversity, so the development sector must learn how to leverage it. The challenge is that such action is high risk, and rarely rewards leaders domestically – the returns are too disbursed and timeframe too distant.

This begs the question of what it takes for a leader to step up and take bold decisions, even in the absence of popular support? The US provides a salient example. In 1947, Secretary of State George Marshall delivered an iconic speech outlining the terms of his post-war European recovery plan, which he likened to a battle "against poverty, hunger and chaos".[9] Having read Chapter 1, we know that this was not the full story; the Marshall Plan was as much about economic opportunity and containing communism as it was altruistic. But it is remarkable how unconditional the plan was, and how unabashed Marshall was in highlighting this:

> It would neither be fitting nor efficacious for this government to draw up unilaterally a programme designed to place Europe on its feet economically. This is the business of the Europeans. The role of this country should consist of friendly aid.[10]

Equally remarkable was Marshall's transparency in asking that the American public trust that he knew best how to deal with the challenge in hand, despite the economic hardships being felt at home:

> The problem is one of such enormous complexity that the very mass of facts presented to the public by the press and radio make it exceedingly difficult for the man on the street to reach a clear appraisement of the situation. Furthermore, the people of this country are distant from the troubled areas of the earth and it is hard for them to comprehend the plight and consequent reactions of the long-suffering peoples[11]

Another standout moment came 20 years later when President Johnson launched his "war on poverty". These social justice reforms were provocative at the time, but ultimately responsible for unprecedented gains in poverty reduction for black and older Americans. What allowed Secretary Marshall and President Johnson to go against the grain was context.[12] In both 1947 and 1964, enthusiasm for and trust in the federal government was at an all-time high. Americans were euphoric that their leaders had delivered victory in World War II, and then pulled them into a period of unprecedented economic growth. Borrowing from Sachs "these epochal events were a great crucible of consensus building...",[13] and it was largely this communitarianism, that allowed these ground-breaking moments for development to take place.

The lesson for development practice is that global leadership does matter, but the moment has to be right. These moments cannot be manufactured, nor can they be depended on to deliver change when and in the forms that are needed. Practitioners can be ready, however, so that when the enabling conditions are present, development gains can be capitalised upon.

3.2 What matters to beneficiary governments?

Donors are not the only player for which aid "mattering" makes a difference. Beneficiary governments are also powerful players in influencing whether aid is – or is not – used for its intended purpose. In exercising this discretion, they will play to their interests, which are not too dissimilar from those described above. They will seek to keep citizens satisfied and avert domestic disaster. They also want to assert leadership on the global stage. The main difference is that constituent needs is not as strong a driver of government priorities, especially where alternatives such as wealth expropriation and power consolidation exist.

This said, when development does matter to them, leaders often go to great lengths to get it right. Turkey, Botswana and India are all examples of how the judicious use of foreign assistance can accelerate growth, reduce poverty and improve access to public goods.

Unfortunately, these experiences are more the exception than the rule. This has not escaped the attention of donors. While they may not give aid strictly or principally for human development, they also do not want to see it squandered or used for nefarious purposes. It's embarrassing when goods provided by taxpayers under the guise of development assistance end up being traded on open markets. When they are exchanged for drugs or guns, it's a scandal.

To avoid these situations, much thinking has been directed into how beneficiary governments might be encouraged, incentivised, or cajoled into committing to use aid prudently. This is a difficult topic to navigate; an education minister is unlikely to disclose to a donor or implementing agency that he would prefer to use aid monies to buy a dozen land cruisers than build a new school. It's easier to accept the money gratefully, engage in some creative bidding and smile naively when the school delivered looks more like a dilapidated corner store than a high-tech learning institution. After all, in high context environments, there are all sorts of reasons why aid programs fail. This places donors or a development agency in the awkward position of having to accuse a fellow government of expropriating funds, or accept a non-ideal project outcome. One senior manager interviewed for this book explained that even in the face of obvious funds misappropriation, non-continuation of a project into a second phase can be interpreted as akin to an accusation, making it almost impossible to even curb losses.[14] Indeed, it's these types of challenges that largely explain why experiments in aid conditionality have had limited success.

A first such experiment – known as the Washington Consensus – took place in the 1980s when international financial institutions introduced policies that predicated aid on recipient governments undertaking economic policy reforms. There is no reason to go into detail about the disasters that followed; interested readers can turn to the many books that have been written on the subject.[15] It is enough to note that for savvy governments, conditionality was a paper tiger that allowed them to accrue millions in aid without having to do very much differently at all. For the weak or diligent governments who did follow the rules, liberalise their markets and remove trade barriers, it was economically ruinous.

But while attempts to coerce governments into action was ineffective, so was relying on goodwill. In 2005, the Paris Declaration on Aid Effectiveness listed local ownership as a lead commitment.[16] The logic was sound – development aid was unduly influenced by outsider thinking, whereas strategies that were domestically conceived and implemented were more likely to respond to local needs, be perceived as legitimate and hence have greater impact and sustainability.[17] Operationalising the local ownership concept, however, proved complex.

The reality of development settings is that they rarely feature genuinely representative and transparent decision-making apparatus. Because of this, development actors devolving responsibility often became a highly politicised process resulting in an inadvertent selection of winners and losers.[18] The UN Transitional Administration in East Timor (UNTAET) – which was applauded at the time for embracing more of a partnership approach to development – learned this lesson early. UNTAET initially consulted through the National Council for Timorese Resistance (CNRT) – a coalition of pro-independence groups. Although this was a logical choice (and the only one for future president Xanana Gusmao), it vested CNRT with unwarranted political influence and, through the process, allowed individuals to advance their agendas and entrench their power.[19]

UNTAET was able to right this ship, largely due to the benevolence and leadership of figures such as Gusmao and his compatriot Jose Ramos-Horta. States that lacked such headship faired far worse. It was becoming clear that in the absence of political will, placing control over programs and budgets in the hands of local authorities was a sure-fire way to obstruct meaningful change. In Afghanistan, a "light footprint" approach was deemed appropriate, due to the country's uninterrupted sovereignty and desire to control rehabilitation and governance.[20] Key areas such as the rule of law, however, were not prioritised by the Afghan interim administration in either financial or programmatic terms, and programs were quickly embroiled in controversy.[21] Even larger dilemmas arose when local strategies contained elements that were incompatible with human rights and other international standards.

As frustrations increased, some donors began advocating a more balanced and pragmatic approach to local ownership. They opined that the principle should not be overstated for the sake of political correctness. Moreover, that development agencies should not shy away from their technical strengths, especially where it was a breakdown in local capacity that necessitated an aid relationship in the first place.[22] The US was the first to put its resources behind these ideas. In 2004, Millennium Challenge Corporation (MCC) was launched, mandated to work in partnership with competitively selected countries that demonstrated a commitment to good governance, economic freedom and investment in their citizens.

The takeaway from these experiments is that while the buy-in of recipient governments is critically important, it is very hard to manufacture. While the

MCC certainly represents the most evolved approach, as explored in the next chapter, it too has downsides and some believe that it has not lived up to expectations. What can be said with more certainty is that, as with donors, there will be moments where recipient state interests and aid goals line up. Again, we can't just wait for these junctures present themselves, but we should be able to recognize them, and step up when conditions for change are ripe.

3.3 Leveraging interests on the ground

In the search for how to get development outcomes to matter to key stakeholders, it is crucial to not overlook the group for which aid matters explicitly – beneficiaries. As discussed in Chapter 2, they have the strongest interest in aid being effective, but lack the feedback loops and power to demand it. The question is thus, not how to get them to care, but how to get their caring to count?

Augmenting the strength and influence of beneficiaries to bring on greater responsiveness in programming is not a particularly new idea. Indeed, when the limits of vesting broad powers in government stakeholders became apparent, the first response was to expand the target of local ownership policies to include this group. This made a lot of sense, perhaps even more than partnering with recipient governments. The commitment of beneficiaries is not in question – they are the uncontested winners of development advances. There is also a pragmatic logic. Beneficiaries understand their context, and this makes them the best architects of solutions that will work for them.[23] Where agencies have embraced these ideas, the results have been impressive. It was a group of young Jordanians who came up with the idea that it would be safer and more efficient for refugees living in their country to make purchases and transactions using iris scanning technology – an innovation that has since been operationalised by some of the largest humanitarian and development agencies.

This is not to imply that empowering beneficiaries as partners in development is a panacea. Power hierarchies and vested interests exist in all social subsets. So just like devolving responsibly to governments can result in winners and losers, the same can take place at the beneficiary level.[24] Translating policy into practice has also proven complicated. The evidence is that agencies tend to underestimate local innovation capacity, and more often than not pay lip service to partnering with them on development solutions. The form this takes is often subtle, including the language development practitioners use, through to their complicated and sometimes opaque bidding processes.[25]

More difficult to overcome is international practitioners' reticence to local engagement. In practice, these processes can be time consuming and frustrating, and they fly in the face of the generally unspoken belief that internationals already know the correct way forward.[26] These tensions are

48

exacerbated by risk aversion and pressure to meet performance targets. Evaluations of the security component of UN Transitional Assistance Mission in Kosovo found that locals *were* excluded from both planning and management. This was less about bias, however, than the fact that international police were being evaluated according to their ability to maintain law and order.[27]

The other way that development programming has worked to strengthen beneficiary power has been by supporting civil society. Such groups serve a range of functions from lobbying for policy reforms, through to acting as a check and balance on the work of the development sector and implementation of aid projects. The logic, again, cannot be slighted. Their vested interest in development outcomes makes them the perfect watchdogs.[28] Indeed, well-informed and politically savvy civil society action has been the force behind some of the most progressive and sustainable development achievements.

But there are limits. First, civil society can only exercise power when it has a voice, which is rarely the case in authoritarian or predatory states. Moreover, because their watchdog power lies in their ability to cause embarrassment, either by exposing scandals or other unsavoury development practices, civil society can develop an uneasy relationship with principals. There is also a risk of this power being hijacked.[29] The oft-cited example is where a civil society group becomes the mouthpiece for an anti-globalisation group – hired at low cost and very effective at protesting anything, from a multinational firm opening a manufacturing plant to UNDP building a water treatment facility. There is no doubt that such action plays an important role in averting local labour market exploitation or risky environmental projects. But there are also cases where a weary principal concludes that it's easier to take their business elsewhere, closing off an opportunity that may have been good in the first place, or could have been better negotiated for an all-around gain. Civil society wins the battle but loses the war. Even if this example is a little sensationalist, it does highlight that the greatest scope for civil society to do good as a sword, is when it is an informed sword.

3.4 Conclusion

If this has been confusing, here is where it all comes together. The previous chapters have set out that as a tool of human development, aid can and does work, but it does so in a sluggish way too much of the time. This is because ineffective feedback loops and incentives working at cross purposes mean that aid outcomes don't matter enough to those with the power to demand impact. Those for whom impact does matter, lack the power to make their voices heard.

The way forward is to stop blaming donors for politicising aid, recipient governments for lack of commitment or development agencies for inefficiency, and to acknowledge that these are *system failures*. With this out in the open it's clear that a much more constructive question is how to make aid outcomes matter more for particular power holders at particular moments.

Opportunities include building evidence that binds aid effectiveness to issues of importance to voters or the realisation of domestic policy goals. Likewise, although we can neither cajole beneficiary governments, nor rely solely on their goodwill, there will be situations where their interests align with a positive development outcome. Leadership opportunities and critical junctures are also moments when development breakthroughs can be made, provided that they are anticipated and acted on quickly and strategically.

This is not a wholesale solution. Indeed, the idea is to move away from fighting underdevelopment in all its forms and concentrate on fighting discreet battles that can be won. If this can be done effectively, such wins may create a weight of demand to do things differently, and thus edge the sector towards something that is more iterative, expert and innovative. The kind of sector that is set up to take on larger and more complex battles.

Such an approach will be complicated, risky and involve more effort. Educating stakeholders on why human development should matter to them, identifying sweet spots where vested interests align, exploiting critical junctures and setting in place enabling conditions so that leaders can make courageous decisions, require that development practitioners play the role of aid professor, politician and innovator simultaneously. Moreover, they need an organizational context where they can act decisively, program flexibly and take calculated risks.

Changes would also be required at the beneficiary engagement level. Practitioners need to create space for local innovation capacity, by making partnering processes less mysterious, discarding biases and sharing rather than acting as the gatekeepers of information. As Duncan Greene explains, this is as much a change in culture as it is in process. Development actors "problematise" by nature – they analyse, identify gaps and then fill them. However, an equally valid approach is to look for instances where locals have got it right and try to replicate it. This is not as unlikely as it sounds; Greene argues that in any community, for any problem, someone will have a solution. But our preference to jump in with a solution is very stubborn – anything else goes against who we are as expert "fixers".[30]

Can development agencies make this kind of change in institutional culture? Of course. Organisations do this all the time.

Indeed, the development sector has changed dramatically over the years; often so slowly we fail to notice it. I often hold up the example of customary justice programming, an area that I have worked on closely for decades. On one of my first postings I was employed to assist in the development of a post-conflict transitional justice mechanism. I brought up with one of my supervisors that while we were struggling to bring perpetrators to the newly established courts, the customary process seemed to be working in overdrive, reconciling families, meting out punishment and facilitating reparation.

Her rebuke was swift and complete. I was told in no uncertain terms that the only justice sector that mattered was the formal one and that renegade "play courts" had no place in UN thinking. How far we have come in two short decades; customary justice programming is now a recognised pillar of the legal development framework, a well-funded programming stream and even a masters level subject at the university where I teach. This is just one of many examples. Today it is standard for civil society to weigh in on program design, the IMF has a gender and inclusion strategy, and local staff occupy senior management roles, not just driver and translator positions. A few decades ago, such norms were unimaginable.

This change has been the result of multiple forces. In some cases, tragic events have pushed the system forward. The human costs of 1980s structural adjustment packages compelled development economists to unpack their strategies and reconceptualise human development as something more complex than could be measured in terms of GDP. Likewise, it was the Srebrenica massacre and Rwandan genocide that drove the international community's policies on human security and Responsibility to Protect. For other advances we need to thank civil society movements. Expansions in development programming around gender in the 1990s and LGBTIQ in the 2000s, took place largely in step with liberalising social norms won domestically.[31]

Does this suggest that we could just wait for the development sector to continue to evolve in terms of its knowledge and practices? Perhaps, but there may not be time. As noted in the last chapter, this is a moment of unprecedented decline in trust around aid, multilateral governance and communitarian thinking. It may be that before development is subsumed by foreign policy imperatives or completely deprioritised, something has to intervene.

The other way organisational reform takes place, of course, is from within. Could agency leaders be the ones to front this change in how the development and humanitarian sectors do business? In the current climate, it's doubtful that they have the political independence, staying power or appetite for risk. But the individuals within them certainly can, and this might be enough to tip the balance. We must remember that principals are not forcing development practitioners into mediocre outcomes; they are just not pushing them to do better. Moreover, institutions are not monolithic. Within each donor agency, development organisation and recipient government, there are tribes with different views, slowly but constantly contesting norms, practices and standards. In short, it's a decision for each program manager, field officer and thematic lead whether to swim with the current, or step up. It is these mid-level managers – perfectly capable of raising the bar, expecting more and pushing their system to do better – that this book is directed towards.

The next five chapters elaborate on these ideas by providing examples of how small but strategic changes in how managers approach development programming and policy making can beget significant changes in outcome. These include the better use of evidence to push past conventional but erroneous "best practices"; navigating around institutional risk aversion to generate and embrace innovation; identifying and exploiting moments of interest alignment and critical juncture; and using data to form constructive alliances with unlikely partners. The key is that practitioners, and in particular middle managers, need to drive this. It will not happen spontaneously.

Notes

1 Aid Effectiveness Land draws much inspiration from the work of Duncan Green; see generally D. Greene *How Change Happens*, Oxford University Press (2016), particularly chapter 12 235–255 and 20–22.
2 D. Greene *How Change Happens*, Oxford University Press (2016) 26, 246–247.
3 J. Sachs *The End of Poverty: Economic Possibilities for Our Time*, Penguin Press (2005) 74–75.
4 M. Buntaine *Giving Aid Effectively: The Politics of Environmental Performance and Selectivity at Multilateral Development Banks*, Oxford University Press (2016) 40–41, 66, 177–179, 183–185, 189–194.
5 M. Buntaine *Giving Aid Effectively: The Politics of Environmental Performance and Selectivity at Multilateral Development Banks*, Oxford University Press (2016) 72–73, 108.
6 M. Buntaine *Giving Aid Effectively: The Politics of Environmental Performance and Selectivity at Multilateral Development Banks*, Oxford University Press (2016) 23, 46–47, 59.
7 A. Noël and J.P. Thérien "From Domestic to International Justice: The Welfare State and Foreign Aid" *International Organization* 49:3 (1995) 523–553.
8 J. Sachs *The End of Poverty: Economic Possibilities for Our Time*, Penguin Press (2005) 329–310; L. Picard and T. Buss *A Fragile Balance: Re-examining the History of Foreign Aid, Security, and Diplomacy*, Lynne Rienner Publishers (2009) 134; J. Sachs *The Price of Civilization: Economics and Ethics After the Fall*, Random House (2011) 35.
9 G. Marshall, speech delivered at Harvard University 5 June 1947.
10 G. Marshall, speech delivered at Harvard University 5 June 1947.
11 G. Marshall, speech delivered at Harvard University 5 June 1947.
12 J. Sachs *The Price of Civilization: Economics and Ethics After the Fall*, Random House (2011) 52–53.
13 J. Sachs *The Price of Civilization: Economics and Ethics After the Fall*, Random House (2011) 68.
14 Interview dated 26 May 2019, by phone, notes on file with author.
15 P. Collier *The Bottom Billion: Why the Poorest Countries Are Failing and What Can Be Done About It*, Oxford University Press (2007) 67; D. Acemoglu and J. Robinson *Why Nations Fail: The Origins of Power, Prosperity and Poverty*, Random House (2012) 446–447.
16 "Paris Declaration on Aid Effectiveness: Ownership, Harmonization, Alignment, Results and Mutual Accountability" (2 March 2005).
17 A. Potter "The Rule of Law as the Measure of Peace? Responsive Policy for Reconstructing Justice and the Rule of Law in Post-Conflict and Transitional Environments" (Paper Presented at the UNU-WIDER Conference on "Making peace Work" Helsinki 4–5 May 2004) 9–10; "Guidance Note of the Secretary-General on UN Approach to Rule of Law Assistance" (2008) 3–4.

18 J. Stromseth, D. Whippman et al *Can Might Make Rights: Building the Rule of Law After Military Interventions*, Cambridge (2006) 379–380.

19 S. Chesterman *Just War or Just Peace? Humanitarian Intervention and International Law*, Oxford University Press (2001) 135–139.

20 Conflict, Security and Development Group (King's College London) *Review of Peace Operations: A Case for Change Afghanistan* (Report) (28 February 2003) 16; J. Stromseth, D. Whippman et al *Can Might Make Rights: Building the Rule of Law After Military Interventions*, Cambridge (2006) 118.

21 S. Chesterman *You, the People: The United Nations, Transitional Administration, and State-Building*, Oxford University Press (2004)150; C. Stahn "Justice Under Transitional Administration: Contours and Critique of a Paradigm" *Houston Journal of International Law* 27:2 (2005) 311, 334; A. Hurwitz "Civil War and the Rule of Law: Toward Security, Development, and Human Rights" in A. Hurwitz (ed) *Civil War and the Rule of Law, Security, Development and Human Rights*, Lynne Rienner (2008) 35; S. Chesterman *Just War or Just Peace? Humanitarian Intervention and International Law*, Oxford University Press (2001)178–180.

22 K. Samuels "Rule of Law Reform in Post-Conflict Countries: Operational Initiatives and Lessons Learned" Societal Development Paper No. 37, World Bank (October 2006) 21; C Call *Challenges in Police Reform: Promoting Effectiveness and Accountability*, International Peace Academy (2003) 4.

23 W. Easterly *The White Man's Burden: Why the West's Efforts to Aid the Rest Have Done So Much Harm and So Little Good*, Penguin Press (2006) 27.

24 See e.g. R. Mani "Exploring the Rule of Law in Theory and Practice" in A. Hurwitz (ed) *Civil War and the Rule of Law, Security, Development and Human Rights*, Lynne Rienner (2008), 29; Stromseth, D. Whippman et al *Can Might Make Rights: Building the Rule of Law After Military Interventions*, Cambridge (2006) 379–380.

25 M. Buntaine *Giving Aid Effectively: The Politics of Environmental Performance and Selectivity at Multilateral Development Banks*, Oxford University Press (2016) 81.

26 S. Chesterman *You, the People: The United Nations, Transitional Administration, and State-Building*, Oxford University Press (2004) 153; UN Development Programme "Strengthening the Rule of Law in Conflict/Post- Conflict Situations: A Global Programme for Justice and Security 2008–2011" 30.

27 C. Rausch "From Elation to Disappointment: Justice and Security Reform in Kosovo" in C. Call (ed) *Constructing Justice and Security After War*, US Institute of Peace (2007) 304.

28 M. Buntaine *Giving Aid Effectively: The Politics of Environmental Performance and Selectivity at Multilateral Development Banks*, Oxford University Press (2016) 60, 111.

29 M. Buntaine *Giving Aid Effectively: The Politics of Environmental Performance and Selectivity at Multilateral Development Banks*, Oxford University Press (2016) 114–115.

30 D. Greene *How Change Happens*, Oxford University Press (2016) 24–26, 94.

31 D. Greene *How Change Happens*, Oxford University Press (2016), 142–143.

4

THE SAMARITAN DILEMMA

Promoting good governance in fragile and poverty-affected states

The lesson from experiments in aid conditionality and local ownership is that when domestic stakeholders have a strong vested interest in maintaining the status quo, development assistance is unlikely to have a significant impact on poverty reduction and related aims. In the worst scenarios, aid resources could be misdirected to reinforce power hierarchies, or as one World Bank employee famously described his project, "develop the capacity of the state to control and repress".[1]

As word of this got out, development agencies were left somewhat between a rock and a hard place. Conversations with recipient states around development funds not being used efficiently are difficult, especially when the insinuation is that they are corrupt, dishonest or unable to get the job done. They are also a bit of a ruse when the recipient government knows that the donor attaches a higher value to maintaining a strategic relationship than to the aid resources in question.

Some proposed that the way around this dilemma was to channel development support towards governments with the capacity and intent to use aid well, even if they were not necessarily the neediest. This is the thinking behind programs such as the MCC.[2] The approach is not without complication, however. A first dilemma is that in the face of stricter accountability around how development support is used, an authoritarian leader might very well decide to reject the aid money and maintain the status quo. These power holders are usually quite good at extracting money from their country and its people – they've been practicing for decades. History suggests that ignoring a population in such circumstances is not something the development community is prepared to do.

Even more complicated is that the forces of political economy are never black and white. The image of an autocratic leader enjoying the spoils of exploited wealth is an oversimplified explanation of how mal-governance works. Even in the most draconian regimes, there will be individuals pushing against the tide trying to secure the best outcomes for the people they serve. At the same time, corruption and rent seeking are not privileges reserved for the elite. These phenomena exist throughout a social system, just in varying degrees of potency. Moreover, such practices may

DOI: 10.4324/9781003376996-5

not be rooted solely in self-interest and opportunity, but also in poverty. Expropriation of funds, bribes, favours and goodwill may be critical components of household income in economies that fundamentally do not work.

What this means is that whether a country's leadership is committed to poverty reduction, or is its chief extractor, is not entirely the point. To be successful, there has to a level of accountability *throughout* institutional layers. Not only is this rarely the case, but these systems are opaque and constantly adapting to changing circumstances, making it difficult to identify pockets of functionality to program around. Duncan Green explains this well. He notes how programming agencies tend to view situations of corruption as "micro-failures" and work to bypass whichever element of the system appears to be broken, for example by skipping over a few layers of bureaucracy and delivering aid more directly. Although this is intuitively sound, it overlooks that just because a system is local or poverty stricken, doesn't make it immune from corruption. As a result, the problem is not overcome, but just moved down the chain.[3]

The upshot is that despite the popularity of initiatives such as the MCC, a majority of aid resources continue to flow into contexts with varying levels of political commitment to the goals of human development. Moreover, this variation in commitment will exist throughout a system. There are not bad governments with benign populations, or vice versa. There will always be a mix of winners, losers, opportunists and altruists existing side by side, and sometimes switching roles. The more constructive question is how to navigate through this patchwork of intent and capacity to achieve positive outcomes.

The development community, not ignorant of these challenges, has sought means of delivering aid that mitigate the risk of expropriation, uphold the doctrine of local ownership, and at the same time address the underlying governance issues that landed countries in trouble in the first place. By the 1990s, somewhat of a solution had been identified – a set of programming interventions broadly classified as democratic governance. Over time, different terminology has been favored, including good governance and institutional strengthening, but the main goals have proven steadfast. Democracy is a core UN value, integral to the mandates of development agencies, and a stated objective of key donors.

The logic behind these interventions is difficult to contest. Freedom of expression, press and assembly mean that badly performing governments will be voted out of office and replaced by ones more willing and able to please their constituents, who will then be rewarded by longer terms. There is an abundance of supporting evidence. Democracy is highly correlated with effective service provision, income and low political violence and is highly resilient.[4] Indeed, when Francis Fukuyama wrote *The End of History* in 1989, it was a widely held belief that a superior form of governance had been found.

But the democracy experiment, when applied to developing countries, has not had the elixir quality hoped for. To flesh out why, this chapter examines three common scenarios where popular dogma around democratic reform, and its main bedfellow, elections, beget programming failures. These examples draw heavily on work of Paul Collier, Fareed Zakaria, James Feron and David Laitin to emphasise a simple point: the enormous gulf between what states need and what the development community tends to give them. This gulf has grown out of an institutional culture that – as explained in Chapter 2 – is not set up to pursue evidence-based programming, and moreover has overcorrected for past wrongs in such a way that crowds out objective discussion around what works and what doesn't.

Fortunately, there is a way around this, but it will be a difficult – although not impossible – pill to swallow. The key point is that it is not a question of whether democracy does or doesn't work. Countries are suited to different forms of governance at different moments. The trick is to know the evidence, be able to read the context and act on cues in a timely and decisive manner.

Moving towards such approaches will involve some unpopular choices – ones that contradict both current thinking around UN reform, and the norms that govern the relationships between donor and recipient states. But political expediency is not a license for continuing down a path that categorically doesn't work. That is irresponsible – to states, taxpayers and future generations. With this in mind, the chapter closes by examining what it would take to transition away from a scenario where outdated norms and political imperatives are holding development back to one where evidence is propelling it forward.

4.1 Democracy or bust

Let's start by challenging the idea that democracy is a sine qua non for peace, development and riches. A first argument is that the democratic model does not preclude the election of someone who is intent on running their country into the ground or trampling on human rights. Let's set aside the late Robert Mugabe, Kim Jong Un and Bashir al Assad, characters who – year after year, catastrophe after catastrophe – still manage to enjoy landslide election victories. The unpleasant fact is that voters may elect a fascist, racist or separatist leader, because this reflects the values and priorities of the majority population.[5] As Fareed Zakaria reminds us, no one can say we were not warned. Alexis de Tocqueville through to James Madison cautioned of the "tyranny of the majority".[6] Indeed, Hitler was elected chancellor of Germany in 1933. These trends have continued through the decades. Whether one regards Yasser Arafat, former president of the Palestinian Territories, as a freedom fighting nationalist or a recalcitrant terrorist – it cannot be denied that he was freely elected.[7]

People voting in "the bad guy" is a particular problem in poor countries divided along ethnic or religious lines. As set out in Paul Collier's masterful book, *Wars, Guns and Votes: Democracy in Dangerous Places*, where individuals identify principally as members of groups, rather than as nationals, voting is mostly an act of identity or self-expression.[8] This has important implications for electoral competition. Because votes are not cast according to policy superiority or capacity to govern well, the easiest way to win elections is to appeal directly to one's group, often by committing to extreme policies that benefit them and/or discriminate against rivals. Moreover, democracy's principal safeguard – that ineffective leaders will be voted out in the next election – doesn't seem to kick in. According to Collier's research, the worse a country is governed, the higher the chance that leaders will be re-elected – from 45 percent in run-of-the-mill democracies to 88 percent in countries with a Polity V Index between negative ten and zero.[9] The upshot is that in divided states, electoral competition pushes leaders into situations where they are incentivised to misgovern and assert group preference.[10] This not only retards development, but also means that they are highly prone to discriminatory policies and ethnic conflict. Again, the proof lies in the data: in states that are small, poor and divided, democracy correlates with slower growth, political violence and conflict, and it doesn't lower the probability of the most extreme human rights violations.[11]

Another situation where democracy can let a population down is when an autocratic regime falls, ushering in a new elected leader who then reverts to his/her predecessor's tactics, and thus an "era of greater absolutism".[12] Such trends are so repetitive and robust that scholars Acemoglu and Robinson have given it a special name – the "Iron Law of Oligarchy". Hugo Chavez, Mohammed Morsi and Daniel Ortega all demonstrate how irresistible the honey pot of absolutism can be, especially when the legacy of authoritarianism means that there are few checks and balances in place to stop them.[13]

To be fair, democracy doesn't only malfunction in developing states. Its limitations – particularly how systems can exclude and be co-opted – are also observable in countries that enjoy stability, wealth and reputations of good governance. In the US, special interest groups such as big industry (especially oil, agriculture and pharmaceuticals), pro-Israeli lobbyists and Wall Street are so powerful that it is pragmatic for policymakers – even the well-intended – to privilege these outlier interests. Such forces repeatedly thwart policy proposals that might have resulted in civic wins, such as improved access to low-cost renewable energy and affordable healthcare. These failings do not go unnoticed. Perceptions that the system isn't responsive to the common interest have eroded trust and participation, ironically leaving more space for special interests to dominate.[14]

These risks, challenges and setbacks beg an interesting question. If the evidence suggests that democracy is unsuited to poverty-stricken and unstable states (and in some cases even makes things worse), why does it remain such a popular programming stream? Could it be that the development sector fell victim to confusing correlation with causation?[15] Western democracies are indeed rich, robust and seemingly immune from political violence, but this does not mean that they got there *because* of democracy. As Fareed Zakaria explains, historically, economic freedoms came first, followed by a middle class, who then demanded institutions that offered increasingly higher levels of political freedom. Democracy – the way the government is formed – actually came as a final step. This suggests that it is not *democracy* that works, but what lies beneath: strong institutions, held up by a broad coalition of people united by evenly distributed wealth. These institutions are stronger and more resilient than the people that run them.[16] They also provide checks and balances – caps on power – that prevent mini-failures from breaking down the organs of governance.

Another theory (which does not necessarily preclude the first) is that democracy works, but only at certain income levels. As set out by Adam Przeworski and Fernando Limongi, democracies where the per capita income sits below USD1500 have a very short lifespan of around 8 years before being overturned or falling into conflict. As income grows to USD1500–3000, democracy starts to become safer, surviving for around 18 years, until they hit USD6000 at which point a state is highly resilient to regressing.[17] This suggests that the medicine might be right, but in some cases it's being administered too early.

Both of these explanations have merit. But the development sector's penchant for democratic reform may be more than just a misreading of the evidence. Against the imperative of "doing something", democracy might not be the effective solution, but it is the *least unpalatable* solution.

To unpack this, let's go back to the academic evidence. It seems that for democracy to work its magic, states need to develop strong institutions and a plan to reach a base level of per capita income. Herein lies the problem. Institutional development is a tough, expensive and lengthy process, and the sector has not found an unambiguous means of delivering it in a way that is effective and affordable, respects local ownership and ensures accountability. A first approach – the one preferred by both donors and recipients – is budget support (a fancy term for giving governments money). As we know, funds given in this manner tend to get misused. Other scholars advocate for a model of "cost sharing". Indeed, it feels more like a partnership with a strategy and less like charity when the recipient state picks up at least some of the tab. Results have been patchy, however. These projects seem to start off well, but soon run into challenges. Most practitioners would be familiar with new health clinics that look great but have no stocks of medicine; vehicles that sit idle because there is no money for fuel or repairs, or courts with computerised case management systems that no one knows how to use. A third approach is that the sector (or an agent) *takes on* the tasks that governments in these situations perform most poorly on. These are generally services such as health care, sanitation and education – the stuff that people need to get their countries up and running but that bad leaders attach less importance to. The problem is that this is unpopular.

Direct programming is messy and high risk, sits uncomfortably with the principle of local ownership, and attracts high administration costs.[18]

Setting in place an enabling framework for economic growth is even more challenging. Prerequisites include capital infrastructure with long-term economic value such as ports and roads. Although this is usually the domain of IFIs, some economists argue that it is a good use of development monies, and a necessity when countries are too poor to acquire loans. Big infrastructure, however, rivals only direct implementation in terms of unpopularity. These projects are expensive and risky, and their impact is difficult to quantify within a programming cycle. They also break informal rules around competing spheres of interest within the development sector. In practice, individual agencies, INGOs and civil society each lobby for their issue and thus their share of the development budget, and are unlikely to concede ground to initiatives that threaten their programming ambit.[19] As one former UN Resident Coordinator commented to me; "getting consensus around a PRS (poverty reduction strategy) should neither be a democracy nor preschool, but it feels like both".[20]

So here we have it. A solid list of highly unpopular entry points: resource-heavy financial support, robust oversight with associated administration costs, unsexy projects and potentially a rioting UN Country Team. The conclusion: democratic institution building is popular, not only because of a misreading of the evidence, but because what the evidence suggests as an alternative, *no one wants to do*.

The point is not to advocate a new blueprint approach for governance in low-income or divided states. It's to highlight that there can be a gulf between what we do and what the evidence tells us we should do, and moreover, why moving to a more evidence-based approach is so difficult. In short it would mean doing things that are unpopular, push conceptions of political correctness and stamp upon heavily guarded conventions in the development sector. These are uncomfortable ideas, but we are left with a question – what if a bit more oversight, spending and dull projects are what's needed to safely transition to a sustainable democracy?

4.2 Promoting good governance in post-conflict states

If promoting good governance is complicated, doing it in post-conflict states is an even greater challenge. This is probably because the stakes are so high. Wars have horrific consequences. They cause fear, death and suffering, the heaviest share of which is shouldered by society's most vulnerable members. Wars are also devastating on national economies. On average, civil conflict reduces a country's growth by 2.3 percent per year, with a typical 7-year war leaving a country 15 percent worse off than it would have been without conflict.[21] The World Bank has found that investor risk perception in the first year of a war can reduce trade by between 12–25 percent, and up to 40 percent for severe civil wars (those with a cumulative death toll greater than 50,000).[22]

The influence of these factors lasts long after fighting subsides; recovering to original growth paths takes around 14 years of peace.

These costs of conflict – both economic and humanitarian – spill over onto neighbouring countries. A country making development advances loses an estimated 0.7 percent of GDP every year for each neighbour in conflict; border countries also host nearly 75 percent of the world's refugees.[23] Then there is a phenomenon called conflict contagion: the presence of a civil war in an adjacent country increases the probability of conflict outbreak domestically.[24] Research by the United Nations Economic and Social Council for West Asia suggests that the concept of neighbourhood may be more extensive than originally thought. They find that "neighbours" are not only geographical, but can also be countries that have cultural, ideological or economic connections.

Finally, conflicts cause spillovers that are global in nature. The instability, weak rule of law and unreliable law enforcement associated with conflict provides these countries with a "comparative advantage in international crime and terrorism".[25] Criminal networks are better able to mobilise, recruit and gain strength in such environments, and public assets and resources can more easily be seized. Organised crime and radical groups thus not only feed off the conflict economy, they accelerate its growth.

Given these outcomes, when a conflict does end, no one wants to backstep. Unfortunately, post-conflict states are highly vulnerable to collapse within the first decade, at around 40 percent.[26] It follows that guarding against this risk needs to be the number one order of business; development and humanitarian actors need to coalesce around this goal.

Populations generally get on board with this quickly and easily. War is so terrible that as long as there is reason for confidence – signals and demonstrations that life is improving – people tend to rally around the new normal.

The greater risk is spoilers. One such group is the select few who benefit from war – those dealing in arms or other illegal goods such as drugs. The other group of spoilers are the political losers. They will pull out all the stops to bring a new state to its knees – usually in a last-ditch effort to win back support, or simply as an act of revenge. Political losers are not inevitable in a post-conflict context. In fact, a majority of conflicts end with a negotiated agreement rather than being won outright through military prowess. One move that is guaranteed to create political losers, however, is elections. Indeed, the risk of political violence increases drastically following an election. The takeaway is that in any post-conflict situation, the safest arrangement will be a muddy, inclusive sharing of power, for as long as possible while governance structures are built and the economy rebounds.[27]

But without an election, who will run the government and protect the peace? In terms of security, what seems to work is peacekeeping – and the more of it, the more successful the result.[28] Paul Collier and Anke Hoeffler's research suggests that investing USD100 million per year into peacekeeping reduces the 10-year risk of recidivism from 38 percent to 17 percent; at

USD200 million the risk falls to 13 percent, and at USD500 million it's 9 percent.[29] Scholars James Fearon, David Laitin and Steve Pinker provide different explanations for this. Most probably, it is because peacekeeping boosts the confidence of the population, increases the costs of violence for spoilers, and reduces the need for new governments to spend money on military (another thing that statistically increases risk of recidivism).[30]

In terms of policy making, the evidence suggests large amounts of technical assistance, especially in the first 2–4 years. Ideally, these responsibilities would fall to a national coalition, and sometimes this is possible. However, the needs of a post-conflict state are very specific and contingent. In most cases, it is more strategic to import such skills.[31]

The third thing that post-conflict states need is steady economic recovery, which boosts confidence, provides jobs, and reduces human capital flight. It may also encourage diaspora to return, bringing their skills and assets with them.[32] This is best facilitated by a large development program geared towards skills building in reconstruction followed by infrastructure and building projects.[33]

The process described – delaying elections, heavy peacekeeping and technical assistance financed under a generous aid program rolled out over the time it takes for the risk of recidivism to abate (around 7–10 years) as opposed to a program cycle (2–3 years)[34] – sits in direct contrast with the rule book. The popularly accepted approach is to restore order and develop a democratic constitution, followed by an election. The international community can then withdraw, safe in the knowledge that the new leadership was installed by way of a legitimate and inclusive process.[35]

The reason for this gulf should come as no surprise. No one wants to take the medicine prescribed by academics. New states do not want babysitters; they want to lead. Donors and aid agencies are equally resistant. UN transitional administration is as close to an expletive as it gets in the development sector – it's not just considered passé; many view it as a throwback to colonialism. The only thing that's less popular is perhaps peacekeeping. Even though it is paid for and effective, for those primed to start governing, the best demonstration of their leadership is for them, not someone else, to provide the ultimate public good: security. For everyone else, peacekeeping is a headache the UN system created that they would sooner leave behind. It is resource heavy, scandal ridden and plays terribly back home whenever a soldier fighting someone else's war is harmed or bestows harm on someone else. So consistent has this hostility towards peacekeeping been, that its coordinating branch – UNDPKO – has been restructured, streamlined and (so rumour has it) slowly disempowered.

The question that remains is – once again – what if the academics are right? What if the comparison is between an approach that works but is expensive, risky and pushes boundaries around political correctness, and one that is less expensive, diplomatic, but sends an already weak country back to the drawing board every few years?

Experience from the field is telling. The closest this combination of heavy peacekeeping, delayed elections and long periods of heavy technical support has come to being put to the test was during the 1990s and 2000s when "UN transitional administration" was momentarily in vogue. We need only look to the stability of these states today. Both Kosovo and Bosnia-Herzegovina are upper-middle income states and prospective EU candidates, while Timor Leste is classified as lower-middle income but with significant untapped oil and gas reserves. Although each have experienced moments of political instability, all recovered while avoiding a coup. These experiences might be contrasted to Iraq; here, sovereignty was handed over to an interim government led by Prime Minister Iyad Allawi only 15 months after the US–led invasion in March 2003. Elections for a transitional national assembly and then a full-time government took place hastily, both against a backdrop of electoral ambiguity, ethnic violence and instability that has carried forward until today.

As a thought experiment, let's imagine what it might take to modify this rule book and take on a new set of engagement procedures. One might argue that this should not be too hard. The benefits to be reaped by donor states are significant: reduced long-term costs (and the political headache when a heavily invested-in peace process fails); safeguards against the spread of terrorism, extremism and transnational crime; and more stable international trade markets. Electorates might also be convinced; I cannot imagine the stress and pain that must come from being the parent of a peacekeeper; but I hope I would appreciate the logic in him or her participating in one longer tour, than having to say goodbye a second, third or even fourth time.

If there is residual scepticism, just roll in the economists. According to the Institute for Economics and Peace, armed conflict cost the world USD519 billion in 2019.[36] Although by far the single biggest expenditure item on the UN's budget, the cost of peacekeeping hovers around USD6 billion annually. From this we can say that the amount spent on peacekeeping works out at around 1 percent of the annual economic losses attributed to armed conflict; considered differently, even if the entire UN peacekeeping budget was spent on a single state for an entire decade (when it is most vulnerable to recidivism), this would still be significantly less than the cost of this state failing. In short, building a post-conflict peace is expensive, but compared to the costs of recurrent civil war, it's a bargain.[37] This should, at minimum, give everyone pause. But before we turn to the nitty gritty of what steps would be needed to realise this kind of course correction, let us consider one more scenario.

4.3 Keep your autocrats

One of the mistakes that the outside world makes is to think that their enemies should be our enemies.

Nelson Mandela, 22 June 1990

A final place the development sector loves to promote democracy is autocracies, and for obvious reasons – these are the places where leaders rule by fiat, crush their opposition and have terrible records in minority protection. The opportunity to intervene in such states, however, is infrequent. Those in control have usually crafted out quite a good existence for themselves, and so have a huge incentive to maintain the status quo. Neither sticks nor carrots are likely to change this, and safe exit strategies are hard to come by – they have watched too many of their friends eventually be indicted by the ICC or meet some other unfortunate end. Because they have no interest in giving up power voluntarily, the only scope for change is where it is taken forcefully.[38]

On these rare occasions where a dictator is overthrown, practitioners should be wary about bringing out the champagne. There's no guarantee that things won't go from bad to worse. Because of the way autocracies work, the structures of the state are seldom developed enough to support a liberal reform agenda, or – without a strongman at the helm – contain violence. Saddam Hussein's Iraq is a prime example. With his ousting, the tools used to maintain order (and instil fear and commit terrible human rights abuses) were very deliberately disposed of. Unfortunately, it was these tools that made the system work. Thus while Iraq in many ways looked like it had the systems and institutions of a serious state, this was largely a façade. As this architecture crumbled – unable to carry the weight of what Iraqis, the international community and the US expected from it – fissures were exposed, hope was overtaken by historical divisions, and the country descended into political violence.

An equally bad scenario is if free elections bring in a figure who is more extreme, less predictable and has a greater capacity for violence. There are a few countries that analysts believe need to be watched carefully, not because there is much chance of them falling, but because of the population's appetite for a more extreme flavour of governance. Jordan is a good example; here the executive leadership is objectively more progressive and modernist than policymakers and their constituents. This can be observed in reform trends. Proposals to expand freedoms, such as making it easier for women to obtain passports and pass on nationality to their children, while generally supported by senior royal family members, tend to be voted down by the more conservative legislature.[39]

This data has led some academics to conclude that autocracies are often better off being left alone, especially when populations are relatively homogeneous. Let's consider the work of Fareed Zakaria. He argues that if the goal is to transform autocracies into thriving democracies, the international community has been using the wrong tools. The more effective and peaceful route is not elections, but instead economic liberalisation.

This is certainly how most of the post–WWII democracies came to be. In 1945, President Syngman Ree set about modernising South Korea's economy, but without democracy. This was remarkably successful, but it could not last forever. Expanded economic freedom had created a new class of people with power independent of the state, which they leveraged to negotiate small changes, first around the rule of law and then socio-cultural freedoms. Eventually leaders had little left to concede, and thus to lose, from a full democratic transition. Against the possibility that the people might take the decision for them, they opted in, survived, and landed themselves on the right side of history.[40] A similar pattern was followed in Taiwan. It may also be playing out in Singapore. Today, Singaporeans enjoy unfettered economic freedom, but there is "a limited free press, an even more limited political opposition, and no free elections".[41] However pressure is building. Globalisation, Internet access and a growing middle class are trends that leaders cannot insulate the country from. This makes holding onto the status quo increasingly difficult and costly. Who else to watch: the United Arab Emirates and China, both of which have managed – through sound and deliberate economic policy – high rates of growth, while maintaining a strong hold on power. Before it's illegal invasion of the Ukraine, some even included Russia on this list. Despite how he governs (and how this represents an increasing threat to international security), it cannot be denied that Putin wants a modern Russia, nor that he hasn't delivered in terms of economic policy and huge reductions in poverty.[42]

Common to each of these scenarios is that the decision to introduce economic freedoms was made by a liberal autocrat serious about reforming their country. In fact, as Zakaria points out, "over the past 50 years, almost every success story in the developing world has taken place under a liberal authoritarian regime".[43] Perhaps this should not be all that surprising; these are the kinds of painful processes that only leaders who don't need to worry about being re-elected can carry off.

What does this mean from a development policy and programming perspective? One suggestion is that rather than promoting elections and political reform, the international community might be better staying out of the way. These countries are not usually in dire need of money. Indeed, those that have progressed down this track rapidly and peacefully have done so with minimum or no external assistance. But while these states may not need financial help, they do want respect. More than anything else, this is the tool that could be used to encourage the liberal autocrat to push their country down a path of reform. They want to be safe in the knowledge that when things get hairy – which at some point they will – Western powers won't shoot in, take advantage, and tip the balance in favour of their discontents. In other words, the only way leaders will have the confidence to do what is needed is for it to be on their own terms. This message – that you can keep your autocrats – would need to be strong and clear.[44] And it would have to be genuine; after all, their iron-fisted leadership is key to getting the job done.

This is where things get complicated. Supporting autocracies to modernise their economies while turning a blind eye to restrictions on free speech, discrimination and other breaches of recognised norms, is a lot to stomach.

The development sector would have to let go of the conventional wisdom that a democracy – struggling or illiberal – is preferable to dictatorship – benign or not. Moreover, that in contexts unsuited to democracy, the benevolent autocrat is not always the problem. Sometimes, they might even be part of the solution. Even if we could come around to this, could we – in the context of a state descending into failure – ignore long-oppressed citizens requesting assistance to install a liberal, rights-upholding, democratic government? Perhaps; but what if the soon-to-be ousted leader, sensing that time was running out, decided to put the brakes on the reform process by disappearing a few hundred of those citizens? Could the international community sit back and trust that the leader would – just like in South Korea – eventually concede?

I don't think we could, and I don't even think we should. For all the things that the development community of practice cannot do or does badly – it is one of the few bodies set up to be able to consistently take a strong stand on human rights, social justice and participatory governance. At a time where few are willing to play that role, red lines are needed. To do anything else might result in a breakdown of the system as we know it, and at a time when there is no appetite to rebuild.

But this is not to say that the argument isn't sound. And this is the point. To do better, we must be able to see the grey, messy complexity of these situations. Ultimately, decision-makers have to come down on one side, but unless we can internalise all the evidence, prudently and untainted, there will be scope for error.

4.4 A three-point plan for better strategies

This chapter opened with a commonly cited argument – that political economy and competing vested interests are the greatest obstacles to human development. These impediments have proven so resilient that some donors have changed track, preferring to prioritise middle- and lower-middle-income states with better governance, and thus the capacity, policies and interest to use aid monies well. For the most part though, the development sector has refused to give up on struggling countries and continues to support them in terms of basic needs and institutional capacity building.

In this work, democratic governance is both a programming tool and a fundamental pillar of the development theory subscribed to. As such, it will never work easily or completely. Simply put, these interventions are built on a misunderstanding of why fragile and developing states do what they do, and the role political economy plays in this.

This is by no means an argument against democracy. But we should acknowledge its limitations, and accept that it works best at particular moments when it is accompanied by other enabling conditions. It especially does not work in small, divided states, where it incentivises mal-governance; in post-conflict states where it increases the risk of recidivism; and in autocracies where underlying structures are too weak to shoulder reform or prevent violence. This suggests that it's perhaps not only the vested interests of rulers that is capping development outcomes, but also that the development community sometimes proffers the wrong type of help.

The challenge is that what states actually need, the international development sector finds really hard to give. This includes large development programs that come with long-term time commitments and heavy doses of technical assistance; peacekeepers; and strategies where development actors take pro-active roles in governance.

I'm going to try to put forward an explanation for how demand and supply have managed to diverge so acutely, and how this happened without anyone raising the alarm. It comes back to that thorny issue of an institutional culture that doesn't reward innovation or mandate upwards learning. Without strong empirical evidence on which to base engagement, it's almost impossible for practitioners to see when and why an approach isn't working. Everyone is just doing their best in difficult circumstances with what always seems to be insufficient resources vis-à-vis needs. These micro-failures built upon themselves incrementally, until questions around impact-effectiveness began to arise and trust began to decline.

Because it's unclear where the fix lies, donors demanded what intuitively seemed to be the best solution: time-bound assistance, heavy on local ownership, and light on administrative costs. It almost became a mantra: get in, do a bunch of stuff, and get out. Compounding this, with no one able to present evidence to the contrary, donors were highly sensitive to what looked bad, felt bad and played bad: peacekeeping, approaches that could be labelled paternalistic, and playing nicely with autocrats. The reverse is also true. A UN mission pulling off a country's first democratic election following the fall of a dictator is as newsworthy as it gets, with the result that this kind of work gets promoted.

One might argue that these are the political realities of development programming. This is a fair comment. The problem is that the battle around how to "do better" was lost without being fought. At present, there isn't a sophisticated enough discourse around these dynamics to communicate back to donors (and recipient states) that there may be a different reason why we're not seeing better outcomes. Donors may still be unwilling to sign up for longer programs and new leaders may refuse to delay elections, but such decisions need to be taken in the context of an evidence-based discussion around the known limits of certain types of programming, possible outcomes and alternatives. Irrespective of whether these conversations are not taking place because of political correctness or because people don't know what to say, it's a dereliction of responsibility. To alter this, three changes would be required.

First, a solid, constantly evolving body of empirical evidence would need to be generated. It's unlikely that academics working alone could come up with the kinds of pragmatic solutions that would both work in context-rich environments and that agencies would embrace. But they would need to be part of the solution; agencies simply do not have the requisite research capacity. To this end, it should be acknowledged that as far as vested interests go, academics are not too complicated. They don't have much to prove apart from their theories, and the idea that one might be taken seriously, inform UN policy and then fail is akin to career suicide.

Armed with evidence, agencies could apply more complex thinking to development questions and take this case to donors and local decision-makers. This step is critical, because we actually need more UN and INGOs, not less, but in the areas they are value adding and useful.

A final change relates to the institutional culture around political correctness. It is certainly true that decades of development assistance took place in a context where beneficiary insights, preferences and aspirations were ignored or worse. But the system has overcorrected in such a way that it is now preventing objective discussion around issues like the suitability of different governance approaches, aid effectiveness through a lens of power relations, or the right combination of local and external decision-making. This may allow practitioners to feel better about the work they do, but it does nothing to repair the mistakes of the past. Moreover, a widespread fear of being labelled a neocolonialist or antidemocratic has, at least to an extent, facilitated norms that coddle bad governments more than they reform them.[45]

What is needed is balance. The UN is not equal to any government, but it has expertise and carries the consequence of failure onto all member states. It should be incumbent upon them to use this expertise wisely. In doing so, they will need to embrace genuine partnership, but also be willing to push the envelope when necessary. For example, one of the challenges of getting technical support into a failing state is that there is rarely demand for it. Aid recipients understand that one expatriate salary buys a score of local jobs. This means that when technical assistance is what's required, the development community is the only player likely to lobby for it, and lobby for it they must. There will likewise be times to push back, using both the available evidence and opinion, for example in the case of premature elections or an ill-thought-through devolution of security responsibility. Having detailed the costs of war and the danger of recidivism, readers should see that the risks associated with sitting on the fence are simply too great.

I have experienced how complicated this can be. In 2018, I was invited by UNDP to assist the Ethiopian Supreme Court to develop a justice sector reform strategy. It was a very peculiar moment, imbued with opportunity. Abiy Ahmed had just been elected Prime Minister on a commitment to bolster peace and stability, strengthen the multiparty system and stabilise the economy. True to his word, reforms were swift – within a few months Parliament had been reconfigured, political dissidents were released from prison, and the controversial Charities and Societies Proclamation had been recalled and amended.

The Prime Minister's reform agenda presented the Supreme Court with an unprecedented mandate to close longstanding deficits in service delivery, independence and accountability. But UNDP had a problem. The court was determined to base its strategy on a decades-old assessment. The judges expressed confidence, both that nothing had changed and in their familiarity with key deficits and how to resolve them. UNDP and I were on the same page – of course things had changed. If nothing else, thinking around how best to undertake justice sector reform had changed. The solution had to be an in-depth research project, upon which to craft a plan that could be sold to donors, hence ensuring the necessary input of resources. It was unspoken, but we also thought we knew stuff they didn't. I had seen these processes go south before and believed I could help avoid those mistakes. Luckily, UNDP had an ace up its sleeve. The newly appointed Chief Justice had a long and impressive career within the UN system; talk on the ground was that she was "one of them" and that she "got it".

By the time of my first meeting with the Chief Justice, the research strategy was almost complete and just needed her signoff. She was tall and stylish, while I was obnoxious and irritating. And she sure let me know it. I was perhaps five minutes in before she explained that she had no interest in more research, and no intention of waiting while the UN ticked its boxes and her window of opportunity closed. Her trump card: the US had already given the court the equivalent of a blank cheque to get the justice system back up and running with a modicum of efficiency.

The subsequent UNCT meeting was disastrous. No one seemed willing to accept that programming could be built on anything but the carefully crafted UN needs assessment they were advocating. My fellow reform strategist – more experienced than me – tried to salvage things with a statement I have always remembered: good plans are made up of many things, but a key one is momentum. That we had, and maybe we should run with it.

I'm not sure how, if at all, the situation was resolved. But with hindsight it is clear that the Chief Justice was betting on her deep knowledge of the justice sector, including how volatile and dynamic the country's appetite for change was. Perhaps she also knew that while her team didn't have all the answers, development advances also come from "learning by doing". All of this is to say that none of this is easy. There is a lot of grey and all sides have a lot to learn. Real partnership is about putting evidence ahead of image, but also allowing space to make mistakes and learn from them.

4.5 Practical steps towards an evidence-rich environment

These three changes – a solid evidence base, programming driven by evidence and a more nuanced understanding of political correctness – are hardly groundbreaking. Far more complex is developing a realistic plan on how to get there. I put this question to the helpful group of retired senior UN staffers and ambassadors mentioned in Chapter 1. Their answer:

Possibly not much. All it might need is a few people stepping up and asking why, against existing evidence, things are being done the way they are. The thing about evidence is that it's sticky; once it's out there, it's hard to refute except by presenting counter evidence. Suddenly, you're on a moving train and it's hard to get off.

And it may be that we are at the exact right moment for this to happen. There is a growing appetite for change, and even some indicators that less-orthodox solutions might form part of this. The past two years have seen an unprecedentedly analytical discussion of the democracy concept at senior policymaking levels. Indeed, in the UN's Sustainable Development Agenda 2030 and enabling General Assembly Resolution, the word *democracy* is used only once.

This leaves us with a question: who will be these brave individuals and how will they shake things up? The "who" should come as no surprise; it is everyone that chose to pick up this book. As to how this this form of disruption might be realised, let's close with some ideas to ponder.

Behavioural psychology tells us that the most expedient way to move towards evidence-based approaches is to eliminate cognitive bias, and the easiest way to remove bias is to know how it works and be able to spot it.

Illustrations can be found throughout this chapter. One reason we have a preference for elections and democracy is that humans like familiar and coherent narratives – stories that fit nicely together and that are consistent with our lived experiences. We even accept/seek out or ignore/downplay evidence to the extent that it fits with or contradicts these preferences. Experts call this the "exposure effect". It is especially relevant for development practitioners, humanitarian workers and diplomats, who tend to be ideologues – they believe in human rights, democratic governance and fundamental freedoms as sacred rites. This works well; it would be no good to anyone if they flipped around believing in something different every other day. But while this might seem fairly harmless, it means that we naturally repel ideas that make our world seem less coherent and navigable – for example, that a crazed autocrat might be a population's choice in a free and democratic election. This can leave us blindsided, and thus liable to missing good opportunities when they present themselves.[46]

Another important bias is the availability heuristic – a tendency to believe information based on how easily an example comes to mind. One reason we are averse to peacekeepers, for example, is because we are more likely to hear about one being killed in theatre or embroiled in a scandal. The takeaway is that what we believe, and thus how we program, is highly influenced by the media. This is not a problem that can be solved by regulation. At the end of the day, while the evidence is that strong democracies develop slowly and incrementally – not by way of overthrows or elections – this is not a story any news station wants to run with.[47]

Just understanding these biases offers a relatively high degree of protection from them. The key is to find ways to talk about them. When I was

Director of the West Asia-North Africa Institute – a politics and security think tank in Jordan – we introduced a non-conventional method for making decisions. At our weekly brainstorming meetings (or whenever a significant decision had to be made), we avoided the typical "tour de table". Instead, everyone would write their ideas on a piece of paper and place them in what we named the "bias box". We would then transfer them to the white board for discussion according to whichever came out of the box first. We did this because humans have a strong bias towards whoever speaks first and/or most assertively.[48] I have no doubt that this allowed us to make better decisions, but what was perhaps more remarkable was how rapidly the idea caught on. I quickly lost count of how many times I needed to explain the rationale behind our box – to passers-by, donors sitting in on meetings, or visiting scholars. And this started in-depth and probing discussions about bias, how inescapable it was, and its tendency to crowd out evidence-based thinking. One of my fondest memories from my time at WANA is knowing that bias boxes have made their way into new offices, carried forward by staff who moved on to bigger and better things.

"Skin in the game" is another highly effective anti-bias trick. People who have – or think they have – something invested in an outcome make profoundly more informed and rational decisions. This is why decision-makers need to be made aware of the evidence on how vulnerable a recovering state is to conflict recidivism, peacekeeper effectiveness and conflict contagion.[49]

A further tool disruptors might draw on is a basic knowledge of statistics. The chief of evaluation at the World Bank once told me that he had identified the two most frequent mistakes causing programmatic failure. First is when managers confuse correlation with causation (correlation does not imply causation).[50] Second is when managers do not factor in a phenomenon called in regression to the mean (mistaking a normal pattern for improvement). When these mistakes feed into programming, the result is an over-attribution of our actions to outcomes – good or bad. On their own, the consequences of this are rarely dire. The problem, he said, is that development and humanitarian programming attaches a strong bias to outcomes. This means that the quality of a manager's decision-making tends to be evaluated according to the outcome (which programming may or may not have had any bearing on), as opposed to an objective reading of the cause-and-effect forces in play. This drives risk aversion and one-off events morphing into "best practices".[51] To push back against this, readers might try making appropriate use of one of the above-mentioned statistical concepts – preferably at a well-attended staff meeting. My bet is that even the most evidence-deaf managers will know what they mean and how they might be used by the following morning.

A final point is how we use data in our day to day. A colleague I have known for more than a decade has been lamenting (for close to a decade) that she is the only economist working in that capacity at a large UN (let's leave it nameless) humanitarian organisation. I found this so difficult to believe that I started to do some digging. In fact, she might be right. It seems that the number of deliberately employed economists, statisticians and econometricians at programming agencies is very low. I'm pretty certain I could have counted them on two hands. This is a critical failing. Humanitarian and development programming takes place in high-context, low-validity environments – the environments where people lack the statistical background necessary to interpret their data meaningfully, regardless of how much experience they have or how expert they are.[52] In these contexts numbers are our friends, and we should use them more. In fact, so powerful are algorithms that it is a growing good practice in the private sector for managers to have to demonstrate why – if their gut or experience points them in a different direction – the data should be set aside.

The takeaway for budding disruptors is that data is a tool of reason, and its judicious use can protect decision-making from some of the most destructive cognitive biases. Making statisticians and econometricians parts of development teams is the best move. Outside of this, knowing the basic concepts, talking about them and employing a few tricks, is something even the most junior staff can do, and it will make a difference.

Notes

1 Human Rights Watch "Development Without Freedom: How Aid Underwrites Repression in Ethiopia", Human Rights Watch, New York (2010).
2 M. Buntaine *Giving Aid Effectively: The Politics of Environmental Performance and Selectivity at Multilateral Development Banks*, Oxford University Press (2016) 10–11, 26. See also W. Easterly *The White Man's Burden: Why the West's Efforts to Aid the Rest Have Done So Much Harm and So Little Good*, Penguin Press (2006) 46–47. For counterarguments see J. Sachs *The End of Poverty: Economic Possibilities for Our Time*, Penguin Press (2005) 217.
3 D. Greene *How Change Happens*, Oxford University Press (2016) 131–133.
4 W. Easterly *The White Man's Burden: Why the West's Efforts to Aid the Rest Have Done So Much Harm and So Little Good*, Penguin Press (2006) 117–118, 130–131; W. Easterly *The Tyranny of Experts: Economists, Dictators and the Forgotten Rights of the Poor*, Basic Books (2013) 142.
5 W. Easterly *The White Man's Burden: Why the West's Efforts to Aid the Rest Have Done So Much Harm and So Little Good*, Penguin Press (2006) 119.
6 F. Zakaria *The Future of Freedom: Illiberal Democracy at Home and Abroad*, Norton (2007) 105–106; see also W. Easterly *The Tyranny of Experts: Economists, Dictators and the Forgotten Rights of the Poor*, Basic Books (2013) 142–143.
7 F. Zakaria *The Future of Freedom: Illiberal Democracy at Home and Abroad*, Norton (2007) 17–20, 106–109.
8 P. Collier *War, Guns and Votes: Democracy in Dangerous Places*, Vintage (2010), 51–57.
9 P. Collier *War, Guns and Votes: Democracy in Dangerous Places*, Vintage (2010) 26–28, 36–37, 44–49 F. Zakaria *The Future of Freedom: Illiberal Democracy at Home and Abroad*, Norton (2007) 114.
10 P. Collier *War, Guns and Votes: Democracy in Dangerous Places*, Vintage (2010) 40, 44, 49.

11 W. Easterly *The White Man's Burden: Why the West's Efforts to Aid the Rest Have Done So Much Harm and So Little Good*, Penguin Press (2006) 120; P. Collier *War, Guns and Votes: Democracy in Dangerous Places*, Vintage (2010) 20–22; F. Zakaria *The Future of Freedom: Illiberal Democracy at Home and Abroad*, Norton (2007) 113.

12 D. Acemoglu and J. Robinson *Why Nations Fail: The Origins of Power, Prosperity and Poverty*, Random House (2012) 217–218.

13 D. Acemoglu and J. Robinson *Why Nations Fail: The Origins of Power, Prosperity and Poverty*, Random House (2012) 436; W. Easterly *The Tyranny of Experts: Economists, Dictators and the Forgotten Rights of the Poor*, Basic Books (2013) 143.

14 F. Zakaria *The Future of Freedom: Illiberal Democracy at Home and Abroad*, Norton (2007) 162–179, 184; see generally A. Gore *The Assault on Reason*, Penguin (2007).

15 W. Easterly *The White Man's Burden: Why the West's Efforts to Aid the Rest Have Done So Much Harm and So Little Good*, Penguin Press (2006) 130–131.

16 F. Zakaria *The Future of Freedom: Illiberal Democracy at Home and Abroad*, Norton (2007) 33.

17 A. Przeworski and F. Limongi "Modernization: Theories and Facts" *World Politics* 49:2 (1997); referenced in F. Zakaria *The Future of Freedom: Illiberal Democracy at Home and Abroad*, Norton (2007) 69–70. See also P. Collier *War, Guns and Votes: Democracy in Dangerous Places*, Vintage (2010) 20–21.

18 P. Collier *The Bottom Billion: Why the Poorest Countries in the World are Failing and What Can be Done About It?* (2007) 118–120, 199; W. Easterly *The White Man's Burden: Why the West's Efforts to Aid the Rest Have Done So Much Harm and So Little Good*, Penguin Press (2006) 189–190. I note that this view is not shared by all scholars. See for example M. Buntaine *Giving Aid Effectively: The Politics of Environmental Performance and Selectivity at Multilateral Development Banks*, Oxford University Press (2016) 11–12.

19 P. Collier *The Bottom Billion: Why the Poorest Countries in the World Are Failing and What Can be Done About It?* Oxford University Press (2007) 122.

20 Interview dated 21 August 2019, notes on file with author.

21 Research by Collier based on cross-country panel date in the last 50 years suggests that the cost of civil wars range from 1.6 percentage to 2.3 percentage of GDP per year of violence; P. Collier *The Bottom Billion: Why the Poorest Countries in the World Are Failing and What Can be Done About It?* (2007) 27.

22 World Bank *World Development Report* (2011).

23 P Collier *The Bottom Billion: Why the Poorest Countries in the World are Failing and What Can be Done About It?* (2007) 31–37.

24 Y. Chaitani and F. Cantu *Beyond Governance and Conflict: Measuring the Impact of the Neighborhood Effect in the Arab Region*, Economic and Social Council for Western Asia (October 2014) http://www.escwa.un.org/divisions/ecri_editor/Download.asp?table_name=ecri_documents&field_name=id&FileID=272

25 P Collier *The Bottom Billion: Why the Poorest Countries in the World are Failing and What Can be Done About It?* (2007) 31.

26 P. Collier, A. Hoeffler et al "Post-Conflict Risks" *Journal of Peace Research* 45:4 (2008) 461–478.

27 P. Collier *War, Guns and Votes: Democracy in Dangerous Places*, Vintage (2010), 81; P. Collier *The Bottom Billion: Why the Poorest Countries in the World are Failing and What Can be Done About It?* (2007) 151–153.

28 J.M. Quinn, T.D. Mason et al "Sustaining the Peace: Determinants of Civil War Recurrence" *International Interactions* 33:2 (2007) 167–193. See also V. Page *Does Peacekeeping Work? Shaping Belligerents' Choices After Civil War*, Princeton University Press (2008).

29 P. Collier *War, Guns and Votes: Democracy in Dangerous Places*, Vintage (2010) 96; see also S. Pinker *The Better Angels of Our Nature: Why Violence Has Declined*, Penguin (2011) 313–314.

30 S. Pinker *The Better Angels of Our Nature: Why Violence Has Declined*, Penguin (2011) 314–315.

31 Collier argues that investing in local capacity to perform the highly specialised tasks associated with the initial stages of post-conflict institution building does not make a lot of sense. Training to the required standard is expensive and lengthy, and the expertise acquired will only be relevant for a short period of time. It is more efficient to import these skills in the form of international development specialists to get a country through a particular moment in time and then send them on their way P. Collier *The Bottom Billion: Why the Poorest Countries in the World are Failing and What Can be Done About It?* (2007) 111–112.

32 J.M. Quinn, T.D. Mason et al "Sustaining the Peace: Determinants of Civil War Recurrence" *International Interactions* 33:2 (2007) 167–193.

33 Collier explains that, while this is ordinarily the domain of IFIs, there are benefits to donors paying development actors to lead on this. Foremost, unless the country is sitting on unexploited resources, the economy is likely to have been bankrupted by conflict. This means that additional debt is not ideal. Moreover, unlike a loan, aid takes the form of a direct and unadulterated stimulus that might be used flexibly, rather than cost effectively. This means that rather than importing cheap labour, aid monies might instead be strategically "wasted" investing in skills building and jobs for locals. P. Collier *War, Guns and Votes: Democracy in Dangerous Places*, Vintage (2010) 88–95.

34 P. Collier *The Bottom Billion: Why the Poorest Countries in the World are Failing and What Can be Done About It?* (2007) 106.

35 P. Collier *War, Guns and Votes: Democracy in Dangerous Places*, Vintage (2010) 80.

36 The Institute for Economics and Peace "The Economic Value of Peace: Measuring the Global Economic Value of Violence and Conflict" The Institute for Economics and Peace (2021) 5. See further P. Collier *War, Guns and Votes: Democracy in Dangerous Places*, Vintage (2010) 98–100.

37 For an iteration on this experiment, see P. Collier *War, Guns and Votes: Democracy in Dangerous Places*, Vintage (2010) 97–100.

38 D. Acemoglu and J. Robinson *Why Nations Fail: The Origins of Power, Prosperity and Poverty*, Random House (2012) 86–87.

39 F. Zakaria *The Future of Freedom: Illiberal Democracy at Home and Abroad*, Norton (2007) 120–121.

40 D. Acemoglu and J. Robinson *Why Nations Fail: The Origins of Power, Prosperity and Poverty*, Random House (2012) 71–75; F. Zakaria *The Future of Freedom: Illiberal Democracy at Home and Abroad*, Norton (2007) 71–72.

41 F. Zakaria *The Future of Freedom: Illiberal Democracy at Home and Abroad*, Norton (2007) 85–86.

42 F. Zakaria *The Future of Freedom: Illiberal Democracy at Home and Abroad*, Norton (2007) 86–87, 94–96, 153, 260–264.

43 F. Zakaria *The Future of Freedom: Illiberal Democracy at Home and Abroad*, Norton (2007) 251, 55–56.

44 F. Zakaria *The Future of Freedom: Illiberal Democracy at Home and Abroad*, Norton (2007) 151.

45 F. Zakaria *The Future of Freedom: Illiberal Democracy at Home and Abroad*, Norton (2007) 16–18.

46 D. Kahneman *Thinking, Fast and Slow*, Penguin (2011) 111–118, 65–70, 87

47 S. Pinker *Enlightenment Now: The Case for Reason, Science, Humanism and Progress*, Allen Lane (2018) 201.

48 D. Kahneman *Thinking, Fast and Slow*, Penguin (2011) 85–86, 245.
49 N. Taleb *Skin in the Game: Hidden Asymmetries in Daily Life*, Random House (2018).
50 A related but slightly different fallacy is "After this therefore because of this", familiar to scientists in the Latin: post hoc ergo propter hoc.
51 Interview dated 12 April 2020, notes on file with author; See further D. Kahneman *Thinking, Fast and Slow*, Penguin (2011) 203–204.
52 S. Pinker *Enlightenment Now: The Case for Reason, Science, Humanism and Progress*, Allen Lane (2018) 367–369; D. Kahneman *Thinking, Fast and Slow*, Penguin (2011) 221–228, 240–242.

5

INNOVATING HUMANITARIAN RESPONSE

The previous chapters described a system where regulatory forces operate imperfectly, creating scope for poor outcomes to go undetected. Part of this stems from a misalignment between the objectives of donors, implementing agencies and beneficiaries. Another factor is that donor governments are rewarded by their constituencies, as opposed to the recipients of aid. Such rewards can push them towards strategies where resources are misallocated and opportunities are overlooked.

It was posited that development practitioners – in particular middle managers – are best positioned to interrupt this pattern by presenting evidence, thinking critically about how and why engagement trajectories are set, and asking questions. In such an environment, it is easier to identify where political niceties and domestic imperatives are crowding out the evidence. Once out in the open, key actors would be forced to make decisions about where their priorities lie. They might still decide that peacekeeping – although it is highly effective – is not worth the headache, but without the smoke screen, space is created to identify alternatives or a middle ground.

Will this be enough? Probably not. The preceding is just an articulate way of saying that we need to stop doing dumb stuff. We also still need a strategy for how – in an era of populism, financial austerity and flailing humanitarian values – to score wins. How to innovate.

I have not been living under a rock. I realise that innovation is the international development system's *mot de jour*; trailed closely by its bedfellow "outside-the-box thinking". But even with this rhetoric, there are not many ideas that can genuinely be classified as new and innovative. We see a lot of repackaging, at best. As a member of WFP's innovation unit told me, "Scaling up a good practice is not innovation. It's common sense".[1]

This should not be all that surprising. Even in the private sector, innovation is problematic and contested. We've also known about this for a long time. Professor Everett Rogers released his dissemination of innovation theory in 1971, and it is still well regarded today. He describes innovation capacity as sitting on a bell curve. In any organisation there will be innovators (2 percent), early adopters (14 percent), early majority (34 percent),

DOI: 10.4324/9781003376996-6

late majority (34 percent) and laggards (16 percent). The upshot is that true innovators are scarce, and vastly outweighed by discontents and spoilers.

The aid and humanitarian sectors face additional challenges. The beneficiary population is usually highly vulnerable. This means that the worst scenario is not a recall of a new product line; it is death. Agencies also do not operate with a lot of "fat" – experimenting means that someone goes without, and that might mean food, shelter or medicine. Finally, they are walking a tightrope. As we discussed in Chapter 2, at this moment there is unprecedented scepticism around the aid sector's capacity to deliver. This is manifesting in funding instability, especially for agencies with less popular mandates; donor governments' development portfolios being subsumed by foreign policy; and the evolution of new players who are less aligned to humanitarian principles than they are willing to deliver a result. What this means is that there is no room for error. Disaster or a scandal could mean an agency's demise. Consider Oxfam, which, following the Haiti sexual exploitation scandal, faced budget cuts in the order of GBP16 million, closed operations in 18 countries and cut 1,500 jobs.

The irony is that the only pathway out of this abyss *is* to innovate – to come up with more impactful, sustainable and cost-effective ways to deliver human development outcomes. So what would it take for agencies to become proper innovators? What conditions would need to be set in place, what incentives? And what challenges would need to be overcome?

To flesh this out we need to enter the world of refugee response and examine the events that brought together the countries hosting Syrian refugees, the agency mandated with refugee protection and the donors funding it (which, serendipitously, also found themselves in the middle of a refugee hosting dilemma). In this example, innovation was realised, but it was by no means clean. It was contested and disrupted before being somewhat foisted onto decision-makers.

An examination of this messiness tells us a lot about how innovation might be generated in the future, and how impediments such as turf battles and geopolitical sensitivities can be diverted to become drivers of change. One of the lessons is that the risks involved are very real. It is not just a matter of agencies gritting their teeth and getting on with matters. Risks need to be understood and managed in order to protect agencies' unique space as mandate holders. This calls for strategic thinking; for example looking for new sources for innovation, outsourcing risk onto entities better situated to handle it, and harnessing the immense power of moments.

5.1 A crash course in refugee response

For readers who are not familiar with the workings of the modern refugee assistance architecture, I'll start with some background. While accounts of refuge being granted to persons fleeing persecution date back millennia, it was the displacement caused by World War I and the conflicts flanking it that impelled states to consider multilateral solutions. Starting in 1920, no less than six organisations were created under the League of Nations framework, each responding to the needs of a discreet group seeking protection outside its country of origin.[2]

By the time the UN was created in 1945, it was clear that stronger arrangements were required. At its first session in 1946, the General Assembly drew attention to the fundamental principle of non-refoulement,[3] followed – two years later – by the Universal Declaration on Human Rights (1948), which recognised the right to seek asylum.[4] It was in these twin principles that a nascent body of international refugee law began to form.

Despite seemingly broad aspirations on the part of the framers, the apparatus created was quite limited. The International Refugee Organization (1946)[5] acted principally as a resettlement agency. Even its successor, the Office of the UN High Commissioner for Refugees, was set up under a three-year term and granted a protection as opposed to an operational mandate. Moreover, although UNHCR's mandate was universal, the definition of a refugee outlined in the Convention was not.[6] Article 1 limited the scope of protection to persons forced to leave their country "as a result of events occurring before 1 January 1951". It would take until 1967 for these geographic and temporal limits to be lifted, and 2003 for the agency to be recognised as a permanent fixture among other UN agencies.[7]

In part, these limitations reflect the optimism of the time – a genuine belief that the United Nations framework would prevent a repetition of World War II's atrocities. They also, however, point to a level of reluctance on the part of states to sign a "blank cheque" concerning the protection and hosting of future waves of refugees.

As time would reveal, whatever role optimism played in these decisions would prove misplaced, and states' reluctance prescient. The year 2020 saw the number of asylum seekers and refugees exceed 30 million globally – more than at any point since the end of World War II.[8] To accommodate such numbers, the support framework has also grown. At its 70th anniversary, UNHCR boasted an annual budget of over USD8.6 billion. Its 18,000-strong staffing pool are dispersed across 135 countries and engage in traditional tasks such protection and durable solutions, as well as a widening array of operational roles including food, shelter, water, sanitation, health care, livelihoods and social services. As at 2020, 150 states were party to the Convention, 106 of which sit on the organisation's Executive Committee. UNHCR is also by no means the only player. In any refugee setting, a broad range of actors – national and international, humanitarian and development – will generally be found.

It might be concluded from this description that the international protection framework is both robust and strengthening over time. Images, however, can be deceptive. Despite its largess, the refugee architecture is fragile. Its efficacy depends on the willingness of states to grant asylum and not refoule refugees until a durable solution – voluntary repatriation, local integration or third country resettlement – is found. While states are technically bound to uphold these principles (they are enshrined in articles 14 and 33 of the Refugee Convention, and in international customary law), enforcement is difficult. In practice, acquiescence depends on a mixture of goodwill, receptivity to pressure and the perceived fairness of the "rules of the game". And herein lies the problem; because these "rules of the game" were written for a different situation in a different era, what they offer host states has become increasingly unappealing.

Let me set out why. Over the past 70 years the nature of conflict has fundamentally changed. When the Refugees Convention was drafted, war was a tool wielded by the superpowers of the day. Today, rich countries don't go to war – with each other, or with anyone else. The conflicts that do take place are predominately intra-state and affect the developing world. Because the vast majority of today's refugees are fleeing conflict (as opposed to individual persecution), it follows that countries of asylum are disproportionately concentrated in the global south. This remains true even considering the current crisis engulfing the Ukraine and spilling over into Europe.

The impacts of refugee hosting on these states can be broad and deleterious. When a population increases unexpectedly, the reach and quality of public services including healthcare, infrastructure, education, and water and sanitation are all impacted. It can also drive price hikes in rent and food, and compound extant challenges such as unemployment, informal economies, institutional dysfunction and natural resource deficits. This lack of balance has evolved into an unspoken partnership; whereby "[d]onors write cheques to support humanitarian relief and host countries of first asylum are expected to provide the territory on the refugees are hosted".[9] These cheques are sizable. Last year humanitarian aid agencies and national humanitarian organisations employed over 570,000 people and spent around USD32 billion.[10]

In theory, this system has the potential to work well. However, a key characteristic of modern refugee crises is their length; more than 6.5 million refugees currently live in protracted situations, and they are likely to do so for an average of 23 years. Over the last decade, less than 2 percent of the global refugee caseload repatriated, was resettled or locally integrated. In short, today's refugees are almost exclusively stationary, and remain that way for long periods of time.

This creates a problem because while states are bound to accept and not refoule refugees, there is no reciprocal or binding rule on burden sharing to offset the associated costs. The situation might be best understood as host states providing a global public good.[11] Like other public goods, some states are able to "free ride" on the provision of refugee protection by host countries as they are not compelled to adequately share the associated burdens. Today, this is manifesting in a "north-south impasse"[12] whereby wealthy developed states are inclined to scale back aid once the urgency of an emergency situation has worn off, leaving host states to assume an increased proportion of the costs – and weakening their capacity to meet basic needs and exacerbating existing development challenges.[13] The term for this in agency parlance is "donor fatigue".

For refugee populations, situations of protraction are even more dire. Because they rarely enjoy labour market access, refugees rely predominantly on savings and humanitarian assistance. The situation is akin to a manufactured poverty trap, whereby a lack of access to capital, credit and other transitional opportunities keeps a population in a state of destitution. The consequences of protracted poverty are well set out in the literature. Such groups perform poorly on a range of welfare indicators, including health, education and indebtedness. They are also more vulnerable to human trafficking, exploitation and negative coping mechanisms such as survival sex, informal and child labour and early marriage. The long-term impact of reduced autonomy and the generational effects of growing up in a refugee context are less well researched but are presumed to be tangible and negative.

A final loser – often overlooked in policy debates – is the future country of return. The implications of protracted displacement in terms of post-conflict recovery and stability are scantly understood. It is clear, however, that in refugee contexts, education gaps and lack of access to livelihoods opportunities result in skills loss. Similarly, long-term dependency and disenfranchisement are linked to a loss of resilience that impacts a population's ability to recover from shocks. There are also the consequences of human capital loss. As demonstrated in the 2015–2018 Euro-refugee crisis, it is the entrepreneurial, educated and employable that tend to seek irregular migration. It is likewise these profiles that are most likely to benefit from resettlement and have better chances of successful integration. In short, those with the greatest capacity to contribute to post-conflict reconstruction and state building are the ones most likely to leave and not return.

This situation has led many to criticise the Refugees Convention as an outdated tool, and UNHCR as ill-equipped to deal effectively with modern displacement crises. The fix, they argue, is quite obvious. The Convention needs to be elaborated to reflect today's challenges. Specifically, host states need better guarantees of support for as long as they are delivering a global public good. And while the international community is in the business of rewriting, they should probably expand the definition of a refugee to include new forms of persecution such as LGBTQI[14] and causal drivers such as climate change.

What these critics do not see is that changing the rules is far from an easy fix. Rights around asylum and non-refoulement have always been difficult to reconcile with the notion of state sovereignty upon which the UN Charter is based. Regardless of its wealth or power, the idea that one's territory could become home to a foreign population – of an indeterminable size and for an indeterminable length of time – is enough to make any government squirm. The post–World War II political climate was unique in this regard. In the wake of the armistice, the full extent of the atrocities committed were becoming known, in particular the fate of Jews who were prevented from escaping Nazi-controlled areas. This reckoning gave rise to a collective social consciousness whereby states were willing to concede part of their sovereignty to prevent history from repeating itself. There were also fewer players to convince. At its founding in 1945, the UN was made up of 51 member states. The upshot is that of the countries hosting the most refugees today – such as Uganda, Bangladesh, Jordan, Sudan and Pakistan – most were not part of the rule-setting discussion, either because they were not yet states or were otherwise not at the table.

Today's geopolitical climate is very different. Camaraderie, humanitarianism and partnership have been replaced with populism, anti-immigrant rhetoric and policies of protectionism. Angst around asylum is particularly discernible as states find creative ways to bypass their Convention obligations. Offshore processing – where asylum seekers are relocated to neighboring countries while their cases are processed – is one pernicious trend. The start point can be traced back to an early, perhaps unexpected, dissenter. In the early 2000s, Australia introduced the Pacific Solution – a partnership entered into with neighboring Nauru and Papua New Guinea to host would-be asylum seekers attempting to arrive in Australia by boat in exchange for more generous aid agreements. The only Australian destination where boat arrivals could be processed was the remote Christmas Island, which was then removed from the country's migration zone to prevent those subsequently classified as refugees from mainland entry.

The idea of offshore processing was quickly taken up by the United Kingdom in 2003, Germany in 2005 and most recently by Austria. While such posturing did not come to fruition, the EU has adopted increasingly restrictive migration policies. These are best showcased by its deals with Turkey and Libya, which aim to obstruct the movement of asylum seekers bound for Europe (including support to the coast guard to intercept and return refugees leaving by boat). Perhaps most disconcerting, in July 2020 the Trump administration introduced a scheme whereby any person entering the US through its southern border would be returned to Mexico or Guatemala while their cases were considered. This was after it greatly reduced its resettlement quota, defunded UNRWA and refused to endorse the Global Compact on Refugees (2018).[15]

Although the offshore processing scheme was withdrawn by President Joe Biden in February 2021, a budding trend seems unmistakable. Certainly, the Covid-19 pandemic has opened up new opportunities for countries to close their borders, restrict humanitarian access and repatriate unwanted visitors. As the climate emergency worsens and states anticipate increased irregular migration, it is likely that hosts will continue to – if not become more comfortable with – placing security ahead of international stewardship.

Against this backdrop, UNHCR finds itself between a rock and a hard place. For the most part, the states flaunting their Convention responsibilities – Australia, the US and a handful of Western European states – are dealing with a minority of the global asylum seeker caseload. They are, however, important donors and/or resettlement countries. Criticising them or invoking a legal response is therefore imbued with risk. In the current climate, there is a genuine possibility that such states might withdraw from the Convention, potentially causing a riptide of retreat. An equally valid argument is that any attempt to shame or otherwise compel states to act as good international citizens would underscore that UNHCR actually has few legal tools to enforce obligations on states.[16]

The challenges faced by UNHCR thus go far beyond forging better solutions for refugees in protracted settings. Innovation – better ways of doing things – is desperately needed, but the agency has few tools to get there and the path is treacherous. In such situations the only certainty is that something will happen to interrupt the status quo. And in 2014, this is exactly what occurred. It wasn't, as many anticipated, a mass refoulement of refugees or a state party's withdrawal. It was an idea. And it was one that has changed the face of refugee assistance. The purpose of this chapter is to understand this process of innovation and how the lessons can be replicated in the system more broadly.

5.2 An idea is born

There is no better example of the challenges faced by host states than the ones affected by the conflict in Syria. Of the 10.3 million Syrians forcibly displaced, over 2.9 million sought refuge in Turkey, over a million in Lebanon and 66,000 in the Hashemite Kingdom of Jordan.[17] This latter country, although the numbers were smaller by comparison, perhaps felt the worst impacts. With no water or oil, a struggling economy and volatile neighbours, Jordan had little to offer. But true to their proud Hashemite tradition, they opened their borders and shared what they had, just like they did for Palestinians in 1948, Lebanese in 1975 and Iraqis in 1991.[18]

Jordan was also my home for five years at the height of the Syria crisis. I had taken on the mandate of setting up the country's first policy think tank – the West Asia North Africa Institute – under Royal Family patronage. As a start-up, the challenges were enormous. We were dirt poor and smirked at by many, but my team of fiercely intelligent researchers was full of pluck and enthusiasm. One of our priority areas was Middle East economic policy, particularly how rentier states could reorient their factors of production to encourage growth and tackle youth unemployment. Another research theme was displacement and how pressures around movement were impacting human security. The idea that these two issues perhaps had a common solution was posed at more than one staff meeting by our displacement lead, Sean Thomas. Refugees participating in the labour market, however, was a highly sensitive and politically polarising topic. Much to Sean's disappointment, we were strongly encouraged by the local and international refugee focal points to leave the topic alone.

But good ideas are resilient, so I sent Sean off to the library, challenging him to bring me a more convincing argument. He came back with some economic theory posed by Oxford University political economist, Paul Collier. We took to Google to discover what Paul was up to. In fact, his email address was not difficult to find so I decided to put Sean's ideas to him. Without about 10 minutes Paul had written back. His email was professional and directed: interesting idea, do a bit more homework and let me know how it goes.

And work we did. Two research teams were banded together and quickly began to churn out both data and ideas. This was enough to get Paul on a plane, bringing with him the charismatic Professor Alexander Betts who ran the Refugees Studies Centre at the University of Oxford.

That first morning, we squeezed into a library on the upper floor of the palace complex. Paul and Alex listened patiently as we set out our ideas in lead up to what we thought would be a fruitful brainstorming session. However, there is a reason why our guests were known as the best in their field. They hadn't come to brainstorm; they had already come up with an idea. Had it not been so ingenious, we might have all been a bit deflated. I can recall Sean slumping back in his chair mumbling to himself "Dammit, that's just so much better.".

Paul started with an observation that I now regard as pivotal to all development and humanitarian work: states do nothing – nothing well at least – unless it is in their interests. So, they pushed us, what did Jordan need? And whatever that something is, they continued, it needed to wind into a narrative where the refugee population eventually returned to Syria. Indeed, the legacy of offering a home to Palestinian refugees was such that Jordan was sitting on a demographic precipice; the country simply could not entertain the idea of a permanent refugee presence.

We figured that what Jordan needed was a vibrant economy for its youthful population. The government, in fact, already had a plan for this, and it wasn't a bad one. With its small size and no natural endowments of oil or water, Jordan's strategy was to become the Singapore of the Middle East. To enable this, the government had invested in a strong education sector geared towards technology-driven innovation. Significant progress has been made; economic and industrial zones had been set up throughout the country, complemented by investment-friendly policies and a clear legislative and regulatory framework. But there, about a decade prior, the initiative had stagnated. The problem was that no one wanted to invest in Jordan. The country's middle-income status rendered it largely ineligible for IMF or World Bank assistance, whereas private investors were put off by Jordan's less than favourable trade agreements, bureaucracy, negligible resources, limited market access and conflict-ridden neighbours.[19] They were probably right; even with investment, Jordan would struggle to overcome the entry barriers to global trade markets. It would have been competing, for example, with Asia, which enjoys stability, uninterrupted coastlines, plentiful natural resources and a large, low-cost labour force.

Paul explained Jordan's problem as one of conglomerates of scale or, more simply, the need for a "cluster". They needed to identify a product – one that they could make better than other countries, expand to scale and then develop competitiveness. Most of the time, manufacturing clusters develop naturally, sometimes with a bit of luck thrown in. But in the case of Jordan, because its economy faced so many impediments, something more or something different would be needed. And maybe they did have something: refugees.

5.3 From an idea to a plan

What happened next involved a bit of work on both sides. But to be clear, while WANA crunched the numbers, added political nuance and leveraged our connections to pique the interest of the right people, the ideas belonged to Paul and Alex. With their guidance, at the invitation of the Royal Hashemite Court, we published a White Paper in the Institute's name, setting out a fairly unorthodox theory. It went like this.

To attract the investment needed to start a cluster and break into global markets, Jordan needed to provide work permits to refugees. Indeed, a principal reason attributed to the underutilisation of Jordan's development zones was the lack of complementarity between the labour force required and local labour market dynamics. A less politically correct way of saying this is that Jordanians just didn't want to work there. Arab pride mixed with strong investment in education meant that Jordanians were really only interested in white collar jobs. But the refugee population constituted an immediately available, affordable and appropriately skilled set of workers. UNHCR registration data indicated at least 21,208 Syrian refugee builders, many of whom were already working in the construction sector informally. The available data also suggested that there was room for a significant number of relevantly skilled Syrians to be integrated into open sectors within existing foreign labour quotas – particularly agriculture.[20]

If refugees had permission to work, this might attract a set of investors keen to exploit a new profit opportunity. These might include (i) manufacturing companies with consumer markets likely to covet goods produced using "safe" Syrian refugee labour; (ii) energy, manufacturing and pharmaceutical companies forced to leave Syria but looking to re-establish operations in a similar but stable operating environment; and (iii) reconstruction industries seeking to secure a foothold in a post-conflict Syria such as semi-refined and refined raw materials industries.

To push investors over the line, other vested stakeholders might be encouraged to play a role. First in line would be donor governments, who needed to address the humanitarian situation but might prefer for this to be in the form of something more constructive and sustainable than continuing humanitarian aid. As part of a renegotiated aid package, they might also offer more attractive free trade or market access agreements, increasing the appeal of Jordan to investors. International financial institutions – the World Bank and International Monetary Fund – might also be convinced to bend their rules and provide assistance through loans to offset manufacturing development or subsidise plant establishment.

Jordan would secure two wins. First, manufacturing and industrial opportunities would establish new white-collar positions. This would allow the government to begin to address a long-standing tension in the Jordanian economy: the disconnect between the skills sets and ambitions of the bourgeoning youth population, and the number and type of jobs available. Second, because the investment model proposed was based on so-called "footloose industry", Syrians had a sure ticket home. The idea was that following a cessation in hostilities, new companies would have the opportunity to expand operations to Syria, taking advantage of a new market and utilising a trained repatriating worker population. Existing plants, however, would remain in Jordan, the country having established itself as a safe and profitable business environment.

5.4 The London Compact Agreements

The role of the WANA Institute pretty much ended there. The proposal got owned up the food chain and we contentedly watched from the side lines as a fairly incredible process played out. At the Supporting Syria and the Region Conference held in London on 4 February 2016, Jordan, Lebanon and Turkey released strategies for refugee labour market inclusion and job creation conditional upon unprecedented increases in donor funding, concessional loans and agreements pertaining to market access.

Jordan secured the following commitments:

- Pledges amounting to around USD700 million in grants to support the Jordan Response Plan for 2016.
- Additional pledges of around USD700 million in grants for 2017 and 2018.
- Increase in Multilateral Development Bank financing from USD800 million to USD1.9 billion.
- Donor support for job creation programmes for Syrian refugees and host communities.
- Additional pledges of around USD300 million of grant or grant equivalent.
- A plan for modifying EU Rules of Origin.

Against these pledges, the government of Jordan committed to:

- Provide 200,000 work opportunities for Syrian refugees over the following three years and until 2018.

- Commence the required administrative changes to allow Syrian refugees to apply for work permits (renewable annually in accordance with existing laws and regulations).
- Formalise existing Syrian refugee businesses.
- Establish new tax-generating businesses.
- Allow a specific percentage of Syrian involvement in municipal works, through private sector employment on a contractual basis.
- Improve the business and investment climate (the government committed to produce a detailed plan on the reforms and incentives needed to boost the investment architecture with technical assistance from key donors, the World Bank and the IMF, by mid-2016).[21]

While this might appear to have been a streamlined process, a lot had to happen for the cards to fall correctly into place. Paul and Alex remained involved in important ways, including by engaging former colleagues (Shanta Devarajan, then the World Bank's Chief Economist for the Middle East and North Africa) and a former student (Stefan Dercon, DFID's Chief Economist), and placing a carefully timed article in *The Spectator*. These, plus other quiet measures, meant that the Jordanian delegation arrived in London with an extraordinarily strong hand. I would also like to think that in the mix was some forward thinking around how best to support a post-conflict Syria and protect it from recidivism – and perhaps even a subtle acknowledgement by donors that the humanitarian legal framework was inherently inequitable.

But what really drove the deals home was that at the same moment host states were negotiating for a relaxation in Rules of Origin, loans and grants, Europe was desperate to put the brakes on an unregulated flow of non-nationals into its territories. Starting in 2015, irregular population movements into Europe demonstrated that, in the absence of opportunity, refugees and others would seek better conditions elsewhere. It was clear that the most pragmatic way to stop this flow was for host states to offer more and better opportunities to discourage secondary movements.

In short, a deal was brokered. Host states opened up their labour markets in return for new and heightened forms of assistance long sought after to grow their economies. Donor states anticipated that this would provide a sufficient incentive for refugees to remain in neighbouring host states, and perhaps even set in place enabling conditions to buffer withdrawals of humanitarian support over time.

And to a large extent this worked; donors bought their way out of an increasingly desperate situation. But in doing so, European states showed their hand. Despite having international obligations, member states had no interest in hosting refugees on the same scale as Jordan, Turkey and Lebanon. Moreover, they were willing to pay a high price to maintain the status quo ante. How this levelling of the playing field would go on to influence the management of future displacement crises is still playing out.

5.5 Things fall apart

Given these extraordinary events, it was quite hard to watch in the months following the London Conference as slow progress on both work permits and pledges led many to ask: "What went wrong?" To answer this question, the WANA research team was led back to the table by an innovation-leaning Swedish NGO named Spark. Armed with more and better data, we were also curious to learn what Jordan's experience meant for Compact Agreements more generally – in short, did they make sense, and if so under what conditions? I will set out our findings in detail, first to highlight some of the core impediments and opportunities in promoting refugee livelihoods, but also because it gives insight into the power that quantitative economics can have in unravelling development challenges.

As to the first question – what went wrong – we found three mutually constituting obstacles that had transformed realising host state and donor commitments from challenging to impossible.

5.5.1 Insufficient demand

First, the appeal of legalised working status for refugees vis-à-vis the status quo was significantly overstated. This was less a result of out-of-touch decision-makers making errors of judgement than it was a simple misinterpretation of evidence. Syrians clearly had a desire to work – this was their overwhelming stated preference in UNHCR protection assessments. Private sector employers likewise stated that they would be likely to hire Syrians with work permits.[22] The available data also suggested that there was room for a significant number of relevantly skilled Syrians to be integrated into open sectors within existing foreign labour quotas – particularly construction and agriculture.[23] The problem was that while there was nothing unreasonable or false about any of these statements, together they did not add up to a demand for work permits. The error was one with which econometricians are familiar – just because a group says they want something, this doesn't necessarily mean that they will do it given the opportunity.[24] In particular, when employers stated that they would likely hire permit-holding refugees, *ceteris paribus* they would still prefer to hire them illegally given the opportunity. The upshot was that providing access to work permits, even at no cost, was not sufficient to facilitate meaningful labour market inclusion. In reality, much of the appeal of Syrian workers lay in their informal status; they could be employed cheaply, and without employers having to pay social security or secure permits.[25] Moreover, legalisation imposed costs that employers were reluctant to bear, including minimum remuneration and fair working conditions. As the weaker party, Syrians were hardly in a position to press their employers to assume these costs.

5.5.2 The cost of integration

A second mistaken assumption was that Syrians could easily be integrated into sectors where there was a known shortage of low-skilled labour. Again, this thinking was neither excessive nor unreasonable. It was only when WANA staff went beyond business owners and investors to speak directly with floor-level factory managers that we began to understand why they were reluctant to employ this category of worker. It turned out that mechanisation trends, particularly in the paper, plastic and packaging and the wood and furniture sectors, meant that employees required significant in-house training – usually 1–2 years – before they could make a cost-effective contribution to the workplace. Businesses were simply not willing to make such an investment for a group that they perceived was likely to repatriate in the near future. And again, for those employers who were willing to make such an investment, or where training was less intensive, it was easier and cheaper to employ Syrians informally.

5.5.3 Data imperfections

A final obstacle was that Jordan's commitment to provide 200,000 working opportunities for refugees was based on a misreading of the data. According to UNHCR registration numbers, Jordan was hosting a total of 649,563 Syrian refugees, including children, as of May 2016. When disaggregated for age and gender, this suggested a working-age population of 291,610, of whom 138,540 were male. Based on these figures, meeting the 200,000 goal would already be challenging; all men would need to find employment, plus around 20 percent of women – a significant increase in the rate at which women worked pre-crisis. But this also assumed that every working-age male and female was *able and willing* to work. Relying on data collected by WANA Institute and IPSOS in 2016, the combined male and female Syrian refugee labour participation workforce in 2016 was 163,050. In other words, even if *all* males and females who were able and willing to work could find employment, Jordan would still only be able to reach around 80 percent of its 200,000 work permit goal.[26]

5.5.4 A perfect storm

Insufficient demand for permits coupled with unrealistic expectations coalesced in such a way that Jordan was unable to muster what was needed to overcome its most difficult constraint: job availability. It took time for all parties to realise that regardless of any consensus around refugees' permission or right to work, goodwill could not create jobs. It was not that those with decision-making responsibility overlooked the stagnation in Jordan's job market. In fact, job creation was a critical component of the Compact Agreements. The plan was that the jobs needed would be created by the stimulus that would follow the combination of pledges, soft loans and ripple-down investment.

In terms of donors releasing funds, a cat-and-mouse game ensued. Formalisation required that incentives be directed at both refugees and employers. This was problematic insofar as donors' willingness to make good on their pledges was somewhat contingent on a level of job formalisation taking place. The heated debates between EU staffers, senior representatives of the humanitarian community and the government will not easily be forgotten by those present. In terms of investment – by far the most difficult challenge – the catalytic process that was supposed to pique the imaginations of the private sector never got started. In retrospect, Jordan's structural deficits, such as poor resource endowments, limited sea access and proximity to conflict, presented too much of a disincentive for private sector companies.

This series of (fairly benign) missteps and incorrect (but well-reasoned) assumptions fuelled criticism that the Compact Agreements were inherently flawed and ultimately not within Jordan's interests. Some even postulated that the Agreements provided a stop-gap solution to Europe's refugee problem, but with such unrealistic expectations placed on Jordan that it could not translate improved market access into any tangible benefit. This is probably an unfair assessment. A more accurate conclusion is that even when all parties are supportive of livelihoods approaches, refugee labour market integration will still be a difficult "two steps forward one step back" process. This is especially the case where unemployment is rife and the informal labour market is strong.

This situation might have been avoided had decision-making been grounded upon a stronger evidence base, particularly around a realistic job permit goal and the kinds of incentives needed to hire Syrians or regularise their informal employment status. Arguably, such corrections might have occurred mid-flight. But this did not happen, and it must be acknowledged that this was in part due to lack of mutual trust and donors' aversion to risk.

5.6 A proof of concept

While all this might reek of missed opportunity, these insights piqued the excitement of the WANA research team. Our reading of this data suggested that it was too soon to shut the door on Compact-type arrangements. It seemed we were not the only ones. While key actors were tripping over each other to distance themselves from the disappointment that had enveloped the Jordan experiment, progress was being made elsewhere.

Seven months after the London conference, in September 2016, the New York Declaration for Refugees and Migrants was signed by all 193 UN member states. Annexed to this Declaration was the Comprehensive Refugee

Response Framework (CRRF) – a road map setting out a new way of approaching protracted refugee situations. Key objectives included easing pressure on host states and facilitating refugee self-reliance – a clear acknowledgment of the need for greater equity in burden sharing. Moreover, by highlighting the need for a longer-term approach, early engagement by development actors, and a widening of stakeholders to include the private sector and IFIs, it seemed that pragmatism had risen to the fore. Finally, there was talk that UNHCR was prepping to launch a series of pilot Compact-type experiments with support from the World Bank. Quietly, the latter agreed to support WANA to come up with a more sophisticated proof of concept. We were not aware until much later, but the Bank was running its own numbers and wanted a parallel process against which to compare its findings.

Before I present the data, let's recap the logical appeal of supporting refugee livelihoods and self-sufficiency. From the perspective of most refugees, access to livelihoods opportunities is vastly preferable to material assistance. Jobs provide a degree of autonomy, dignity and relief from boredom, eliminating some of the criticisms associated with food vouchers and direct assistance.[27] They can also protect against more insidious consequences. Long-term unemployment and poverty are associated with domestic abuse, survival sex and child labour. Particularly in the case of young men, lack of opportunity, hopelessness and marginalisation are precursors to several forms of violence.[28]

Investing in livelihoods should also work for donors, who are keen to avoid sunken costs and the criticism levelled when they eventually withdraw support.

But the most compelling argument is perhaps the least discussed. Readers should recall from the last chapter the devastating and broad-reaching consequences of war, and moreover that the best way to avoid war is to prevent defused conflicts from reigniting. It follows that among the things a post-conflict Syria would need was young, able-bodied men (to rebuild), the educated (to intellectually contribute) and the financially privileged (to reboot the private sector). This is the precisely the demographic that left for Europe; indeed it is where half of the Syrian population with a university degree is currently located.[29] Although it sounds Machiavellian, what host states needed to create was a situation where refugees were both not too desperate to leave, but not content enough to set down roots. Certainly, the evidence is that had this group enjoyed opportunities close to home – where they spoke the language and had family ties or cultural links – most would not have got on boats.[30]

So far, investing in refugee livelihoods seems to be a no-brainer. The only player left to convince is host states – arguably the most important player in terms of programming feasibility. The evidence is that in *certain contexts*, host-state economies can benefit from an injection of refugee labour. The most obvious example is in countries with ageing populations or negative population growth rates. Another example is in economies with labour gaps that nationals cannot or are not willing to occupy. When new market entrants fill such gaps, they stimulate sectorial growth and provide nationals with the conditions needed for upward occupational mobility. This is important for reasons beyond sectorial sustainability and national productivity. The presence of newcomers in these roles opens inroads for the creation of new, value-added opportunities, which nationals are better positioned and motivated to fill. There is even some evidence that an increasing proportion of professional positions available to nationals vis-à-vis low-skilled and labour-intensive jobs encourages nationals to invest in education and skills building. A final example is where the host economy's comparative advantage is the production of low-cost exports. Here, an increase in labour supply can promote formalisation among low-skilled nationals and facilitate market expansion, including into horizontal value chains. Indeed, a productive, sustainable industrial base has long been hailed for creating jobs and expanding a state's export base. Moreover, where a labour supply injection brings new skills, this can facilitate diversification, or start a process of structural change to shift production towards more value-added and knowledge-intense activities.[31] In each of these growth contexts, the weight of evidence is that while local wages may fall, over time economies are flexible enough to absorb additional labour and wages recover to their initial levels.[32]

Unfortunately, these are rarely the contexts in which refugees find themselves. More likely, these economies will be stagnant or contracting.[33] In such situations, where the skills of refugees compete with existing labour or the influx is large relative to the size of the economy, wages and employment tend to be negatively affected. This impact will be felt by both refugees and nationals, and may persist for many years.

The only way to remedy this situation is to provide economic stimulus. But how much stimulus, when and from who remain unclear. This was certainly where things fell apart in Jordan, so it was an important question. Important enough, we decided, to test it.

Our theory was that if a proportion of the resources spent on long-term refugee hosting (humanitarian funds) was invested in labour-intensive livelihoods projects at an early stage of a displacement crisis, this would allow a proportion of the refugee population to become self-sufficient. We wanted to know if a break-even point could be detected, or even a point after which cost savings might accrue. The numbers were getting pretty complex, so in 2017 we partnered with the Institute for Economics and Peace to examine the impact that different levels of investment would have had on economic growth and employment in the context of the Jordanian economy. Using a regression model, these outcomes were compared to the costs of supporting refugees currently borne by the host state and the international community.[34]

A first step was to properly calculate the cost of hosting refugees. The methodology used took into account eight categories of direct and indirect costs, including interest on debt, food subsidy expenses and increased trade deficit losses, as well as erosion of environmental capital and reduced social cohesion resulting from prolonged displacement. It also took into account the benefits accrued, such as the impacts of increased demand and external investment. The findings estimated the combined direct and indirect cost of hosting refugees in Jordan from 2011 to 2016 at USD22.5 billion. Of this amount, USD15.25 billion was borne by Jordan (68 percent) and USD7.25 billion by the international community (32 percent). Conservatively assuming that the current humanitarian unit costs remained constant, the model projected that this cost would rise to USD27 billion for the period 2016–2020, with a cumulative cost of over USD71 billion by 2025.

The second step was to calculate the impact, in terms of GDP growth and employment, of investing different amounts of capital relatively early in the crisis (we used 2014). Perhaps not surprisingly, in all cases the investment approach proved to be more economically efficient when compared with humanitarian assistance. For example, an investment of USD3.1 billion (around half of the 2016 hosting cost) was estimated to have created 125,300 jobs in the first year, with Jordan seeing an annual increase in the economic growth rate of 0.45 percent over the next decade. In short, the impact of refugees entering the labour market and becoming self-reliant made the "investment approach" more economically efficient than the "humanitarian approach" within four years.

This modelling process was admittedly imperfect and relied upon various assumptions.[35] For example, fiscal stimulus has the potential to increase economic growth and employment when an economy is performing below its capacity and potential growth level. This was true in the case in Jordan, but would not necessarily apply to other economies. The model also assumed that as refugees became employed and self-sufficient, a proportional amount of humanitarian assistance and its delivery architecture could be eliminated. In practice, some refugees will require ongoing protection and assistance, and moreover, even if self-sufficiency was possible for a proportion of a refugee population, the associated "humanitarian architecture" can be impractical to scale back. The results did, however, offer a sound argument for the efficacy of investing in self-sufficiency vis-à-vis supporting basic needs over the long term. This left only one question – who might supply such funds?

5.7 Show me the money

5.7.1 The devil you know

The most reasonable answer is that this stimulus would come from donors. The economics certainly makes sense – donors make large resource contributions early on in a crisis, rather than in small amounts over a longer timeframe. In essence, all that is being requested is a reallocation of funds. The pragmatics, however, are complicated. Humanitarian funds are generated, earmarked and administered differently from development funds. Such an approach would likely be complicated by domestic rules, priorities and public sentiment, not to mention the protests that would ignite from within the humanitarian and development establishments. Perhaps more importantly, the approach is risky. It requires that donors speculate on whether a refugee situation is likely to become protracted or not. If refugees return home relatively quickly, more money will have been spent than necessary.[36]

An evaluation of the initial years of the CRRF seems – unfortunately – to reflect this. By September 2018, 15 countries were applying the new framework and UNHCR should be credited for its efforts to build momentum around the initiative, variously labelled a "game changer", "minor miracle" and "a once in a lifetime opportunity". From the Leaders' Summit on Refugees (2016) to the Global Compact on Refugees (2018) and Global Refugee Forum (2019), UNHCR has pulled out all the stops to garner attention and engage new stakeholders. The upshot is that if anything was going to get donors to the table, it was this. But while donors are supportive of the CRRF (as they should be – it makes far more sense than what came before it), they have not opened their wallets. UNHCR's traditional donors remain the same and although some are directly supporting CRRF projects or related initiatives, there is no evidence that this is new (as opposed to reallocated) funding or that the organisation's overall financial health has improved because of the CRRF.[37]

5.7.2 *The new kid on the block*

What about the complementary sources of funding identified under the CRRF framework – international financial institutions (IFIs) such as the World Bank, International Monetary Fund and regional development banks?

IFIs extending their loan and grant-making facilities to refugee host states actually predates the CRRF, although not significantly. The International Development Association's (IDA) financing arrangements for the period 2014–2017 (IDA-17) channelled funds to interventions supporting refugee and local communities through a regional window entitled "Development Response to Displacement Impacts Projects". In April 2016, the Global Concessional Financing Facility (GCFF) was launched – focused principally on Jordan and Lebanon – to support projects co-benefiting refugee and host population groups. Then in December 2016, IDA-18 was negotiated – a USD2 billion regional sub-window specifically to support refugees and host communities. In practice this meant that financing support (low or zero interest loans and grants) was made available to 14 low-income countries (including three CRRF countries), contingent upon refugee protection frameworks and policy action plans being set in place.

Multi-donor trust funds have been a further source of financing. The USD500 million Ethiopia Jobs Compact (a set of industrial parks to support the creation of 100,000 jobs, 30 percent earmarked for refugees) was financed by the World Bank, European Union Investment Bank, DFID, the Netherlands government and the European Union.

That IFIs were engaging with host states prior to the CRRF, or that the CRRF does not seem to have led to a significant elaboration of these arrangements, should neither be regarded as a criticism nor a disappointment. Indeed, the real coup is the alignment and cooperation between UNHCR and IFIs. There is no doubt that the CRRF has led to better outcomes for refugees in the participating host states. In Kenya, the Refugee Bill (2017) extended working rights to 500,000 refugees; in Mexico and Djibouti reforms have granted refugees better access to identification, employment and financial services; while in Panama and Costa Rica, groups of refugees are being included in vocational training and national employment programs respectively. The CRRF enabled these wins, and countries signed onto the CRRF – at least in good part – because of the carrot that was potential access to financing.

5.7.3 The devil you don't know

It is also not to say that there are not more opportunities if we are willing to move a little further outside the box. One such opportunity might be found in leveraging the enormous wealth – around USD250 trillion – held in global capital markets.[38] A particularly ripe source of untapped funds is the current account surpluses held in Gulf States, much of which accrued following oil price surges in the early 2000s. With ten sovereign wealth funds and USD1.7 trillion worth of assets under management, Gulf States have emerged as the world's largest net supplier of financial resources. But this capital rarely flows into low-income and fragile states. Arguably, this is not because there are no good opportunities. Quite the contrary, emerging markets currently offer the highest rates of return. The explanation – as realised by Jordan – is that capital flows are conservative, and shy away from geopolitical risk, uncertainty and bureaucracy.

> Emerging markets private equity has earned 11 percent over the past 10 years after fees, according to advisors Cambridge Associates. Large public equities funds with more than 50 percent of their assets invested in the Middle East and Africa show similar returns, according to Morningstar. Emerging markets are growing at an annual rate of 5.8 percent; the Middle East and North Africa is growing at more than 3 percent annually, according to the World Bank.[39]

Kito de Boer, former special envoy of the Madrid Quartet, has presented a strong argument on how this situation might be turned around to benefit struggling host state economies. First, mechanisms need to be created to diffuse risk and overcome the bureaucratic hurdles that dissuade investors from deploying their capital. This might be done through intermediary entities that "grease the wheels" and thus connect capital to markets. They might negotiate with authorities, secure approvals, and ensure that purchase agreements won't be blocked. They can also mitigate the greatest risks – those associated with underdeveloped legal systems – through on-the-ground teams with the experience and connections to avoid corruption and advocate for strategic advances in law and regulation. He presents the example of Shurook as a proof of concept. Shurook is a not-for-profit entity that works with the private sector to create investible projects in solar power, water treatment, low-cost housing and healthcare. Its most value-adding role is to "walk the hard yards of early-stage project development"[40] by identifying available land, negotiating grid accessibility with the government and managing discussions with IFIs on how to reduce political and operational risk.[41]

Second, motivated investors need to be identified. These might be found in the growing market for impact investment, or in diaspora communities (who have always been willing to invest but have lacked investible opportunities where the risk is managed).

Third, new public–private investment institutions need to be built that provide finance to frontier markets through mechanisms other than debt financing. One option might be a regional bank structured along the lines of the European Bank for Reconstruction and Development or the Asian Development Bank. Such a bank would act as a linking agent, by redirecting capital to match finance for projects that are most needed and strategic for host state development. Such capital might come from the Gulf sovereign wealth funds mentioned earlier, *zakat* contributions or public–private sector partnerships. Such an arrangement would – borrowing a term from the impact investment sector – allow capital owners to "do well and do good", and at the same time liberate donors to support and add value in ways that others cannot. Examples include technical assistance on regulatory reform, labour-intensive but low-profit infrastructure projects, or an overhauling of vocational education systems.

5.7.4 *Insuring against risk*

A final high-potential but unexploited means of injecting money into a host economy is by transferring risk to the insurance sector. The discourse around risk outsourcing has mainly focused on how the humanitarian sector can improve its efficiency in responding to natural disasters and disease outbreaks. Currently, funding is largely connected to tipping points such as deaths or numbers of infected persons, as opposed to supporting an early response geared towards containment. An examination of how the international community intervened in the Ebola epidemic is a case in point. A month after Ebola was detected in Guinea in March 2014, experts estimated that USD5 million was needed in emergency funding to contain the virus. By October, this figure was USD1 billion. Readers might recall that when funding did start to flow, it was not necessarily because experts' advice got stronger or clearer; it was a combination of bureaucracy, that the threat had developed increasingly global overtones, and media coverage. Similar scenarios have played out in cases of famine: "despite urgent warnings of food insecurity in Somalia in 2010, donors waited eleven months to scale up assistance.".[42] As stated by the Centre for Global Development, this state of affairs is systematic of a model that finds it easier to mobilise resources for response than for planning or prevention. In fact, their research estimates that only 10 percent of emergency aid spent between 2010 and 2015 was attached in advance to predictable future emergencies.[43]

Innovative steps have been taken to mitigate such inefficiencies. The Caribbean Catastrophe Risk Insurance Facility (CCRIF) is a regional insurance pool established in 2007. In the last decade, the CCRIF has made 22 payouts worth USD69 million to ten member governments, all within two weeks or less of a claim. The vast majority of Haiti's USD8 million payout from the CCRIF was available just 19 hours after the 2010 earthquake struck.

The World Bank's Crisis Response Window (CRW) operates in a similar way. The facility allows countries affected by disaster to borrow on an accelerated basis from the International Development Association (IDA), the World Bank's soft loan window. Since its establishment in 2010, the CRW has issued concessional financing to Guinea, Liberia, Sierra Leone, Malawi, Nepal, the Solomon Islands, Tuvalu and Vanuatu for disasters ranging from flooding, storms and earthquakes to commodity price slumps driven by the Ebola outbreak. Loans do not have to be attached to a specific, predictable risk, and while they take months not hours, they are still faster than most IFI or donor processes.[44]

There is no reason that the logic of risk outsourcing could not be extended to refugee situations. As in the case of disasters, most funding for displacement emergencies comes when needs are acute or become visible, as opposed to when it could be most effectively and efficiently used. Insurance policies or expedited loan facilities have three principal advantages. The first is speed – money is paid out quickly as it is tied to a contract and not a slow and unpredictable fundraising process. Such funding could go directly to governments or, if premiums are offset by donors, to a jointly administered fund that could be expended according to a pre-agreed plan of strategic disbursement and investment prioritisation. The second is capital depth – the insurance industry can underwrite much more expensive losses than aid budgets can; today's insurance industry covers more than USD300 billion in annual global catastrophe risks. The third advantage is efficiency – because resources flow as a single, larger grant, a unified response plan could be implemented as opposed to the current approach of funding many small projects. Some innovation is happening in this regard. Index-linked securities, including catastrophe bonds, are a recent innovation that enables risk to be transferred from the insurance industry to global capital markets.

Bringing all this together, it can be said with a fairly high degree of confidence that Compact-type arrangements do make sense. But they need heavy financing, and this is unlikely to come from traditional sources. Creating jobs is costly, and even if issues of trust and risk aversion could be overcome, donor governments simply do not have the depth of pocket. IFI and private sector engagement seems unavoidable, and the CRRF should be recognised for the steps it has made in this regard.

But there will still be countries that are not resilient enough to assume debt burden, where markets are difficult to penetrate or that are simply too high risk. In such cases more radical solutions will be needed. Wheel greasers that can direct capital towards sensible investments, insurance, and new types of financing that allow capital owners to "do well and do good" may be the answer. Donors would then be freed up to support the specifics where they have value added, such as technical assistance, low-profit but strategic infrastructure projects, or vocational education or by offsetting insurance premiums.

5.8 Where to from here – the future of UNHCR?

At the beginning of this chapter it was posed that one of the impediments to better development programming outcomes was that agencies do not fight and compete for them. This is either because of a lack of incentives, or that the risk-imbued climate in which they operate eschews innovation. In the case of the agency charged with refugee protection, it is a bit of both. On the one hand, they are caught between the hand that feeds them, host states and beneficiaries – each of which have a different vision of success. On the other, in a geopolitical climate marked by anti-migration rhetoric, the agency has little negotiating power to promote fairer deals for host states and better conditions for refugees living in situations of protraction.

Against this backdrop, the Compact notion *was* a breakthrough innovation. It may not have been fully effective in Jordan, but this is how innovation works. An idea is born and tested, tinkered with as better information became available, modified, and then applied again with greater success. Today, the CRRF is being rolled out in 18 states. This is an unprecedented recognition of the roles played by host states, a more concrete joining up of humanitarian and development assistance, and an ushering of new players into the refugee policy architecture. Broader financing solutions must still be found, but significant progress in access to livelihoods and education have been achieved and the approach is broadly well regarded.

The most important achievement is perhaps the least discussed. The need for more equitable burden sharing and the idea of refugee employment rights – words barely spoken a decade ago – have become part of our parlance. It is in these, seemingly small and incremental but "sticky" wins, that development progress is made.

There are important lessons to glean from these events. Despite being the *mot de jour*, genuine innovation is rare. This is because such processes are disruptive, risky and create losers. The Compact Agreements were no exception.

Let's go back to Jordan when the first draft of the WANA White Paper was being circulated in mid-2015. Donors were sceptical. One European ambassador questioned the legitimacy of host states "exploiting" the Syrian refugee situation to gain enlarged market access.[45] They were also steadfast about the stringency of their own policies. The Deputy EU Ambassador at the time told me directly that "European rules of origin will never be negotiated in the case of Jordan".[46]

Also resistant were the humanitarian actors who, theoretically, should have been jumping up and down. While UNHCR laid low almost throughout the process,[47] others were more vocal. At a roundtable of humanitarian and private sector actors convened in April 2015 by the WANA Institute and the Jordan Strategy Forum, one INGO director spoke of the dangers refugees could be exposed to if they were permitted to work, along with the diversion of limited resources this "scheme" would draw in terms of monitoring.[48] At a briefing offered to the NGO Working Group, fears centred around the possibility of a flood of refugees from other parts of the country, other host states and even Syria, if work permits were made available.[49] I have no doubt that these concerns were genuine, but an element of self-interest may also have been in play. Donor calls for a better joining up of humanitarian and development goals have been sounded over many years. These had largely fallen on deaf ears, in good part because they flew in the face of vested interests around funding allocations, coveted mandates and egos. Insofar as the Compact deals echoed these calls, a negative reaction might have been anticipated. As far as the humanitarians were concerned, any "joining up" served one group of agencies, and it wasn't them.

Then there was the government. The day before WANA's White Paper was released, with Paul Collier, Shanta Devarajan, and Stefan Dercon literally mid-flight en route to Amman, we met with the Deputy Minister for Planning and International Cooperation. He asked me plainly, "If this proposal is so win-win – why didn't UNHCR or someone else come up with it before?" We all understood; Jordan didn't want to be anyone's guinea pig. And indeed, the country had much to lose. Refugee hosting was already a polarising issue and any indicators of permanence were a potential conflict flashpoint. Many were also set to lose face. Jordan has been battling high levels of unemployment for more than a decade. In fact, the chief aim of the 2012 *National Employment Strategy* was to nationalise the workforce by replacing migrant workers with Jordanians in key sectors.[50] Then there were the several ministers who had been quoted committing to the population that Jordan would "never open its labour markets to Syrian refugees."[51]

In this environment, that only 10 months later a system of refugee labour permits would be in place, along with a waiver period on the regularisation of informal labour, *was* exceptional. And because the principal players (local and international) have mostly rotated, it is easy to forget how insurmountable these policy imperatives appeared at the time, in contrast with how quickly and easily they fell away. It is also perplexing. Given all the talk around innovation, why was it not UNHCR that came up with the Compacts idea in the first place? Moreover, why – once the idea had caught the attention of DFID, the World Bank and the Jordanian government – did they not assume centre stage? What does this say about agencies' innovation capacity? And how many other ideas might be lying dormant, waiting to be discovered and acted on?

If we dig a little deeper, the situation is actually not perplexing at all. There are two reasons why UNHCR was never going to be the energy behind the Compacts experiment idea. These need to be fleshed out, not to attribute blame, but because they provide important insight into the relationship between innovation, humanitarian response and aid effectiveness – and moreover, how institutional systems and norms can obstruct advancements in thinking and how such complications might be overcome.

A first explanation concerns short-term gains and losses. Let's walk a mile in UNHCR's shoes back in 2015. At that time, more than 3 million refugees had left Syria and there were no signals that the conflict was abating. The agency had been here before. They knew that it was only a matter of time before donors would tire of the crisis, and that a complex political tug of war would ensue with a vulnerable refugee population at its centre. The balance of power was not in UNHCR's favour. Jordan and Lebanon were not parties to the 1951 Refugees Convention or the 1967 Protocol, and even in the case of Turkey which was, the agency had little power to exert in the event that the government decided to backtrack, double down or close borders. Their armoury comprised goodwill and trust, and they intended to protect it at all costs.

Against this backdrop, was UNHCR really in a position to propose a solution that lay in Jordan, Lebanon and Turkey opening up their labour markets to refugees in return for loose commitments around new donor funding, investment and trade deals? Add in the World Bank – an entity long associated with forced austerity, protests and civic unrest; and the UK – whose meddling in the region still bore an air of distrust – and the proposal was as close to a fishy deal as could be imagined.

A more realistic assessment is that UNHCR pushing the Compacts initiative would likely have secured its failure. Laying low may therefore have been a well-calculated move; the risk in terms of protection losses almost certainly outweighed the benefit that might have accrued.

This insight also highlights that an essential ingredient in the proposal gaining traction was that it came from a local source, and one tacitly aligned to – and therefore trusted by – the Royal Hashemite Court. This is not to sing WANA's praises too loudly. Local legitimacy was critical, but being small, mostly unknown and relatively unimportant was also key. This meant that if the plan ended badly, a scapegoat was close at hand. The other essential ingredient was the academic authority and neutrality that came from Oxford University. The UK may not have been the most trusted country, but the involvement of one of its country's most prized academics played perfectly to Jordan's fixation with class status and gaining respect on the international stage.

The second reason it would have been difficult for UNHCR to have been the brainchild behind the London deal cuts to a deeper and more sensitive dilemma. The features that make Compact Agreements logical – the reality of protraction and Western states' unwillingness to share in the hosting burden themselves[52] – also signal that the international refugee architecture is unsuited to deal with the scale and complexity of modern displacement. Facing up to this might seem logical, except that the proposal on the table was by no means a guaranteed fix. If it didn't work, UNHCR would have laid bare that the system governing refugee cooperation was in trouble.

UNHCR would also have been aware that forging "deals" around anything other than a state's customary and legal obligations was a one-way street. Once a package was negotiated with a host state, the next one would inevitably want the same. UNHCR's operating premise – that states open their borders on the basis of good international citizenship – would be compromised with limited scope for backtracking. As we noted earlier, a fairer system that takes into account this changed reality is a non-starter – the political forces that allowed states to come together to forge the Refugee Convention in 1951 are not present today. Against this, UNHCR should be seen as having important legal and humanitarian reasons to closely guard and resist any weakening of its protection mandate.[53]

This puts a new spin on UNHCR's role and participation around the time that the first Compact Agreements were being negotiated. By the London conference in February 2016, the agency was faced with a tough choice. It could stand firm as the agency lobbying for refugee protection on the basis of states responsibilities as set out in the 1951 Convention, or it could move with the tide and mould itself to a new reality in an effort to remain relevant. After all, a defunct refugee agency is helping no one.

UNHCR may also have been thinking about the many stakeholders that would prefer to see the agency scaled back or disappear altogether. Indeed, if it did not step up to claim its seat at the table, there were other agencies – IOM and UNDP for example – ready to do so. Also on its leadership's mind was the certainty that another crisis moment would present itself, perhaps sooner rather than later. The refugees of the future will not be fleeing conflict, they will be driven from their homes by climate change and loss of livelihoods. When this happens, drawing on the principles of the convention, goodwill and trust might not even be an option.

The takeaway is that sometimes for innovation to occur, there needs to be a push. When this happens, organisations can be forced into a choice: to lead, or get out of the way and make room for one of the numerous other entities willing to take their space. Leading, however, can also be a gamble. To play this role they must evolve, but in doing so, they risk conceding their space, role and authority. It reminds me of an insightful quote by Chris Patten, the last governor of Hong Kong: "Sometimes things have to change to remain the same."

The World Food Program (WFP) faced this dilemma a few decades ago. Created in 1961, WFP's mandate was to disseminate food aid through the auspices of the UN system. It is one of the more unique agencies as its work naturally spans the development and humanitarian spheres – providing food in the aftermath of disaster, during periods of famine, through to school lunch programs in poverty-ridden states. WFP appeared to be doing a decent job. Beneath the surface, however, the picture was less rosy. The main donors of food aid – the US and Europe – produced it under heavily subsidised agriculture systems driven by special political interests. In laymen's terms, this means that what these countries produced didn't make economic sense – they could purchase the equivalent cheaper on international markets. But farmers in these countries are powerful and lobby hard for subsidies to keep them in business. This interrupts an economy's functioning in many ways, including by discouraging investment in sectors that have higher profitability and sustainability. A further consequence is that because production is not driven by market forces, supply exceeds demand, that is, there is an excess that cannot be sold. This turned out to be quite convenient, as producing countries could give this food to WFP in the form of aid, simultaneously riding off their compulsory UN contribution.

This worked well for the US and Europe (and WFP), but it harmed those developing countries for which agriculture did make economic sense. Subsidies narrowed their profit margins, making it harder to compete and expand production. Moreover, unlike in the West, these countries often had few or no alternative sectors from which to generate export income. Country recipients of food aid fared the worst. Free food over the medium or long term drove local producers out of business. Such countries became increasingly dependent on food aid, or were forced to purchase food on global markets, leaving them vulnerable to financial shocks.

In an ideal world, this problem should have been called out and dealt with. To be fair, scientists and policy specialists did, but their voices were drowned out by powerful players profiting too well under the status quo. And why did WFP not blow the whistle – after all their mandate was to protect poor and disaster-affected populations from starvation and malnutrition? The reason should now be obvious. The system may have been flawed, but their *raison d'etre* depended on it.

Just like in the refugees example, what shook up the system was an intervening event. Technological advancement in the late 1990s gave those countries producing excess food a new and better option for what to do with it: they could convert it to ethanol fuel. States liked this idea; they might have to start paying their UN dues, but it was a step towards reducing their dependency on the Middle East for oil as well as a cleaner way to create energy.[54] WFP suddenly had a problem. Without food to distribute, what purpose did the agency serve? At that point the irregularities inherent in the WFP model had started to become known – food aid was damaging local economies, promoted food dependency and was undignified for beneficiaries. With the exception of sudden-onset emergencies such as natural disasters, it made far more sense to invest in states' capacity to produce their own food and give those in need the cash to purchase it.

I am skipping over a great deal of complex politicking, but in short WFP was forced to make a choice: to adapt or risk redundancy. It chose the former. This transition – which took place over a couple of decades – was painful and contested, but ultimately successful. Today, largely thanks to the leadership of its twelfth Executive Director, Ertharin Cousin, WFP is a robust organisation which defines its mandate around food security, as opposed to food aid. It is a leader in the field in terms of delivery technology, with 38 percent of the organisation's food assistance portfolio provided in cash.[55] In 2020, these achievements won it the highest accolade: the Nobel Peace Prize.

Turning back to UNHCR, a similar trajectory can be detected. It seems that they have also chosen to embrace a new reality and try to assert a level of control over their direction. It has not been easy. The organisation has been criticised for "cutting deals" with IFIs and ceding to pressure to deal with refugees and migrants under a common framework.

Only time will tell if this transition will be successful, although what UNHCR does in the coming years may prove instructive. Transformation must go beyond holding forums and launching framework agreements. If WFP's experience is anything to go by, for UNHCR to become the kind of agency that comes up with Compact-like deals and manages the political brokering needed to see them home, much would need to change. The composition of the staffing pool will need to shift, new partnerships will have to be forged, and an enabling environment that engenders innovation would need to be mainstreamed throughout the organisation. If this could be pulled off, it might work. With a leaner and more effective UNHCR, the deceits in the Convention become far less of an issue.

As it starts down this path it should be remembered that UNHCR has been this agency before. In Africa in the mid-1960s, the organisation's modus operandi was all about inter-agency cooperation, refugee livelihoods and linking hosting to rural development projects. These projects were commonly referred to as ICARA, from the International Conference on Assistance to Refugees in Africa. A decade later, after it became clear that refugees were unlikely to repatriate, the narrative switched to integration, led by UNHCR and UNDP in partnership. The basis was mutually beneficial bargaining; host states would enable refugee self-reliance, and donors would assist them in the form of development assistance. Similar inter-agency partnerships were repeated in South America (CIREFA) and in Asia under the Comprehensive Plan of Action (CPA).[56] Admittedly, these events took place in a different time and political context, but the world was no less complicated.

How well the organisation pivots will likely be informed by its middle managers. This was the case in the examples of ICARA, ICARA II, CIREFA and the CPA, which were driven by figures such as Sergio Vierra de Mello, Kofi Annan and Erika Feller – all quite junior at the time, but forward think-ing, brave and hungry for results.[57] Those occupying their roles today will need to step up with fresh ideas and enthusiasm, and reminders that innova-tion has been part of the organisation's DNA before, all the while subtly pointing to the competition that UNHCR now faces. This will need to back-stopped by strong academic partnerships, and staff that are able to grit their teeth as they work with econometricians, development partners and policy brokers under very different rules of the game. Most importantly, they will need to engender an environment where innovation is promoted, risk is tol-erated and mistakes are accepted. After all, no one ever believed that Syrians would live in camps, that Jordan would allow them to work or that the EU would negotiate Rules of Origin. But they did. So let's not place boundaries around what might be imagined or discourage that imagining from taking place. The future of the humanitarian system might depend on it. As for the broader development apparatus, what lessons can be taken?

5.8.1 Towards an innovation culture

Innovation is imperative. It is where the biggest wins accrue, and might be how the development and humanitarian sectors navigate through this cur-rent era of distrust, insularity and populism. But agencies need to be much smarter about how they encourage and facilitate it. Inserting the term into documents and creating innovation units will not cut it. For innovation to become embedded in institutional culture, significant changes need to take place.

The literature on organisational transformation suggests that for the agencies that have successfully embraced innovation, a key step was over-coming risk aversion and changing how failure was perceived and dealt with. Such transformations require time, deliberate effort and leadership from the top. In almost all cases, they occur during periods of boon (where there is some "padding") or catastrophe (where there is little left to lose). Where these conditions do not apply, in the short term some risk can be outsourced, which is why agencies like UNHCR should take seriously ideas such as insurance and made-for-purpose multilateral banks.

Innovation-centric organisations also accept that change will be resisted, contested and, in many cases, lead to conflict. Measures need to be set in place to bypass or overcome such resistance, as well as to diagnose the drivers of it. Battles over budgets, turf wars and hurt egos need to be distinguished from genuine threats to an organisation or its beneficiaries.

Finally, it is important to acknowledge that not all innovation can, or should, be produced in-house. We have set out why UNHCR could not have been the driving force behind the transformation that ultimately enveloped it. Some of this was grounded in altruism – a genuine risk that "deals" would erode the authority and legitimacy of the principles holding up refugee protection globally. Other concerns – such as conceding ground or funding to rival agencies – were not. The takeaway is that innovation potential must be viewed through a much wider lens. Domestic think tanks, which enjoy local insight, political nuance and trust, are a particularly important source of new thinking, along with academia. Agencies need to be able to form relationships with these entities, as well as partnerships when the situation calls for it.

5.8.2 The power of data

The Compacts experiment is another call-out for how agencies invest in, use and understand data. No one envisaged that Jordan would take on the political risks and loss of face that accompanied the deal brokered in London. But they did. And in large part this was because the economic data spoke louder vis-à-vis these other concerns. Moving forward, we should keep in mind Paul's wise words: "States do nothing, nothing well at least, unless it's in their interests". Such "interest" will comprise, inter alia, financial gain, political positioning, status among allies (and adversaries), security imperatives and humanitarian objectives. Currently, development and humanitarian agencies rely on just one of these interests to get its work done: the rhetoric of good international citizenship. As the world gets more complex, insular and cash strapped, this may not be enough. They will also need to draw on numbers, data and facts to support their arguments.

Beyond forging plans that appeal to states and serve humanitarian purposes, the proper collection, management and interpretation of data will be a prerequisite to effective refugee livelihoods programs. Indeed, the missteps that derailed the Jordan Compact agreements might have been avoided through the involvement of staff with experience in surveying and behavioural economics.

Equal to this is understanding the limits of data – what numbers cannot and should not be expected to do. In the months following the London conference, WANA enjoyed a small moment of notoriety. We were contracted by a handful of UN agencies and INGOs, each hoping for a similar win. One agency (which I'm sure would prefer to remain nameless) contracted us to calculate the costs borne by Egypt as a result of the large numbers of undocumented migrants who were making their way to Europe from the Sahel and had become "stuck". Despite data deficits, it was clear that these costs were significant – certainly in the hundreds of millions of dollars annually. We suggested that this was a sound platform from which Egypt could leverage better aid, especially from European donors. Unfortunately the contracting agency didn't see it that way. They had been hoping that – as in the case of Jordan – migrants could be sold as an economic benefit, and thus underwrite their policy objective which was to convince the government to recognise them. Unfortunately they had promised such a finding to their own donor, which created quite an uncomfortable situation with respect to us getting paid. The lesson should be obvious – data is data, and the story it tells will not always be a kind one. But if it is to remain a powerful tool, it must be used properly and not manipulated. Academia and think tanks operate under strict ethical rules in this regard, which development and humanitarian agencies, if they want to engage, will need to embrace. Anything less risks compromising the integrity of all players.

5.8.3 The power of moments

A final thing that must be understood about successful innovation is the power of moments. The Compact Agreements only worked as well as they did because of the irregular entry of refugees and others into Europe starting in 2015. Before then, Europe could pressure traditional host states to uphold their international obligations from a fairly safe standpoint, helping out just enough to both sleep well and keep the system intact. But as soon as the situation spiralled out of control, their limits were exposed. As Europe's bulwark states buckled under pressure, Syrians, Afghans, Iraqis through to Eritreans began to dissipate into countries with less appetite for diversity and disorder. Sweden halved its aid budget and closed its border, Denmark introduced a policy of confiscating all refugee assets valued above USD1000 and Switzerland followed suit.[58] Host states in the Middle East were instantly handed a powerful negotiating line: why should they keep their borders open when rich, strong and resilient countries would not do the same?

This moment could have gone one of two ways. Wealthy states – which did not wish to host refugee populations in large numbers – forging bargains with traditional hosts, and thereby somewhat levelling the playing field by offering them more protection against fatigue-induced withdrawals of funding. Or rich states closing their borders with no mitigating actions – something that might have spelled an unravelling of the norms that unpin the humanitarian system.

In fact, the die was cast the moment Europe cut deals with Jordan, Lebanon and particularly Turkey, hence putting a value on how much it would pay to stop irregular migration into its territories. How much of a game changer this was finds proof in how quickly and easily Kenya, far removed from the Syria crisis, managed to secure its own deal by threatening to close Dabaab refugee camp, and the *al-Shabaab* threat contained within it.[59]

So moments, and how they are handled, matter. This can be done from a platform of fear, protectionism and realpolitik. Or it can be informed by a spirit of cooperation and a shared vision of what the future should look like. No one can claim that this story was all about white hats acting for the greater good. But that the end solution moved the international community towards a system that is more fair, predictable and safe – if nothing else – proves that the humanitarian framework is not dead.

Notes

1 Interview dated 3 February 2019, by telephone, notes on file with author.
2 In 1920, Fridtjof Nansen appointed as a League of Nations High Commissioner for Prisoners of War. The following year he was also appointed as the High Commissioner for Russian Refugees. In 1923, the word Russian was dropped, reflecting that the mandate had been extended. Indeed, over the next decade the office would help process Russians, Greeks and Armenians, Turks, Assyrians and others. Other refugee mandates included: the Nansen International Office for Refugees (1931–1938), the Office of the High Commissioner for Refugees coming from Germany (1933–1938), the Office of the High Commissioner of the League of Nations for Refugees (1939–1946) and the Intergovernmental Committee on Refugees (1938–1947).
3 "No refugees or displaced persons who have finally and definitely ... expressed valid objections to returning to their countries of origin shall be compelled to return" Resolution 8 (I) of 12 February 1946.
4 Article 14.1.
5 Resolution 62 (I) of the UN General Assembly (15 December 1946).
6 See paragraph 1 of the Statute annexed to Resolution 428 (V) Statute of the Office of the UN High Commissioner for Refugees (14 December 1950). The Convention Relating to the Status of Refugees (1951) will hereafter be referred to as the "Refugee Convention".
7 Initially set up for three years, the High Commissioner's mandate was regularly renewed thereafter for five-year periods until 2003, when the General Assembly decided "to continue the Office until the refugee problem is solved"; Resolution 58/153 (22 December 2003) paragraph 9. See further, G. Loescher, A. Betts and J. Milner, *UNHCR: The Politics and Practice of Refugee Protection* (2013) 133.
8 <https://www.unhcr.org/figures-at-a-glance.html> accessed 22 July 2020.
9 P. Collier and A. Betts "Help Refugees Help Themselves: Let Displaced Syrians Join the Labor Market", *Foreign Affairs*, November/December 2015.
10 ALNAP (2018) "The State of the Humanitarian System 2018" ALNAP Study, London ALNAP/ODI 16.
11 A. Suhrke "Burden-Sharing During Refugee Emergencies: The Logic of Collective Action versus National Action" *Journal of Refugee Studies* 11:4 (1998) 396–415. See also G. Loescher et al (eds.) *Protracted Refugee Situations; Political, Human Rights and Security Implications*, UNU Press (2008).
12 A. Betts and G. Loescher (eds.) *Refugees in International Relations*, Oxford University Press (2011) 61.
13 A. Betts *Forced Migration and Global Politics*, Wiley-Blackwell (2009) 87; A. Betts and P. Collier *Refuge: Rethinking Refugee Policy in a Changing World*, Oxford University Press (2017) 76.
14 Note that the eligibility of new groups to claim refugee status is discussed at the Annual Executive Committee meeting ("ExComm").

15 J. Crisp "UNHCR at 70: An Uncertain Future for the International Refugee Regime" *Global Governance* 26 (2020) 359–368.

16 Unlike other the other core Conventions, the Refugee Convention has no associated Committee (akin to the Committee on the Rights of the Child, or the Committee on Economic, Social and Cultural Rights) mandated to receive complaints around member state violations. There is scope, however, for such complaints to be referred to the International Court of Justice, or other Committees as violations of international customary law.

17 This is deemed an underestimate by the Jordanian government, which sets the number closer to 1.4 million; Jordan Response Platform, *Jordan Response Plan for the Syria Crisis 2015*, MOPIC (2014). As at 2015, there were also over 241,000 Syrian refugees in the Kurdistan Region of Iraq, and over 122,000 in Egypt; UNHCR et al, *3RP Regional Progress Report* (2015) <http://reliefweb.int/report/syrian-arab-republic/3rp-regional-progress-report-june-2015> accessed 28 July 2015.

18 W.L. Ochsenwald, "The Vilayet of Syria, 1901–1914: A Re-Examination of Diplomatic Documents as Sources" *Middle East Journal* 22:1 (1968) 73–87.

19 A. Betts and P. Collier *Refuge: Rethinking Refugee Policy in a Changing World*, Oxford University Press (2017) 104.

20 WANA Institute, "Providing 200,000 Work Opportunities for Syrian Refugees in Jordan: A Viability Assessment", unpublished paper (2016).

21 "The Jordan Compact: A New Holistic Approach between the Hashemite Kingdom of Jordan and the International Community to deal with the Syrian Refugee Crisis", final statement, Supporting Syria and the Region conference, London, 4 February 2016 <//2c8kkt1ykog81j8k9p47oglb-wpengine.netdna-ssl.com/wp-content/uploads/2016/02/Supporting-Syria-the-Region-London-2016-Jordan-Statement.pdf> accessed 16 October 2019.

22 Meeting notes, roundtable organised by WANA Institute and Jordan Strategy Forum, King Hussein Club, Amman, May 2014.

23 WANA Institute, "Providing 200,000 Work Opportunities for Syrian Refugees in Jordan: A Viability Assessment", unpublished paper, 2016.

24 Explanations in behavioral economics include gratuitous concurrence (a tendency to tell an interviewer what they want to hear) and social desirability response bias (providing an answer that is perceived to be utilitarian). Thus, it is not contested that Syrians stated that they wanted to work. It is certain that many did. But others may have so answered, for example, because they believed that this was the "correct" answer, because they supported refugee working rights more generally, or because this was their way of communicating that they needed additional material assistance.

25 Note that at the outset of the program, work permits were not completely free of charge – refugees needed to obtain a health certificate at a cost of JOD40. This charge was later abolished.

26 Data collected by the WANA Institute and IPSOS in 2016 revealed the following: employed females: 12,246, female labour force participation (employed and looking for work): 45,921; employed males: 81,739, male labour force participation: 117,759. Of males, 59 percent are employed, 26 percent looking for work. Male-female employment total: 93,985, total labour force participation: 163,050.

27 The idea that refugees experience positive material outcomes when they have access to labour markets finds support in academic scholarship on migration. In most cases, despite a short-term disadvantage in terms of employment participation, wages and occupational ranking, over time these differentials narrow and migrants ultimately earn and save more than they would have by not migrating. However, see also arguments by Collier that such outcomes do not

necessarily outweigh increases in overall social wellbeing; P Collier *Exodus: How Migration Is Changing Our World*, Oxford University Press (2014) 146, 171–173, 245. Refugees, although the body of evidence is smaller, follow a similar trajectory, albeit with slightly less-positive outcomes; see J Woetzel et al, *People on the Move: Global Migration's Impact and Opportunity*, McKinsey Global Institute (2016) and E. Ott, *The Labour Market Integration of Resettled Refugees*, UNHCR (2013).

28 E. Harper, *Examining Psychological Drivers of Radicalisation in Jordan*, WANA Institute (2016).

29 A. Betts and P. Collier *Refuge: Rethinking Refugee Policy in a Changing World*, Oxford University Press (2017) 118, 229.

30 A. Betts and P. Collier *Refuge: Rethinking Refugee Policy in a Changing World*, Oxford University Press (2017) 133, 155.

31 United Nations Economic and Social Council for Western Asia, *Measurement and Analysis of Poverty in Jordan*, ESCWA (2014) 25; and generally, J. Woetzel et al *People on the Move: Global Migration's Impact and Opportunity*, McKinsey Global Institute (2016).

32 How these short-term impacts are distributed depends on the extent to which newcomers transform the skill composition of the domestic labour supply. However, in the most typical scenario (the entry of low-skilled workers), the groups most impacted are low-wage national labour and recent generations of immigrants, whose skill sets closely mimic those of new entrants to the labour market. D. Roodman, "Why a New Study of the Mariel Boatlift Has Not Changed Our Views on the Benefits of Immigration" The GiveWell Blog, 20 February 2017. The literature examining the impact of migrant and refugee labour on local wages is extensive and beyond the scope of this paper, but see generally M. Clemens and J. Hunt, "The Labor Market Effects of Refugee Waves: Reconciling Conflicting Results" Working Paper 23433 NBER (2017).

33 J. Woetzel et al *People on the Move: Global Migration's Impact and Opportunity*, McKinsey Global Institute (2016) 67.

34 The model was based on Keynesian economic theory, which holds that when an economy is performing below its potential, a sufficiently large increase in government spending will stimulate aggregate demand and return the economy to its potential growth path. In theory, the scale of this stimulus should be easy to calculate: the maximum cost of stimulus should be no higher than the cumulative returns to the benefiting parties.

35 For example, it was assumed that all jobs created would be filled by refugees, whereas in reality, a majority would likely go to nationals. Moreover, these jobs are standard jobs in the formal economy as opposed to the low-pay ones that refugees currently hold. A further assumption was that once a refugee gains meaningful employment, they and two dependents no longer require humanitarian assistance. Finally, the model absorbs the stimulus as a single investment in 2014 that is spread evenly over the economy's different sectors (in reality, most stimulus packages are rolled out over time and target specific sectors). Like the costing analysis, the model is conservative and looks solely at the economic benefits of the stimulus. In fact, investment-induced employment has knock-on effects for the wider economy and society more broadly, such as bolstering social cohesion, reducing poverty and minimising skills atrophy. Finally, the model is based on historical data and thus is indicative only. However, various robustness checks were conducted, which revealed consistent results dependent on the level of stimulus injection.

36 To overcome this forecasting challenge, the WANA Institute developed an empirical model for predicting refugee protraction using a Probit regression model and based on a definition of at least 25,000 refugees being displaced

for a minimum of five consecutive years. The findings will not be detailed here due to the significant protection challenges and ethical concerns such modelling creates.

37 UNHCR "Two Year Progress Assessment of the CRRF Approach September 2016–September 2018" ES/2018/07 (2018) 25.

38 R. Kersley and A. Koutsoukis "The Global Wealth Report 2016" Credit Suisse, 22 November 2016, <www.credit-suisse.com/corporate/en/articles/news-and-expertise/the-global-wealth-report-2016-201611.htm> accessed 2 April 2019.

39 K. de Boer "The Trillion-Dollar Pipeline in the Mideast No One Is Talking About" CNBC, 5 October 2016, https://uk.finance.yahoo.com/news/trillion-dollar-pipeline-mideast-no-132600954.html.

40 Kito de Boer "Guest Post: 'The Trillion Dollar Pipeline in the Mideast No One Is Talking About'" CNBC, 5 October 2016, https://uk.finance.yahoo.com/news/trillion-dollar-pipeline-mideast-no-132600954.html.

41 Another positive example is Leap Frog Investments which has roughly USD1 billion under management invested in 21 portfolio companies in Africa, Asia and Latin America.

42 T. Talbot and O. Barder "Payouts for Perils: Why Disaster Aid Is Broken, and How Catastrophe Insurance Can Help to Fix It" Policy Paper 087, Centre for Global Development (2016).

43 T. Talbot and O. Barder "Payouts for Perils: Why Disaster Aid is Broken, and How Catastrophe Insurance Can Help to Fix It" Policy Paper 087, Centre for Global Development (2016).

44 For other examples of donors experimenting with emergency relief windows, see L. Picard and T. Buss A Fragile Balance: Re-examining the History of Foreign Aid, Security, and Diplomacy, Lynne Rienner Publishers (2009) 257.

45 Interview dated 18 June 2014, (redacted) Embassy, Amman, notes on file with author.

46 Interview dated 3 September 2014, EU Mission, Amman, notes on file with author.

47 A. Betts and P. Collier Refuge: Rethinking Refugee Policy in a Changing World Oxford University Press (2017) 106, 217.

48 Meeting notes, roundtable organised by WANA Institute and Jordan Strategy Forum, King Hussein Club, Amman, May 2014.

49 Briefing to NGO UN Working Group, Amman, August 2014.

50 Ministry of Labor National Employment Strategy 2011–2020, Ministry of Labor (2010), http://inform.gov.jo/en-us/By-Date/Report-Details/ArticleId/36/National-Employment-Strategy.

51 Interview dated 18 June 2014, (redacted) Ministry, Amman, notes on file with author. Interestingly, the only group that seemed receptive to the idea was private sector actors. At the above-mentioned roundtable, they noted the hardworking nature of Syrians, their entrepreneurialism and their specialist skill sets. Although not representative of the sector as a whole, the general consensus was that Syrians would be a skilled and competitive addition to the labour force.

52 A. Betts and P. Collier Refuge: Rethinking Refugee Policy in a Changing World, Oxford University Press (2017) 8.

53 In terms of modifying the existing humanitarian architecture, it is important to highlight that the use of the orthodox policy framework in protracted settings is not the result of an oversight or a lack of creative thinking. The factors driving this have complicated legal and mandatory roots. Under the 1951 Refugee Convention, UNHCR's core mandate is to ensure the international protection of uprooted people worldwide. Its founding statute specifies the functions of protecting refugees and promoting durable solutions, and only over time did this mandate evolve to include the provision of material aid; see UNHCR Statute,

UN General Assembly resolution 428(V) of 14 December 1950. The point is that the manner in which refugees are currently supported has legal and historic roots. Modifications would undoubtedly be complicated by recent increases in populist and nationalist sentiments among UN member states.

54 There was also mounting pressure from entities such as the OECD for less "tying" of aid.

55 www.wfp.org/cash-transfers accessed 22 September 2020.

56 A. Betts and P. Collier *Refuge: Rethinking Refugee Policy in a Changing World*, Oxford University Press (2017) 146–150.

57 A. Betts and P. Collier *Refuge: Rethinking Refugee Policy in a Changing World*, Oxford University Press (2017) 220–221.

58 A. Betts and P. Collier *Refuge: Rethinking Refugee Policy in a Changing World*, Oxford University Press (2017) 88–89, 228.

59 A. Betts and P. Collier *Refuge: Rethinking Refugee Policy in a Changing World*, Oxford University Press (2017) 152.

6

EXPLOITING THE SWEET SPOTS

At the beginning of this book, it was argued that a key impediment to better human development outcomes was the rules of the game under which programming takes place. Under these rules, the mechanisms that would usually operate to link incentives to performance work imperfectly. Driving this is that the principals of the system (donors) fund development work principally as an exercise of statecraft. This creates a disconnect between the work they mandate and the reward they are seeking, creating scope for programming failure and inefficiency to go undetected. The recipients of development aid might be in a position to correct this. Here too there are impediments, however. Beneficiary states often fear the levelling of power relations and redistribution of wealth that development brings. Direct beneficiaries – those most invested in good outcomes – lack both the power and a feedback loop to signal their satisfaction and close performance gaps.

It was posited that if the goals of donors and/or beneficiary states aligned with development objectives, the sector would operate in a very different manner. Might it be possible then, to seek out development pathways that fall in everyone's interests? In fact, such win–win situations do exist, but they are rare. The good news is that if we can spot them, and work creatively to exploit them, the gains are there for the taking.

Although it might seem an odd choice of development challenge, the story of this chapter is terrorism, and the violent extremist groups who perpetrate these acts. The destructive nature of this phenomenon is typified by the group born as Al-Qaeda in Iraq in 2004, but that came to be known as the Islamic State in Iraq and Syria (ISIS).

The consequences of this group's operations have been felt world over. Its rise deepened and protracted the civil war in Syria, compromised state building in Iraq, and created a context for neighbouring states to engage in proxy wars. Outside the conflict theatre, between 2014 and 2018, ISIS was responsible for 143 attacks, killing 2,043 individuals across 23 countries.[1] Against such threats, states expanded the ambit and power of their security agencies, often encroaching on citizens' due process rights and exacerbating minority–majority tensions. Even today, years after the group's so-called military defeat, the impacts linger. As at July 2020, around 30,000 children were

 DOI: 10.4324/9781003376996-7

being held in camps or detention facilities on suspected ISIS association or terror-related offenses; the number of Syrian refugees sits at 5.5 million; and almost everyone has had to adjust to a new security "normal".

While the international community has dealt with terror groups throughout its history, ISIS begot an unprecedented reaction, not just in terms of budget, but also in scope. Since 2006, 27 separate Security Council Resolutions have been passed concerning the group. In 2017, the UN Office of Counter-Terrorism was formed, and is currently monitoring 208 projects, implemented or overseen by 18 UN or quasi–UN agencies across 72 countries.

The scope and comprehensiveness of this response is interesting. Violent extremism is nothing new. Modern history is littered with religiously motivated violent extremist groups such as the Ku Klux Klan and groups formed to advance liberation such as the Irish Revolutionary Army and Tamil Tigers, as well as groups that have sought to establish a new state order, such as the Red Brigades. The pragmatist might also point out that against other threats, the risks posed by terror groups is small. In 2015, the world saw 11,884 deaths attributable to terrorism outside of war zones; in the same timeframe, 2,250,000 died in car accidents and 437,000 by murder.[2] This "overreaction" is part and parcel of how terrorism works; its lethality lies not in the objective risk it poses, but the fear it engenders and the havoc it reeks on systems and values.

But ISIS was different. The group brought the brutality of terrorism livestreamed into our living rooms, freely accessible and to an extent inescapable. Its use of children as soldiers, executioners and suicide bombers breached the most basic of social norms for the purposes of propaganda.[3] Significantly, although terror groups have always been disproportionately stocked by youth, ISIS attracted not just any youth, but what Western powers saw as "their youth". Indeed, around 20 percent of recruits hailed from Western states, confounding scholars and practitioners alike.[4] In short, ISIS provoked the reaction is did in large part because of how personal it was for the West, and how cleanly it exposed a lack of social cohesion in seemingly resilient societies.

It was not only the West that had a strong interest in neutralising ISIS and its splinter groups, but also the states upon whose territory it had set up shop: Iraq, Syria, Lebanon, Nigeria and others. Terror groups leave local populations vulnerable to attack and threaten the state's monopoly over power. Herein lies another feature that distinguishes the terror phenomenon – apart from the groups themselves, basically everyone is united against them. The logic runs that if there was ever something that the international community should have been able to get right, fighting off ISIS was it.

In many respects this played true. The response was far from perfect, but broadly speaking it was expeditious, grounded in self-learning and results orientated. Insofar as terrorism, underdevelopment and weak governance are interconnected, important steps in our thinking have been made.

This is exciting, as it shows what the system is capable of when motivation is strong and the key players are invested.

Unpacking what this means for development programming more broadly is critical. In those moments when interests coalesce around the search for a solution, spaces open for policy shifts and programming gains that would not otherwise be possible. But to capitalise on these, development actors cannot stand idle. They must use their expertise to situate a challenge within a context that is broader than an election cycle, and encourage solutions that address underlying development imperatives. In short, these are windows of opportunity to be exploited, but only if we choose to take on that responsibility. This is not cheating; it's called making progress.

6.1 Responding to violent extremism: a brief historical overview

To get to the lessons on win–win pathways, we need to immerse ourselves in the phenomenon of violent extremism. This story benefits enormously from research undertaken by the WANA Institute. Our human security team was composed of five fiercely intelligent young researchers, who overcame enormous challenges to ensure that the Institute's research and ethics standards won out over donor rivalries, corruption and competing security ends. Much of their work is cited here and can be read in full; it remains among the most innovative and thought-provoking work on violent extremism published to date.

6.1.1 Countering violent extremism mark 1: bad ideas, even worse programs

Starting immediately after the 9/11 terror attacks on the United States, and gaining momentum again with the rise of ISIS, the emergent threat of violent extremism impelled comprehensive security responses both within and between states. This trend strongly favoured governments expanding the powers and reach of the security sector with a view to disrupting terror networks and thwarting acts of extremist violence.[5] Examples include states revising legislation to widen the definition of terrorism[6]; elaborated powers of arrest and pretrial detention; empowering law enforcement to monitor private communications; and revoking the citizenship of persons who engaged in terrorist activity.[7] Such measures were complemented by softer "PVE" (preventing violent extremism) approaches that aimed to eliminate or ameliorate the causal drivers of the phenomenon.[8] Popular activities included awareness raising, religious counter-messaging, and expanding access to livelihoods.

These responses reflected how violent extremism was thought to work at the time. By 2011, scholars had dismissed the idea of a terrorist neurology or gene (yes, at one time this was an accepted, if not dominant, theory) and settled on the idea of a "radicalisation process". This process was driven by push factors – including poverty, lack of opportunity, injustice and political exclusion; and pull factors – such as indoctrination and inducement.[9] It was believed that recruiters worked through online fora and mosques, using religious propaganda to target young, male Muslims who were either financially impoverished or had little scope for upwards social mobility.

But as the ISIS phenomenon entered a fifth year with no signs of abating, this theory came under increased scrutiny. The human security team at the WANA Institute was on the case: Neven Bondokji, Leen Aghabi, Barik Mhadeen, Adel Sparr and Kim Wilkinson had designed a comprehensive research project targeting youth in four radicalisation hotbeds in Jordan. They wanted to understand how pressures around education, relationships, religion and governance influenced their thinking and led some to cross the border into Syria. In 2017, we published a paper suggesting that the commonly referenced push-pull factors were too generic to adequately or consistently explain radicalisation.[10] The argument ran that while unemployment, political marginalisation or religious ideology may have driven individuals to join ISIS, these phenomena were broad reaching, leaving models unable to explain why a majority of those affected neither radicalised nor behaved violently. A second point was that even if a set of drivers could explain radicalisation, radicalisation did not seem to explain violent extremism. It was increasingly clear that many individuals ascribed to radical ideology and/or justified the use of violence to achieve set goals, but never went on to join extremist groups or engage in extremist behavior.[11]

We were not alone in this thinking. In Europe, experts had begun to worry that treating radicalisation as a form of pre-terrorism risked alienating particular groups, and was exacerbating the feelings that did feed extremism, such as identity polarisation and marginalisation.[12] Soft approaches, such as awareness-raising, counter-messaging and skills-building were likewise criticised as inappropriately targeting youth and/or Muslims. Certainly, the signs identified by policymakers (and to an extent scholars) as indicative of budding extremism closely mimicked normal adolescent behavior. These included searching for role models, introspective behavior, feelings of grievance, emergent political engagement, and the exercising of self-expression or dissent.[13] Where "Vulnerability Checklists" included characteristics such as feeling discriminated against, regularly visiting mosques, or engaging in regular prayer, it was easy to see that Muslim youths were being doubly typecast.[14] The child protection and psychology community of practices issued damming condemnations. They argued that basing preventative interventions not on acts but on markers of future behaviors as well as latent stereotypes was driving existing perceptions, as well as discrimination against specific ethnic, religious and socio-economic groups.[15]

Similar arguments were levelled against emboldened security arrangements. Practitioners, scholars and civil society groups all agreed that when such measures encroached on basic rights, this drove existing angst and/or created new grievances. Prime examples included "stop and search" and "surveil and sanction" powers, which disproportionately impacted Muslim youths and Muslim-run businesses respectively.[16] It was further observed that individuals who had their livelihood compromised, citizenship revoked, or right of entry denied were becoming potent icons for ISIS propaganda.[17]

Finally, new partnerships came under intense fire. Our findings were that in Jordan, engaging Imams in counter-messaging and restricting the operation of mosques had worked mainly to de-legitimise these actors within their communities.[18] Perhaps more importantly, a new level of "us and them" identity politics had been breached. Muslims from a variety of backgrounds were incensed that their religion was being cast as the culprit, and co-opted by the state, to deflect what they perceived to be a social contract or geopolitical problem.

6.1.2 Research-rethink-reprogram-repeat

During this initial wave of programming, academic research, empirical studies and field testing were taking place at warp speed. This included WANA's own work, which boasted a highly sensitive study of returnee fighters and a mapping of the psychological factors driving young people to join extremist groups. From this, a more sophisticated understanding of violent extremism evolved – one that was almost unrecognisable from that which dominated just a few years earlier. Four insights are particularly noteworthy.

First, there was robust evidence linking Adverse Childhood Experiences (ACEs) to future extremist tendencies. Field research conducted by UNDP, for example, identified a link with micro-level experiences, including lack of exposure to other religions and ethnicities, violence, poor access to education and low civic engagement. Their findings placed particular emphasis on a child's relationship with his or her parents and how this influenced the socialisation process and formation of identity. It seemed that when individuals were later exposed to challenging life circumstances, such experiences were refracted to influence a world view where extremism was more likely to present as an attractive or logical option.[19]

This provided a powerful new lens through which to view individuals exposed to chronic marginalisation, conflict and disempowerment. It suggested that in some cases individuals joined a violent extremist group to seek change or exact revenge. Certainly, WANA's work with returnee fighters found no evidence that their decision to join a violent extremist group resulted from brainwashing or coercion. In most cases, individuals left their family, jobs and other commitments and/or outlaid significant personal resources to join ISIS.[20] That the "pull of the fight" outweighed these responsibilities and emotional commitments suggested that for individuals who were determined to "do something", neither opportunity – such as employment – nor enhanced securitisation was likely to be persuasive.

Another insight was that extremism could be understood as a form of subgroup behavior taking place against a broader context of identity politics. Experts highlighted that within subgroups, certain types of deviant behavior can become normalised. In criminal gangs, for example, theft or vandalism can be an understandable and logical form of aggression that requires no explanation or deconstruction unless it threatens group cohesion. It followed that joining an extremist organisation might well be regarded as a rational form of dissent or self-expression, consistent with the broader subculture. Subgroup culture also explained how a relatively peaceful group might turn violent or its members undertake acts that were not wholly reflective of their ideology. Research by Ginges et al., for example, showed that the norms aligning a subgroup often lie dormant and only became apparent, operative or acted upon when it is questioned, threatened or attacked. When this happens, the need for group cohesion allows individual members to take more extreme positions, a phenomenon called "extremity shift". The result is that individuals with varying degrees of ideological commitment can be influenced by an individual with a strong moral imperative to commit violent acts that they would not commit singularly.[21]

A fourth shift was the almost full transition in how experts viewed state-led counterterrorism responses, from vehicles of frontline protection to drivers of extremist behaviour. As noted, states largely approached extremism as a security problem to be managed, replete with heavy-handed tactics and encroachments on previously enjoyed freedoms. Some came to view this as governments waging a battle of relative power – pitting state prowess against those groups perceived to be high risk. The implication was clear: to the extent that extremism was an act of dissent, further acts of state oppression were more likely to exacerbate tensions than assuage them.

A final point was the consensus around what *did not* drive violent extremism. Early scholarship drew a clear line of causation between religious ideology and extremist goals. This relationship was now viewed as more complicated and variable, with religion acting as a proxy or pathway enabler in a majority of cases.[22] The Internet also turned out not to be as potent a driver as first imagined. Undoubtedly, it played a role for certain individuals at certain stages, but mainly by exploiting pre-existing rifts as opposed to a recruitment or indoctrination tool. To the extent that the Internet did serve the extremist agenda, it was as a carefully tuned, highly effective propaganda machine. Footage of civilians killed by US drone attacks, Shia militias in Iraq, and the corpses of tortured Syrian children all worked to validate the perception of Sunni marginalisation while simultaneously portraying ISIS as the only political group capable of countering Shia influence in the region.[23] Perhaps most shrewdly, messaging tapped into would-be recruits' feelings of deprivation and limited social mobility before their governments were even aware that this was a problem. In offering to fill these extant deficits with immediate employment, future opportunity and a spot on the "winning team", ISIS highlighted the paucity of strength exercised by their home states. Against this, the narrative offered by the West came across as trite and condescending. Professor Scott Atran sums this up well, opining that while the West has always been very good at saying what it is against, it is yet to craft a powerful message about what it is for.[24]

Let's take a moment to reflect back on this story. At the outset, the threats posed by violent extremism invoked fear-induced reactions that manifested in poorly conceived policy responses. These errors were identified and debated. Mistakes were conceded. Thinking and analysis continued, allowing a more sophisticated understanding to evolve. Such insights facilitated moderate improvements in how programs and policies were designed and implemented. This process was reset and repeated through much of the 2004–2017 period, supported by multi-stakeholder partnerships, research and discreet information sharing.

In short, there were significant shifts in thinking. What was first perceived as a security threat was reconceptualised as a religious phenomenon with links to internet-indoctrination, and then into an even more complex phenomenon connected to childhood experiences, a form of group behaviour, through to an act of dissent against a predatory government.

This turnaround may strike some as curious, perhaps even disconcerting. Such a conclusion is probably too harsh. Transitions in thinking – even wide ones – are customary. We also used to believe in aid conditionality, that condom distribution would promote homosexual promiscuity and that children should not participate in decisions concerning their welfare. Foolish ideas have always existed, including in the aid sector. It's just that debunking them takes place over such a long timeframe, we don't usually notice.

In the current case, what is remarkable is that instead of reckoning taking place over a period of decades, it occurred in five short years. This tells us a lot of things, but one undeniable takeaway is that this all happened because *it mattered*. Key stakeholders were invested, not just in an answer, but in the right answer, so they funded evidence generation, corralled experts, listened to them, and changed tack. The United Kingdom went through so many counterterrorism strategies in one year that even the intelligence community struggled to keep up. This is a good thing. What is even harder than thinking seriously about a problem is admitting when a current approach is not working, accepting some costs as sunk, and adopting a new approach. The gulf between the ISIS response of 2014 and today's best practices should be celebrated.

6.2 Towards a more effective framework for fighting violent extremism

By 2017, the sector was in a much better position in terms of its knowledge. These insights, however, had somewhat unwelcomed implications for programming. The absence of discreet drivers suggested that targeted or quick-impact interventions were unlikely to work. Moreover, if religion and the Internet were not wholesale drivers of extremism, some questioned how they could be wholesale responses. This cast doubt onto the efficacy of efforts such as counter-messaging and alternate narratives.

New thinking also put a cautionary spin on the logic underpinning the West's broader strategy for fighting extremism. If joining a group was an act of agency to assert power or exact revenge, then eliminating the group was unlikely to be the answer. The same could be said for interventions aimed at teaching young people to better appraise risk, eschew violence or "just say no". Perhaps most worrying was the possibility that programs aimed to interrupt opportunities to engage, dissuade membership, or counter-instruct might actually be exacerbating feelings of powerlessness and angst.

The WANA research team suspected that the answer lay in accepting the uncomfortable idea that participating in extremism contained an element of agency – an active rejection of injustice, religious alienation, despondency, exclusion and other grievances.[25] If correct, it followed that preventing people from exercising such agency was going to be fraught with difficulty. Certainly, if there was one lesson learned from the previous five years of programming, it was that modern recruitment networks were very difficult to quash and to the extent that people want to join the fight, groups will find ways to engage them.

We figured that if the decision to join a violent extremist group was the result of a cost-benefit analysis, a more effective approach might be to adjust the risk-return assessment in favour of non-extremist options. More simply, if the causal drivers could not be eliminated, and agency can/should not be revoked, then the only way to compete with extremist groups was to offer more attractive alternatives. The question then became, what kind of environment did youth need in order to reject violent extremist groups?

To answer this question, we teamed up with Terre des Hommes (TdH) – a Swiss non-government organisation agency boasting a broad child protection mandate and decades of experience working in conflict zones. One of the refreshing things about TdH is that they know what they do not know and aren't afraid to ask for help. They liked our research and wanted to explore how they could tweak their programs to bolster young people's resilience against extremism. This kickstarted a two-year investigation that brought together child psychologists, protection actors, juvenile justice workers and programming agencies. We published our findings, marketed as a resilience framework for preventing violent extremism at the individual and community levels.[26] Three entry points in particular, are worth calling out.

6.2.1 A safe space for dissent and radical ideology

TdH had long been engaged in youth empowerment, particularly by using sport, vocational training and extra-curricular activities as a tool to divert at-risk youth away from gangs, criminality and drug use. We were particularly impressed by their "FabLabs" – innovative open spaces where vulnerable and difficult-to-reach youth could create their own projects using advanced technological and production tools.[27] There was no doubt that these activities were successful in vesting users with skills in problem solving, promoting creativity and building social capital. But was this enough to prevent them from joining a violent extremist group?

The child psychology scholarship suggests that young people don't just need something to do, they need something meaningful to do – action geared towards the structures and processes that have relevance to them.[28] It followed that anything TdH put on offer would need to deliver on an individual's needs and desires more easily and effectively than joining an extremist group. We decided that sport and extracurricular activities might not "cut the mustard" insofar as these youth were looking for a way to assert power, effect change or channel their grievances. What made more sense was to make available alternative pathways for "would-be" fighters and ideological radicals to constructively, but non-violently, address their concerns.

The idea that frustration and radical thought are positive impulses that can be constructively rechanneled away from violent ends was a novel one. We also thought it had strong logical appeal. Few would deny that chronic social injustice in Arab states, Sunni geopolitical marginalisation and the Syrian war are all valid sources of angst that had largely been ignored in PVE response strategies to date. It was also clear that some of those who ventured into violent extremism had altruistic intentions, perceived their actions to be utilitarian, or were looking to attach themselves to structures that allowed them to feel empowered.[29] We recalled that several of the returnee fighters profiled by WANA had attempted to engage their cause – either at the political level or through community service, but were unsuccessful or rebuffed. This all suggested that entry points such as public debate, opportunities to engage in peaceful protest, civic action and community service might prove cathartic and/or constructive.[30] Such opportunities would need to deliberately extend to those with radical inclinations – offering them alternate forms of expression that did not involve joining a group, or that group turning to violence to make itself heard. In short, societies needed to be sufficiently inclusive for subgroups – even those harbouring non-mainstream beliefs or dissenting views – to feel that they have a safe space to exist, albeit with clear red lines.

Our field research also suggested that projects engaging youth in peacebuilding and strategy co-creation rarely went beyond the usual suspects – educated youth from privileged backgrounds who shared a common, progressive narrative. Moreover, most felt that programs were geared more towards mollifying angst than taking it seriously. It seemed that what was needed was genuine, sustained dialogues that lifted youth from a variety of ideological positions, together with leaders, professionals and community leaders. Chronic disempowerment may have actually made it easier to achieve wins in this regard. Authorities acknowledging the validity of certain widely held perceptions (even if this fell short of endorsing them) may have had transformative impact by generating goodwill.

6.2.2 From counter-messaging to critical thinking

A second entry point related to messaging. By this point, criticism of counter-indoctrination strategies had reached a high-water mark. Muslims believed that their religion was being coopted for political purposes, and memes portraying Islam as a religion of peace seemed to be most frequently invoked as a punchline than a call to action. There was also growing concern that so-called sensitisation programs were being interpreted by young people as yet another example of the state telling them what to do and how to think.

These observations sat comfortably with the scholarship on juvenile justice and youth psychology. The message from experts was that youth do not want to be persuaded; they need to be informed, and to be provided with tools to make better, non-violent decisions.[31] This had always been a challenge, but one made more acute by identity politics and changes in the way young people receive and process information. The upshot was that modern youth (both in the Middle East and the West) increasingly lacked the practical skills needed for living in a cohesive and context-informed society. These include critical thinking, problem analysis, and values such as tolerance and peaceful conflict resolution. Changing this would require both school curricula reforms and improved pedagogical techniques – away from doctrinal approaches and rote learning and towards environments that promote creative thinking and safe idea experimentation.

We were not the first to stumble on this of course. UNESCO has led significant research and advocacy geared towards expanding educational objectives to include critical thinking, conflict diagnostics, tolerance and capacity for self-reflection. Although there are deficits in comparative and longitudinal data, their findings suggest that engaging learners in critical reflection on topical issues can increase open-mindedness about gender and ethnicity and modify the way students respond to conflict. Pedagogical techniques such as peer-to-peer, team-based and experiential learning also show promising outcomes, as do "de-biasing" courses and computer games, debating (especially when students are made to take counter-intuitive positions), and programs aimed to reduce mal-attribution.[32]

6.2.3 Assuaging a heavy-handed state

A third entry point concerned what states needed to do (or stop doing). The evidence is that positive interactions between individuals and government officials build trust and mutual regard. Examples include efficient health and education services, equal access to livelihoods opportunities, and guarantees around the security of people and their property. In fact, even neutral interactions – where state goods are provided without violence or corruption and with a modicum of efficiency – signal a bi-functional relationship with reciprocal obligations. Good governance in the political realm pays the most dividends. Observing people participate in elections, political parties lobbying freely, and representatives being held to account signals that individual power can be asserted through one's vote. For countries with burgeoning youth populations, this huge wielding of latent power might be highly placating.

The opposite of good governance is unregulated violence. Individuals are most commonly exposed to violence in homes, schools and institutions like prisons. Violence can also be structural. It can be embedded in educational curricula (for example the characters depicted as heroes), social culture and the content of entertainment. The most malign form of violence, however, is state levelled: denials of due process rights, human rights violations and abuses of power. It seemed that the linkages between violence and vulnerability to extremism should be marketed as a clarion call for states to strengthen the rule of law, crackdown on corruption, and reboot the relationship between citizens and the state organs mandated to protect them.

6.3 A critical juncture

This has been a long – although hopefully interesting – discussion to get to where we need to be. In response to a new, multifaceted threat, scholars, practitioners and policymakers worked at double pace to design responsive programs, learn from errors, realign, and program more effectively. But as quickly as that happened, it stopped. There was a game changer.

On 9 December 2017, Iraqi Prime Minister Haider al-Abadi announced that Iraqi security forces had liberated the last ISIS–controlled areas along the Syrian border. This followed the retaking of Raqqa, ISIS's de facto capital by Syrian Democratic Forces (SDF) in October and the Syrian government forces' seizing of Deir Ezzor in December.

With ISIS "defeated", all the thinking that had been directed towards these evolving threats largely halted. For those educated about the group and its operating strategy, this was a grave mistake. The group was not gone; it had been pushed underground, and because the causal drivers remained, it would return stronger and more resilient. Even if it didn't, a new form of extremism would grow, as has taken place throughout history. What was actually needed was to use this time wisely, to build understanding and consensus, pilot more impactful solutions, engage in experiential learning, and forge new compacts between the young people most vulnerable to extremism and the stakeholders mandated to protect them.

Luckily, some people with foresight spoke up. By this time I was no longer with the WANA Institute, but still working actively on security issues, including as an advisor to the SRSG on Violence Against Children, Dr Najat

Maalla M'jid. Najat was extremely interested in the resilience approach WANA had published with TdH, and concerned that the issue had been somewhat dropped from the international agenda. As a medical doctor, she knew that this was a disease lying dormant, and that we had to prepare for the next epidemic. On a snowy afternoon in Geneva, she asked me to come up with a way to make it happen, and not to worry about who I offended in the process. Indeed, what makes Najat most effective is that she has little time for bureaucracy, semantics or diplomatic niceties. She just wants results.

It didn't take us long to realise that operationalising a resilience approach would not be easy. Although knowledge on what was needed had reached a high point, insofar as such interventions involved tough and risky choices, enthusiasm was scant.

The issue was that the pathways the evidence supported were problematic for both donors and recipient states. Promoting family-unit cohesion, peaceful dispute resolution and values such as tolerance are all sensitive, incremental interventions that require highly trained professionals. Donors are often reluctant to fund such work due to its resource intensiveness, unclear outcomes that are difficult to qualify, and potential for political backlash. Even where funding is available, professionals with the relevant psychosocial intervention experience are rare, both at the international and national levels. Programming for critical analysis and systems thinking is another unfamiliar area for the development sector. Perhaps more importantly, it is an area often challenged by communities who consider it an importation of Western influence. Violence reduction programs have been equally resisted, especially where norms around corporal punishment, discipline and authority are deeply embedded in the social fabric.[33]

The most significant challenge, however, was in the area of resilience-building. Creating opportunities to build social interest, especially in the forms of civic activism or participation in policy processes, was deemed high risk for states whose governance models depend on exclusion and heavy-handedness. Indeed, the social contracts that keep these states stable relied upon limited political freedoms and space for dissent. Irrespective of a causal link, any move oriented towards giving young people more power and freedom was likely to be a tough sell. Key Western donors – who also want a stable Middle East – were sensitive to such arguments. They raised a valid concern that any interventions likely to weaken existing power distributions risked a diminution in stability, which might prove more costly in the overall fight against extremist violence.

Simply put, authoritarian states don't particularly want a generation of youth armed with critical thinking and analytical skills, nor to open up space for greater political expression, engagement or protest. Support for this line of thinking is not difficult to find. In May 2020, Hong Kong's pro-Beijing leader Carrie Lam vowed to overhaul the city's education system. She lamented that of the 8,000-plus individuals arrested in the 2019 pro-democracy protests, 17 percent were secondary-school students.

Moreover, she said that the education curriculum was to blame. At the centre of her argument lay Hong Kong's liberal studies program, introduced in 2009 as a means of fostering critical thinking in students. This system had won the city state praise from educators and helped elevate Hong Kong's global ranking, but had long been criticised by Beijing who worried about this exact type of scenario.

6.4 The power of the superpowers

At the beginning of the chapter I promised that this story would lead us to some exciting development pathways. We now need to pull the key elements together. A first thing to note is that when a global challenge strikes, if the wealthy and powerful have an interest in solving it, solving it is what will likely happen. Indeed, the investment made – not just to militarily defeat ISIS but to understand the phenomenon and its drivers – was nothing short of impressive. Funding flowed into research, pilot programming and lessons-sharing conferences. This work was interdisciplinary and cross border – it brought together military, psychology, youth, livelihoods, cohesion, geopolitics and intelligence. Participants had to learn to speak a common language, listen to each other and coordinate. We also saw unprecedented levels of cooperation – between sectors and between states. Even in the coveted world of military intelligence, behind the scenes, statespeople talked – about what they knew, what they didn't know, revelations and mistakes. All this combined to form a robust, efficient and highly productive learning machine.

This is a win in and of itself. For those development workers who were engaged in this fast-moving, results-driven, mistake-eschewing process, the experience was impactful. Staff at UNDP – one of the agencies leading on PVE – likened the pace and pressure to an election campaign or fighting a bushfire. These lessons are also sticky. The development sector might be known for being risk adverse and siloed, but there is also something inherently appealing about being part of a team that is working towards something important, making progress and achieving wins. There is a good chance that those – especially early-career workers – who experienced what a lean, robust, forward-looking workplace feels like will expect this in the future. Sometimes such expectations can be enough to change workplace culture.

This was not a one-off. As the saying goes, history does not repeat, but it does rhyme. The all-hands-on-deck approach bears striking similarity to how the COVID-19 pandemic has played out. I was in China in January 2020, the week the disease was first reported in the international media, and I followed the administration's response with cautious interest. Back in Geneva my children told their classmates stories of streets overflowing with people whose faces were hidden by masks, having no idea how prescient their experience would prove. The first Swiss case was reported on 25 February, but it was another two weeks before schools, restaurants and non-essential shops were closed. Initial advice was terrible, but reflected how little scientists knew about the disease at the time. In America, masks were discouraged. We now know that this was not because the evidence was lacking, but because officials feared that panic buying would cause essential care workers to go without. It is now clear that honesty and transparency would have been better. Masks protect everyone, and could easily have been made at home or quasi-measures fashioned.[34]

But as better data flowed and understanding grew, the world reacted. Most of Europe was locked down from spring until the beginning of the summer, only to pay the heavy price come autumn as cases soared and hospitals quickly became overwhelmed. Ironically, I wrote this chapter from isolation in my own home, being diagnosed with COVID-19 only a week after Pfizer-BioNTech announced the world's first vaccine on 18 November with a claimed efficacy rate of 95 percent.

By the month's end, two more vaccines – by Oxford-Astra Zeneca and Moderna – had completed their phase three trial endpoints. On 2 December the United Kingdom authorised the use of the Pfizer-BioNTech, the government reassuring its population that an estimated 10 million doses would be available by year's end.

Without making light of the 6.5 million individuals who lost their lives to this illness, this is an incredible achievement. COVID-19 is a complex and mutation-prone virus; many experts predicted that a vaccine might never be found. But global superpowers, anticipating what this would mean for the economy, health systems and social cohesion, switched gears to overdrive. The world's leading scientists were corralled; some were even pulled out of retirement. Funding was no object. Operation Warp Speed was set up with an initial USD10 billion, and special dispensations were granted to roll out expedited clinical trials. And the result: in less than a year, the world had not just one viable vaccine, but three.

This achievement should also give us pause. There is still no vaccine for Malaria, which kills over 400,000 annually, mainly in Africa. There is also no vaccine for dengue fever; it kills 25,000 each year, or trypanosomiasis (African sleeping sickness), or Chagas disease.[35] The reason there is no vaccine is because the companies that make them are for-profit, and there is no profit to be made in diseases that affect the poor. Even for ailments that have vaccines and are preventable, the poor are dying. COVID-19 killed 1.5 million in 2020, but a roughly equal number died of tuberculosis. The COVID-19 pandemic is an opportunity to start a conversation around this. Do we have a system that only learns when it becomes important, and important for whom? And how do we feel about this?

6.5 The opportunity within – imagining the moment that wasn't

The takeaway of this chapter is that within these moments lie unique opportunities. The same pressures and incentives that facilitate fast and steep learning also create scope to implement creative responses that would not normally be entertained.

We can see this in how quickly and easily the development community engaged in value-based counter-messaging. These early programs directly aimed to influence not only what "brand" of Islam people should ascribe to, but who they were and what they should stand for. These messages were unabashedly steeped in Western liberalism. This was a significant turnaround. Generally speaking, the development sector steers clear of anything that might be labelled an effort to modify attitudes and mores. This is because little is known about how, why and under what circumstances norms evolve, but also because it begets accusations of cultural imperialism. I mentioned this shift in passing to a Belgian minister during a brainstorming meeting on counter-messaging. His response: "any political correctness around religious pluralism was stricken from the agenda the same day our sons decided to strap on suicide vests".[36] This is not a great example given how much criticism counter-messaging programs went on to attract, but it does demonstrate how quickly and easily red lines can shift in times of urgency and where the stakes are high.

Let's extend this reasoning to the kind of programs that might have been realised had the timing been a little different. Think back to the progress made in understanding terrorist recruitment and the types of reforms needed for young people to reject extremism. Ultimately, what rose to the top were critical thinking skills, opportunities to engage in civic action, and a curbing of state-waged violence.

In fact, the development community has been pushing these types of projects for decades. And for decades, they have been resisted by recipient states (and to an extent donors). We learned about this in Chapter 1: human development approaches give rise to many good things, but they do so by dismantling the tools used to maintain elite power. The only thing that interrupts this is a critical juncture. And maybe that's what ISIS (and COVID-19) are: critical junctures. Moments where the cards are reshuffled, and windows of opportunity for development progress opened.

Consider for a moment a scenario where ISIS wasn't "defeated". It's quite possible that target states might have been receptive to the kinds of reforms experts were coming up with. They would not have transformed into rights-loving, egalitarian democracies. But they might have considered rolling back the heavy-handedness of security services, more seriously addressing corruption and nepotism, or modifying the social contract to make it more inclusive and responsive. They would still have had concerns about conceding too much power and the risk this entailed, but ISIS unbridled and on the loose was a threat too. Western powers might have also asserted pressure for reform if they believed that this was what was needed to eliminate the group. In short, all sides may have viewed governance reform as a well-calculated risk, and this might have been enough to make some headway in important areas for human rights, equality and empowerment.

What's more important, such steps forward are sticky and tend to build on themselves.

Evidence in support of this can be found by examining the strategies adopted by states that successfully warded off the Arab Spring. As protest movements heated up across the region, Jordan's King Abdullah II moved quickly to address his people's demands for political and economic reform. In 2012 he introduced Constitutional amendments, created a Constitutional Court, and for the first time allowed the popular election of a Parliament. Morocco, which weathered an even more virulent protest movement, adopted a similar strategy. In early March 2011, King Mohammed VI gave a speech announcing his reform agenda, which introduced formal limits on the monarchy's power, including preventing him from appointing the Prime Minister and from participating in meetings of the lower house of Parliament. The draft of the new Constitution was announced on 17 June and put to referendum on 1 July, passing with 98 percent of the vote.[37] In both cases, the kings avoided violent means of containing protests such as arrests and civil society crackdowns, setting their administrations apart from the tactics employed by other "survivors" such as Bahrain, the UAE and Saudi Arabia. This combination of tangible reforms and restraint in dealing with the opposition undoubtedly played a role in the public's continued loyalty to the royal family. But rest assured, the moves were a considered choice; they conceded just enough to quell unrest, but not so much that risked the status quo. Most incredible: these changes stuck, and have become part of Jordan and Morocco's new normal.

The idea that when interests align, the stage is set for development breakthroughs should fill everyone with excitement. But there is a cruel irony. When superpowers care about resolving a challenge, that challenge gets resolved quickly. So the window in which development gains can be won is short. Security practitioners are facing this today. ISIS remains a concern, but no one would deny that the loss in momentum has made garnering interest in programs, especially more risky ones, more difficult.

We might be seeing the same thing with COVID-19. At the height of the pandemic, not only were scientists working towards a vaccine, there was also debate around broader issues concerning development. The crisis laid bare the inadequacies in national health systems and the world's vulnerability to health crises.

This was demonstrated most clearly by the United States, which despite its global superpower status levelled one of the most chaotic and deficient responses. Despite making up five percent of the global population, the United States accounted for 25 percent of the world's cumulative cases. Perhaps most disturbing was how the pandemic showcased America's deep racial inequality. Disproving popular dogma, COVID-19 discriminated among wealth and class.[38] Black Americans were twice as likely to contract COVID-19 than white Americans, and their fatality rates were around 2.3 times higher. This is because black populations are more prone to exposure (they travel to work because they more rarely telecommute), are less likely to get tested (they cannot risk forced sick leave) and when they do get sick they are more likely to have pre-existing health conditions and less likely to have health insurance. As painfully captured by Fareed Zakaria, there is no spin doctoring – "the COVID divide is also a class divide".[39]

For those in the health sector, the unmasking of these fissures was met with optimism. There seemed to be a genuine reckoning that health systems needed to be "built back better". Driving this was the idea that COVID-19 was a warning, or a "dry run". Indeed, the science tells us that there will be another pandemic, and that it will likely be far more transmissible and deadly. So we must prepare. Looking again to the science, because this next pandemic will almost certainly evolve in a developing country, primary health care systems need to be strengthened. These countries need trained doctors and nurses, equipment and large stockpiles of therapeutic medicine and protective equipment. They also need governance support so that when that outbreak happens it can be contained as quickly and with as little death as possible. Wet markets need to be better regulated (although not shut down because this is where the poor who lack refrigeration access meat) and the trade in exotic animals abolished. Urbanisation needs to be better planned – one reason we are seeing an increase in the rate of diseases jumping from animals to humans is habitat destruction and deforestation. But the biggest challenge will be for the global community, particularly the West and emerging economies, to reduce its consumption of meat. Today, 74 percent of the global meat supply comes from overcrowded factory farms that are "petri dishes for powerful viruses" and antibiotic-resistant bacteria, delivered direct to our dining tables.[40]

Today the optimism of the health community is somewhat muted. Like with ISIS, now that we have a vaccine it is possible that this all will be forgotten. Only time – and perhaps the actions of health workers in the development community – will tell.

6.6 The role of the development sector

All things considered, the lesson from this chapter is a positive one. So much of the human development struggle is that vested interests get in the way of the reforms that people living in poverty need. But every so often there are moments where the players with the power to affect change find themselves on the same page – aligned in their motivation to tackle a global challenge. In that moment, learning will be fast paced and space will open up to implement solutions, even ones usually considered painful or risky.

In the case of ISIS, the idea that effective counterterrorism on the one hand, and protection of human rights and the rule of law on the other, are complementary and mutually reinforcing goals bears all the hallmarks of opportunity. For decades, protection agencies have experienced the limitations of relying on human rights frameworks and international good practice to quell practices that – although critical for development – serve to maintain power hierarchies and wealth holdings. Simply put, these are hard sells. Evidence then that violence against children, state abuse of power or political exclusion plays a key role in propagating violent extremism may be exactly what is needed to overcome obstacles around political economy and garner the commitment needed to make tangible progress.

But for this to happen, development actors cannot sit by idle. They must play an active and deliberate role by contributing their experience in development and humanitarian response to the learning process. A particularly important role is that of the troubleshooter. States' initial response to the threats posed by ISIS was to extend the reach and powers of the security sector, including its powers of arrest and detention, by revoking citizenship and encroaching on private communications. The realisation that such moves were inadvertently facilitating recruitment was late, but when it happened it was largely due to voices in the child protection, juvenile justice and psychology communities of practice.[41]

The next step is more complicated. A comprehensive understanding of a problem doesn't always translate into an obvious pathway forward. Here, development actors need to connect the dots and make a case for a particular course of action. This is especially in cases where the preferred solution involves tough choices. With the benefit of hindsight it is easy to see that the pre-2017 period was a prime opportunity to curry favour around the logic of investing in programmes aimed at critical thinking, corruption control, eliminating violence and security sector reform. Today, such openings no longer exist. Health development professionals should learn from this. The announcement of a COVID-19 vaccine should have signaled that the window for attention and action would shortly begin to close. Now is the time to craft arguments highlighting the scientific inevitability of a future pandemic, the fissures identified in health systems globally and an action plan for closing the gaps. Such arguments should read against the emerging evidence on virus mutation, the risks attached to poorly regulated wet markets and the externalities of habitat destruction. This is not just an idea – it is proven that decision-makers through to voters are more open to evidence and rational decision-making when they have "skin in the game".[42]

Third, building a solid case may involve investing in new evidence. In the case of ISIS, the WANA-TdH research suggested that for states with voluminous, disenfranchised youth populations, moderate concessions in political freedom might be the key to averting more serious demonstrations of discontent. Development actors might have emboldened this case with research on the types of concessions likely to have been particularly impactful, and how possible stability implications might have been managed. Producing such evidence needs to be seen as a core part of development programming, not an indulgence or an optional extra. Previous chapters have outlined steps that the sector needs to take in this regard; staffing structures need to include more economists and statisticians, a stronger investment in research capability – especially predictive analytics – and teaming up with academia and think tanks.

Here, I need to add an important qualification. The aim should not be the production of "package ready" evidence that is used to justify a rigid development agenda. As one donor remarked to me, "evidence isn't a drum that can be used in the same way they [development actors] use human rights conventions; they cannot just bang on them until we sign or go deaf".[43] I think what he meant is that to be effective, research needs to be scientifically grounded and objective. This doesn't mean development actors need to abandon their agenda, but they do need to let the evidence lead, and at the same time be transparent about their development aspirations.

This last point brings up something sensitive among development practitioners. For some, the idea of using data to push through development wins smells fishy. A little like cheating. They might agree that there is a logical link between good governance and fighting terrorism, or between better primary health care and an efficient pandemic response, but still question whether this approach is strategic. Don't we want states to make these reforms, not because it serves their current aim or because they're scared, but because it's the right thing to do? Doesn't this mean that next time around, when there is no security or health imperative to get their attention, the moral force of the argument has been weakened? And what's this about not beating the human rights drum? After all, this is what we do best.

If this sounds farfetched, it's not. In fact it's playing out right now in the debate around repatriating those foreign children held in camps in Iraq and Syria. One more story.

6.7 What to do with all the children?

Between 2009 and 2017, 4,640 foreign children became affiliated with ISIS in Iraq and Syria and at least 730 infants were born to foreign parents in these territories. To date around 1,180 children have been repatriated, leaving more than 4,000 in theatre.[44] What should happen with these children, as well as child affiliates who have already returned or who never left, has become the subject of a polarised international debate.

The UN is advocating that states set in place repatriation and reintegration processes that comply with their obligations under international law as set out in, inter alia, the Convention on the Rights of the Child (1990).[45] To this end, children should be repatriated to their home countries and children born to nationals granted citizenship. Following repatriation, children should be considered as having been recruited by violent extremist groups in violation of international law.[46] This does not preclude criminal liability. Under international law, any child – provided that they have reached the age of criminal responsibility – can be held legally accountable for crimes committed. However, their victim status should be taken into account in assessing their culpability, and moreover, legal processes must adhere to international juvenile justice standards, which provide children with special rights and protections, irrespective of the gravity of the offence. This includes detention being used only as a last resort and for the shortest period of time.

Despite strong advocacy on the part of the UN and specialist child protection agencies, states have been slow and uneven in their approach to repatriation, bucking the expectation that (particularly Western) states would abide by international norms. Some countries of origin have refused to receive adults associated with extremist groups, as well as their children. Others are willing to repatriate only children, only orphans, or only children under a certain age. Similar trends apply to prosecution. Despite encouragement towards a human rights–compliant approach, few states have included child-specific protections in their counterterrorism legislation and regulatory frameworks.

This disconnect between international best practice and state response demonstrates how hard it is to push norm-based approaches when a state doesn't see it as in their interests. Indeed, some governments argue that repatriation sits at odds with their duty of care to protect citizens and others from violence. In part, this is because once on home soil, authorities are constrained by their domestic legal apparatus, as well as available resources. In a majority of cases, and particularly where acts were perpetrated overseas, evidentiary deficits are likely to prevent the prosecution of children. Experts are uncertain, however, how effective existing rehabilitation and reintegration methodologies will be in preventing recidivism. There is no doubt that such concerns have been aggravated by the media. There has been highly publicised reporting around extremist indoctrination processes and the lasting impact this may have on children's capacity for terrorist violence. In 2018, Germany's domestic intelligence chief Hans-Georg Maassen characterised children affiliated with ISIS as "living time bombs" who could "come back brainwashed with a mission to carry out attacks".[47]

This debate has left states and the UN at an impasse. But the trade-off is not between upholding human rights and maintaining security; it is between domestic short-term and long-term security ends. As distasteful as it might appear, states are likely to remain reluctant to take any steps that may expose their citizens to short-term vulnerability, irrespective of international best practice.

The irony is that if we follow the evidence – especially research on juvenile justice and child soldiers – what states need to do to mitigate security risks is quite closely aligned with what the child protection community of practice wants.

While repatriating is a risk, not repatriating is equally, if not more, risk imbued. For the thousands of children being held in administrative, pretrial or post-conviction detention in Iraq and Syria, the evidence is that their exposure to violence is high and the protection of their due process rights low.

These children are highly vulnerable to being drawn back into an extremist group, or driven down another dysfunctional pathway. The same logic applies to repatriated children; punitive treatment or denying them due process rights risks exacerbating or creating new hostility directed towards state authorities on the part of children themselves, their families and/or their communities.[48] These insights echo the research conducted on child soldiers, where recidivism seemed to hang on punitive treatment and unsuccessful community reintegration. The takeaway is that, far from being "soft" on children who have been affiliated with extremist groups, the most effective way to prevent recidivism – either in the form of extremism or variant forms of violence – may be to divert them away from any justice process that exposes them to violence, causes gaps in their social development and education, or introduces new opportunities for stigmatisation or discrimination. The implications for programming are quite clear. Children located in Iraq and Syria should be repatriated to their countries of origin, and states (including Iraq and Syria) need to set in place accountability processes that reflect juvenile justice principles.

The current discourse – insofar as UN stakeholders are advocating solutions that states feel do not reflect their legitimate interests – is not facilitating this. The reality is that in the current climate, children's rights arguments are likely to be trumped by state security interests and voter concerns. It follows that states are going to be less receptive to approaches that are grounded in their international obligations than they are to approaches that will protect their citizens from violence in the short-term and mitigate against recidivism in the long-term.

With no practical means to reconcile these tensions, the result is a level of stasis. Polarisation in the discourse is also diverting thinking away from the kinds of solutions that might best accommodate the needs of all stakeholders. Against the strong evidence that exists on how to prevent recidivism in children in conflict with the law, this should be viewed as a missed opportunity. Arguably, the most constructive role that can be played by specialist agencies is to provide relevant, evidence-based lessons from the juvenile justice scholarship that states can draw on as they balance risks, craft policy and build their own frameworks.

But could the child protection community also have a point? They rightly argue that states are bound by their international legal obligations (true) and that it is UN's role to advocate for this (also true). They are also concerned about alighting a slippery slope. Advocating that states should repatriate, not because this is what the CRC tells us, but because it will prevent recidivism, implicitly concedes that there are situations where state interests and human rights face off. Is it smart to go down this path, especially in the current climate of populism and insularity? We might not be able to climb back up.

There is no easy answer to this dilemma and perhaps it is here that idealists and pragmatists need to go their separate ways. It could equally be argued that the role of the UN is to get the job done, and being picky about when and how this is done is unproductive.

I would push back, however, on the idea that moments where objectives align are one-off happy coincidences. Global challenges such as terrorism and the difficulty of controlling pandemics are rooted in development challenges: poverty, mal-governance and inequality. No one should be surprised by this.

Perhaps we have already stumbled on at least part of the answer, in Chapter 4. A path forward might lie in seeing the development space as a broader playing field. There needs to be room for a sub-set of the development community, perhaps think tanks, to bring the evidence-based pragmatic argument. This would allow for "enlightened pragmatism" to weave its magic but still allow the child protection community to stay true to its messages. We need to be able to work together and move back and forth the way that is needed. At the moment it feels like we are drowning each other out with mixed messages.

Notes

1 Pooling of news data by *CNN*, *Al Jazeera* and *BBC*.
2 S. Pinker *Enlightenment Now: The Case for Reason, Science, Humanism and Progress*, Allen Lane (2018) 191–193.
3 N. Benotman and N. Malik "The Children of the Islamic State" *Quilliam Foundation* (2016) 14–15, 27–28, 41–44; "Extreme Measures, Abuses against Children Detained as National Security Threats" *Human Rights Watch* (2016).
4 N. Benotman and N. Malik "The Children of the Islamic State" *Quilliam* (2016) 21–23; R. Barrett "Foreign Fighters in Syria" *The Soufan Group* (2014) 9, 16–17.
5 E. Rosand "Communities First: A Blueprint for Organizing and Sustaining a Global Movement Against Violent Extremism" *The Prevention Project: Organizing Against Violent Extremism* December (2016) 8; see also UN Security Council Resolution 2178 (2014) which encouraged all states to ensure that their legal systems provided for the prosecution, as serious criminal offences, of travel for terrorism or related training, as well as the financing or facilitation of such activities.
6 "Children and Counter-Terrorism" *UNICRI* (2016) 51–52; "Preventing and Countering Youth Radicalisation in the EU" IPOL PE 509.977 (2014) 20–21; V. Coppock and M. McGovern "'Dangerous Minds'? Deconstructing Counter-Terrorism Discourse, Radicalisation and the 'Psychological Vulnerability' of Muslim Children and Young People in Britain" *Children & Society* 28: 3. doi: 10.1111/chso.12060.
7 "Extreme Measures, Abuses Against Children Detained as National Security Threats", Human Rights Watch (2016); "Children and Counter-Terrorism" *UNICRI* (2016) 36–37, 57–64; V. Coppock and M. McGovern "Dangerous Minds"? Deconstructing Counter-Terrorism Discourse, Radicalisation and the "Psychological Vulnerability" of Muslim Children and Young People in Britain, 3; "Preventing and Countering Youth Radicalisation in the EU" IPOL PE 509.977(2014) 21–26; C. Angus "Radicalisation and Violent Extremism: Causes and Responses" NSW Parliamentary Research Services (2016) 14–15.
8 See generally L. Ris and A. Ernstorfer "Borrowing a Wheel: Applying Existing Design, Monitoring, and Evaluation Strategies to Emerging Programming

Approaches to Prevent and Counter Violent Extremism" Peacebuilding Evaluation Consortium (2017).

9 See generally N. Bondokji, L. Agrabi and K. Wilkinson "Trapped Between Destructive Choices: Radicalisation Drivers Affecting Youth in Jordan" WANA Institute (2016).

10 Neven Bondokji, Leen Aghabi and Kim Wilkinson "Trapped Between Destrictive CXhoices: Radicalisation Drivers Affecting Youth in Jordan" WANA Institute (2017).

11 J. Khalil and M. Zeuthen, "Countering Violent Extremism and Risk Reduction: A Guide to Programme Design and Evaluation" *Royal United Services Institute for Defense and Security Studies* (2016) 8, 11–13, Whitehall Report 2–16; "Preventing and Countering Youth Radicalisation in the EU" IPOL PE 509.977(2014) 11; R. Borum "Radicalization into Violent Extremism I: A Review of Social Science Theories" *Journal of Strategic Security* 4:4 (2011) 8.

12 "Preventing and Countering Youth Radicalisation in the EU" IPOL PE 509.977(2014) 31; J. Khalil and M. Zeuthen "Countering Violent Extremism and Risk Reduction: A Guide to Programme Design and Evaluation" *Royal United Services Institute for Defense and Security Studies* (2016) 6.

13 V. Coppock and M. McGovern "Dangerous Minds"? Deconstructing Counter-Terrorism Discourse, Radicalisation and the "Psychological Vulnerability" of Muslim Children and Young People in Britain, 11–14.

14 C. Angus "Radicalisation and Violent Extremism: Causes and Responses" *NSW Parliamentary Research Services* (2016) 14–15.

15 They also highlighted the strong evidence that when individuals feel targeted by the state, their vulnerability to recruitment into the group that is the broader subject of the intervention tends to increase, usually as a means of securing protection "Extreme Measures, Abuses Against Children Detained as National Security Threats" *Human Rights Watch* (2016). This is consistent with the scholarship on youth delinquency, which sets out a positive correlation between "preventative" youth programming and subsequent misbehavior; the logic is that when youth feel stereotyped and stripped of agency, they follow what is being presented to them as an assumed action pathway, creating a self-fulfilling path.

16 T. Choudhury and H. Fenwick "The Impact of Counter-terrorism Measures on Muslim Communities" *Equality and Human Rights Commission* (2011), Equality and Human Rights Commission Research report 72.

17 R. Borum "Radicalization Into Violent Extremism II: A Review of Conceptual Models and Empirical Research" *Journal of Strategic Security* 4:4 (2011) 50–51; E. Rosand "Communities First: A Blueprint for Organizing and Sustaining a Global Movement Against Violent Extremism" *The Prevention Project: Organizing Against Violent Extremism* (2016) 7–8.

18 C. Angus "Radicalisation and Violent Extremism: Causes and Responses" *NSW Parliamentary Research Services* (2016) 14–15; "Preventing and Countering Youth Radicalisation in the EU" IPOL PE 509.977 (2014) 21.

19 UNDP "Journey to Extremism in Africa: Drivers, Incentives and the Tipping Point for Recruitment" UNDP New York (2017).

20 See generally. N. Bondokji and E. Harper "Journey Mapping on Selected Foreign Fighters in Jordan" WANA Institute (2017).

21 J. Ginges, S. Atran, S. Sachdeva and D. Medin "Psychology out of the Laboratory: The Challenge of Violent Extremism" *American Psychologist* 66:6 (2011) 507–519.

22 This is because the drivers of extremism are often opaque; they are situational, broad reaching and have loosely identifiable targets. Religious narrative bundles these externalities into a clear operational mandate, locus of attack and an obtainable objective. However, see other augments set out in e.g. J. Russell

and H. Rafiq "Countering Extremist Narratives: A Strategic Briefing" *Quilliam* (2016) 3–19; D Gartenstein-Ross and L Grossman *Homegrown Terrorists in the U.S. and the U.K.: An Empirical Examination of the Radicalization Process*, FDD Press (2009) 3–19.

23 For example, see A. Bari Atwan *The Secret History of Al-Qa'ida*, al-Saqi (2006) 44–50; M. Özçelik "The Two Radical Sources of Instability in the Middle East" *Council on Foreign Relations' Global Memos*, 15 August 2014. http://www.cfr. org/councilofcouncils/global_memos/p33347

24 S. Atran "Voice of a Frontline Researcher & Anthropologist" podcast led by S. Green, Centre for Strategic and International Studies (2016).

25 See also Global Open Days, UNAMA "Consultations on Women, Peace and Security: Women's Role in Preventing Violent Extremism" (2016); "Preventing Violent Extremism Through Promoting Inclusive Development, Tolerance and Respect for Diversity" UNDP (2016) 13.

26 E. Harper "Reconceptualizing the Drivers of Violent Extremism: An Agenda for Child and Youth Resilience" Terre des homme and WANA Institute (2018).

27 The FabLab concept was created at the Massachusetts Institute of Technology in 2001, as part of the global "Do It Yourself" movement. FabLabs work as a non-formal education tool, allowing young people to acquire practical digital skills while also bolstering their resilience. While the workplace is open, work-shops are regularly offered, allowing young people to enhance their creativity and implement their own designs. Terre des Hommes now operates FabLabs as part of its programmes in Greece, Burkina Faso, Ukraine and Gaza.

28 M.A. Zimmerman "Psychological Empowerment: Issues and Illustrations" *American Journal of Community Psychology* 23:5 (1995) 581–599; N. Park "The Role of Subjective Well-Being in Positive Youth Development" *The ANNALS of the American Academy of Political and Social Science* 591:1 (2004) 25–39.

29 UN World Youth Report: Youth Civic Engagement (2016) 90–91.

30 Global Open Days, UNAMA "Consultations on Women, Peace and Security: Women's Role in Preventing Violent Extremism" (2016); "Preventing Violent Extremism through Promoting Inclusive Development, Tolerance and Respect for Diversity" UNDP (2016) 22.

31 Global Open Days, UNAMA "Consultations on Women, Peace and Security: Women's Role in Preventing Violent Extremism" (2016); "Preventing Violent Extremism Through Promoting Inclusive Development, Tolerance and Respect for Diversity" UNDP (2016) 21.

32 A good practice comes from the youth-led association Tunisians Against Terrorism, which has made remarkable progress working with the Ministries of Youth, Education and Interior, as well as members of the National Assembly, to develop a curriculum that included critical thinking skills, process analytics and systems thinking, brought into the classroom via practical exercises in gleaning evidential interpretations of Islamic fiqh. "Transforming Violent Extremism: A Peacebuilder's Guide" *Search for Common Ground* (2017) 35. Another good practice from Germany is the Live Democracy program, which aims at rein-forcing tolerant attitudes, anti-violence and all forms of right-wing extremism; N Benotman and N Malik "The Children of the Islamic State" *Quilliam* (2016) 10–13, 78; see also "Children and Counter-Terrorism" *UNICRI* (2016) 74.

33 *Handbook on Children Recruited and Exploited by Terrorist and Violent Extremist Groups*, UNODC (2017) 31.

34 F. Zakaria *Ten Lessons for a Post-Pandemic World*, Penguin Random House (2020) 82.

35 See generally, P. Stevens "Diseases of Poverty and the 10/90 Gap" International Policy Network (2004).

36 Interview dated 20 November 2019, Brussels, notes on file with author.
37 M. Ottaway "The New Moroccan Constitution: Real Change or More of the Same?" Carnegie Endowment for International Peace (2011). http://carnegieendowment. org/2011/06/20/new-moroccan-constitution-real-change-or-more-of-same/6g.
38 F. Zakaria *Ten Lessons for a Post-Pandemic World*, Penguin Random House (2020) 160–161.
39 F. Zakaria *Ten Lessons for a Post-Pandemic World*, Penguin Random House (2020) 92.
40 F. Zakaria *Ten Lessons for a Post-Pandemic World*, Penguin Random House (2020) 16–20, 27–28.
41 Likewise it was UNDP that lifted the lid on the role of livelihoods in terrorist recruitment. Poverty – initially understood to be a key driver of extremism – turned out to play a far more nuanced role, being of less relative importance in the case of ISIS but pivotal in the Horn of Africa.
42 N. Taleb *Skin in the Game: Hidden Asymmetries in Daily Life*, Random House (2018).
43 Interview dated 21 November 2019, Brussels, notes on file with author.
44 J. Cook and G. Vale, "From Daesh to 'Disaspora': Tracing the Women and Minors of the Islamic State", International Centre for the Study of Radicalization (2018) 3.
45 "Key Principles for the Protection, Repatriation, Prosecution, Rehabilitation and Reintegration of Women and Children with links to UN Listed Terrorist Groups", UN Secretary-General (2019); UN Security Council Resolution 2178 (2014), see also General Assembly Resolution 70/291 on the United Nations Global Counter-Terrorism Strategy Review.
46 The legal basis for this is complex, but is grounded in article 4 of the Optional Protocol to the Convention on the Rights of the Child on the Involvement of Children in Armed Conflict (2002), which prohibits the recruitment and use of children by non-state armed groups in hostilities. The Optional Protocol to the Convention on the Rights of the Child on the Sale of Children, Child Prostitution and Child Pornography (2002) criminalises actions relating to the sale of children, including for the purposes of forced labour. See further Paris Principles: Principles and Guidelines on Children Associated With Armed Forces or Armed Groups (2007) para 8.7.
47 A Shalal and S Siebold "'Brainwashed' Children of Islamist Fighters Worry Germany–Spy Chief" <https://uk.reuters.com/article/uk-germany-security-children/brainwashed-children-of-islamist-fighters-worry-germany-spy-chief-idUKKBN1FK1FR> (accessed 12 February 2020).
48 According to the juvenile justice scholarship, rather than punishment and detention, these children need an opportunity to "reboot"; to gain. The aim should be to vest children with the skills they need – whether self-control, conflict resolution or critical analysis – to access alternate pathways and exercise more constructive life choices. These tools and choices act as a bridge to gaining a "stake in society" – an existence based on connectedness and social interest, where there is no need for or incentive to engage in deviant behaviour. See further E. Harper "Solutions for Children Previously Affiliated With Extremist Groups: An Evidence Base to Inform Repatriation, Rehabilitation and Reintegration" Office of SRSG Violence Against Children, New York (2020).

7

PLAYING POLITICS TO WIN

In 1913, the Queen's Hall Orchestra in London hired its first female musicians. Over time this trend grew, but only marginally and only in the case of certain instruments. By the 1970s, women found this untenable, and with the support of labour unions and some forward-thinking music heavyweights, they successfully lobbied for better pay and conditions of service. They also wanted greater transparency in hiring. The management response did not involve affirmative action, a revised Code of Conduct or training conductors in gender sensitivity. Instead, blind auditions were introduced – a curtain that shielded the auditioning musician, forcing selectors to judge, solely, on the music. And things changed. The research of Princeton University's Cecelia Rouse captured this for the world to ponder. Her examination of 14,133 individuals over 592 audition segments found that between 1970 and 1996, blind auditions explained "between 30 percent and 55 percent of the increase in the proportion female among new hires and between 25 percent and 46 percent of the increase in the percentage female in the orchestras".[1]

What combination of forces allowed this remarkable transition? After all, the orchestral community certainly wasn't immune from battles of power, vested interests and patriarchy. It was the simplest of things – a shared desire to make the best music possible. This allowed a community to inwardly examine their biases and overcome them. They just put up a screen, and 60 years of missed opportunity fell away.

This chapter is about whether these kinds of groundbreaking changes – in attitudes or practices – can happen, or be made to happen, for the purposes of human development. Now of course, change is taking place constantly, and oftentimes in significant and positive ways. Nutrition, longevity, conflict and literacy are all trending in a positive direction. But such change is rarely stark, clean or rapid. Usually, it occurs so incrementally that it passes by unnoticed. It's also not to say that those battles – whether ___ won quickly or slowly, or through simple or complicated fixes – ___ cases, the challenges appeared unsurmountable at the ___ mity of the battle quickly becomes lost in a new collec- ___ s. A few decades ago, no one would have believed that smoking at work or in restaurants would be popularly outlawed in Western cultures. Much the same can be said about littering, wearing seat-belts and handwashing.

We cannot wait decades for incremental change to deliver a solution around gender inequality and the climate crisis. The first case presents a chicken and egg problem – gender equality drives development and development drives equality. We need a "screen solution", especially in failing and fragile states where discrimination retards economic growth, drives conflict and caps opportunity. The issue of climate change is perhaps more direct – we're running out of time.

This begs the question of whether enabling conditions can be created, or the regular process of change sped up, to arrive at a point where decarbonisation and equality between the sexes feels as natural as refraining from smoking in public, or putting on a seatbelt. The development community has invested a great deal of time and energy into these questions. Some believe that change accrues fastest and most sustainably by targeting the laws and policies that regulate behaviour, others support targeting people's values and behaviours at the grassroots level.

Perhaps not surprisingly, the most effective treatment seems to depend on the nature of the problem. In the United States, civil rights protections around segregation required federal court intervention and police action until, slowly, a critical mass of ideologically aligned people formed. We are far from a race-blind society, but the rights secured in *Browder v. Gayle* and *Brown v. Board of Education* are no longer in question. Female Genital Mutilation (FGM) by contrast – an abhorrent practice driven by deeply entrenched cultural norms – has proven highly resilient against changes to the law. Oxfam strategist Duncan Green explains how grassroots action has yielded far greater success, each example telling a unique story. In Senegal, what worked was the formation of "anti–FGM clubs", which expanded rapidly and unaided, largely because members needed other members in order for people to marry. In Egypt, reformers homed in on the 3 percent of women who avoided the practice and tried to replicate their experiences.[2]

The problem is that neither of these approaches – top down or bottom up – has been particularly effective when it comes to fighting climate change or gender discrimination. Unlike the problems explored in the previous chapters, there is no clear and obvious stakeholder with both the power and a vested interest to champion the gender cause. The climate battle is equally complex, but the issue is assigning responsibility. As in music, climate is something that holds undeniable value, but no one owns.

This is not to say that change cannot happen, just that we're using the wrong tools. In the case of gender, pressuring governments to bring their policies into line with international standards and strengthening women's capacity to exercise their rights overlooks that this is a problem rooted in power, not misunderstanding. In many areas where inequality prev~'' marginalisation of women serves the interests of tradition~'

in terms of resource control, sexual commoditisation and monopolisation of decision-making. In climate change, the preferred approach has been a brandishing of evidence. However, because this is a fight between opposing ideologies, evidence, regardless of how sophisticated or frightening, is unlikely to move parties quickly or cleanly towards agreement. In short, the development community is fighting *logically*, but *ineffectively*. The answer is a better reading of the problem in play, and with this, a different approach. At the heart of this lies strategic political engagement – the game that everyone else is playing to achieve their objectives. To not use these same tools is worse than apathetic, it is culpable. We need to start playing the political game more subtly.

7.1 Fighting the good fight, and losing

7.1.1 Strategies, good and bad, for closing the gender gap

While gender gaps have been narrowing for decades, males continue to outscore females on a range of development indicators, from educational enrolment and achievement to labour force participation, earning power and infant mortality. This should concern everyone. Apart from its moral indications, equality is a development imperative. An empowered female populous is connected to outcomes ranging from peacefulness to improved health statistics and environmental sustainability. These gains spill over onto growth potential. More equal societies – where women work, enjoy property rights and can access capital – grow faster and more consistently.[3] This is because gender inequality manifests as a labour market failure, imposing costs in terms of productivity and efficiency. Specifically, gender differences prevent the accumulation of human capital and skew the distribution of resources, thus diminishing an economy's capacity to develop.

While the preceding suggests that women's rights are a precursor to development, the correlation is not unequivocal. There is also evidence that economic development begets, or at least grows in parallel to, gender equality, and reciprocally that poverty and lack of opportunity propagate inequality. This raises a serious question. How can the cycle be interrupted when economic development is needed to eliminate inequality, but it is equality that drives development? Today the weight of opinion supports the idea that while development does improve the rights of and opportunities available to women, it is not, on its own, sufficient to deliver gender parity. Specific actions are required to enhance women's opportunities, positioning and agency for a symbiotic cycle of gains to be kick-started.

A first way the development community of practice has sought to action this is through advocacy – using carrots or sticks to encourage governments to bring their regulatory frameworks into line with international standards, or to take specific actions to strengthen the rights held by women. A good example is the support given by the international community to rebuild in the Indonesian province of Aceh following the 2004 tsunami. The force of the two waves resulted in the permanent submersion of around 80,000 hectares of land, with another 7,000 contaminated or rendered unstable. But before reconstruction could start, issues of ownership had to be resolved. Since most land had never been mapped and what government records existed were destroyed, the government initiated a process of community-led land mapping. The risk for women was that they might lose property that was personally owned, inherited, or jointly owned with their husbands, especially insofar as land certificates, sale contracts or bank accounts – which were generally in husbands' name – were relied upon to determine ownership. The UN lobbied hard to include wording in the relevant regulation that all joint matrimonial property should be listed in the names of both the husband and wife. The UN gender advisor at the time told me that convincing the Indonesians was made a lot easier by the fact that the full scope of budgetary support being offered was still under negotiation. The result was heralded as a huge win for women's rights in the *shari'ah*-ruled state. That only 3–5 percent of land parcels were registered jointly was largely glossed over in subsequent reporting.

The limits of top-down policy reform lent to it being overtaken by an alternate approach: women's empowerment. The theory of change is that if women are given information, skills and tools, they will be better positioned to protect their rights, assert their interests and seek remedies for injustices against them. This levelling of the playing field will ultimately bring about the changes in society needed for women and girls to enjoy the same rights, opportunities and protections as men and boys.

I've never really bought into either of these approaches as complete solutions. As discussed in the last chapter, pressuring a government to reform because it's "the right thing to do" is not a particularly compelling way to initiate change. Even where wielding the moral stick of human rights does work, the data suggests that transformation on the ground is generally mild or in the best case, generational. Empowerment approaches have more logical appeal but are equally complicated. As the women's rights campaigner Nabila Kabeer explains, empowerment manifests in an ability to make choices. For there to be genuine choice, however, alternatives must exist, and women in developing countries usually have very few of these. For women to be able to work, continue their education, or exercise health care decisions, a basic level of economic empowerment is necessary. Likewise, women's "choice" to engage in public life may be hampered by a system that is marred by corruption and nepotism. In practice, these challenges mean that a considerable amount of empowerment programming is limited to sensitising women about their rights under the various international conventions. Telling women that they have rights when they have very little power to realise them, however, does very little to improve their situation; oftentimes it leaves them feeling despondent, angry and marginalised. In the worst cases, well-meaning organisations "empower" women to uphold their rights through the justice system, only to see them rejected by their families or communities for having breaching cultural norms. The point is not to discredit empowerment as an entry point but to highlight how rights-centric approaches can obfuscate the realities of living in a patriarchal, poorly governed or poverty-ridden society, and as a result, inadvertently compromise a women's overall safety and wellbeing.

But battles over gender rights have been fought and won. Let us consider changes that have taken place in Morocco, Tunisia, Kenya and others.

7.1.2 When change has happened – clues from the global south

Commencing in the 1980s, women's groups in Morocco launched a unified advocacy campaign to reform the *shari'a*-based Code of Personal Status (1958) known as the *Mudawwana*. As part of this movement, in 1992, the Union de l'Action Feminine established the "1 Million Signatures Campaign".[4] They argued that the law, derived from conservative interpretations of Maliki *fiqh*, privileged the position of men and that a process of reform (*ijtihad*) was required.[5] Such action reached a tipping point in 2000 with street demonstrations in Rabat and Casablanca. The debates that followed polarised Moroccan society, religious organisations and women's groups.[6] Both the government and women's rights organisations appealed to King Mohammed VI to intervene.[7] The following year he did establish a commission on the reform of the *Mudawwana*, but it was the Casablanca attacks that sealed the necessary commitment. Morocco suddenly needed to present itself as a player in the war on terror, and it seized opportunities to be perceived as progressive and democratic. Women's movements latched onto this momentum, presenting their demands as a fence against religious extremism and a pledge of the state's commitment to modernity. Revising the Family Code facilitated this. Promulgated in 2004, it remains among the most progressive in the region.[8]

As set out by scholar Zakia Salime, three features distinguish the Morocco process and, at least in part, explain its success. First, the reform agenda was largely spearheaded by networks of women within the main Islamist political movements. That these movements supported female participation, both in large numbers and in leadership functions, was unique to the region. This work was complemented by an active women's civil society lobby. The composition of these groups may also have been important. While in both cases membership largely comprised younger, middle class, and educated professionals, they actively engaged women more generally. Examples include legal literacy programs and magazines that devoted space to women's issues; gender awareness programs targeting protection agents such as police, judges and teachers; education curricula reform; and women's leadership programs.[9] This facilitated popular engagement, broad consensus and events – such as the protests – that would prove foundational to the reform process.

Second, the movement carefully chose their adversary and adopted a non-threatening approach. They defined their cause as challenging the legal source of women's oppression, therefore pitching their battle with the state (specifically the legislature), but not religious authorities, men, Islam or the king. Their argument was multifaceted: the *Mudawwana* was (i) unconstitutional (the Constitution guarantees full equality for all citizens), (ii) inconsistent with Morocco's international legal obligations, (iii) contrary to Islamic doctrine that upholds the equality of women and men and (iv) represented a misalignment between family structures and law, with practical ramifications for families.[10] This "something for everyone" approach combined with only tacit use of threats, made it easier for the movement to gain support from political power holders.

Third, the movement carefully warded off competition. While women's groups found allies in the UN system, they made a concerted effort to distance themselves and distinguish their movement from Western feminist discourse by presenting it as an Islamic imperative. The struggle was not for women's rights but for family rights, and this required the correct positioning of women in the family unit as envisaged in Islamic jurisprudence.[11] They highlighted that *ijtihad* had previously been used to reform family law in Morocco, and then built legitimacy around these arguments through evidence-based links to Qur'anic verses and *hadith* supporting gender equality, equality of rights and duties, men and women's mutual responsibilities towards each other and their equal responsibilities towards God.[12] So serious was their commitment to ground demands in Islamic doctrine, they removed equal inheritance (an unambiguous issue in the Qur'an) from an early version of the 1 Million Signatures Campaign. This moderate approach limited their exposure to criticism from traditional Islamists as well as secular conservatives.

The Morocco case study is usually cited to illustrate the potential for *ijtihad* as a tool to promote a more comprehensive set of legal protections for women. It is also a story of the legal system being used as a vehicle for social change. It was women's organisations that largely orchestrated this, and they did so not by sidelining Islam, but by making it a partner in their demands for reform. Their success can be seen as a product of strategic planning and then capitalising on a particular moment in time. The Casablanca attacks provided a fertile political climate, which created greater room to manoeuvre. The role of the king was also a key factor, specifically his strategic decision to align himself with women as an affront to Islamist extremism.

Morocco was not a one-off. This pattern of a particular context (often featuring a slow-evolving civil society movement), followed by a critical juncture, creating a brief window of opportunity that is capitalised upon by a patient but well-prepared group, plays out time and time again.

In Tunisia, the critical juncture was street vendor Muhammad Bouazizi, who in December 2010, set himself on fire to protest the humiliating confiscation of his wares. His act ignited a protest movement that culminated in President Zine El Abidine ben Ali abdicating his 23-year rule. With the world's eyes on Tunisia, the transitional government introduced into law a female quota geared towards enhanced gender parity in political representation.[13] Women seized their moment and were elected in over 26 percent of constituencies to the National Constituent Assembly. They also took to the streets to battle the reforms proposed by the Ennahda party (which won a plurality of seats) including around veiling, polygamy and the positioning of women in the family unit. They prevailed. On 26 January 2014, a new Constitution – lauded as the most modern in the Arab world with respect to women's rights – was passed with an overwhelming majority of 200 out of 216 votes. Perhaps most importantly, women's capacity to inform the political debate was no longer in question: gender equality had become a central tenet of Tunisian politics.

In Kenya, political reform was the carrot needed to broker a peace deal and thus quell the violence that followed the re-election of President Mwai Kibaki in 2007. Again, gender groups mobilised quickly to advance their objectives and influence the normative content of the reforms. In 2010, the new Constitution delivered unprecedented gains to women, including a Bill of Rights enshrining the principles of equality and non-discrimination, and a quota mechanism ensuring that neither gender could occupy more than two-thirds of public or elected offices.[14] Realising these gains has been a slow, difficult and sometimes dangerous process, but one unmistakably trending in the right direction. Kenya's 12th national parliament consists of 416 members, 97 of who are women, or 23 percent of the total.

This leaves an important question. Do wins at the top trickle down to impact practice, and if so, how long does this take? We will come back to this, but for now it is important to highlight that progress at the grassroots level doesn't always lag behind constitutional and parliamentary reform. Sometimes the national and local work in concert, singing to the same tune. The Van Vollenhoven Institute's Professor Janine Ubink's fascinating investigation into how traditional authorities in Namibia integrated women into their leadership and dispute resolution structures identifies a key set of drivers.[15] She explains that when Namibia gained independence in 1990, the country experienced a tremendous momentum for change, including in gender relations. Women had played a prominent role in the pre-independence period as freedom fighters, by expressing their opposition to colonial occupation, and by assuming the roles played by men (who were away fighting or working on white-owned farms) in the functioning of rural villages.[16] Namibia's 1990 Constitution rewarded them, guaranteeing equality and freedom from discrimination, including on the basis of sex,[17] and steering them into political roles at both the national and regional government levels. These changes quickly and easily filtered downwards. The people of the Owambo region, for example, who had been highly engaged in the liberation struggle, strongly identified with the new independent Namibia. This, coupled with a desire to assert their relevance in the new political order, impelled them to align their customary laws with the new Constitution and the broader gender equality discourse. Women were integrated into the traditional leadership structures and began to participate in traditional court processes, and customary rules changed to better protect women's rights. Not only were these changes "sticky", they built upon themselves. Today, Namibia ranks 12th globally in terms of its gender gap[18] and seventh according to the number of women in parliament.[19]

7.1.3 The formula behind the success

The lesson from these case studies is that these wins share common elements. Reforms were not driven exclusively by a demand for enhanced gender parity or protection. They also enabled state agendas that made an elaboration of women's rights politically appealing. In Tunisia and Morocco, there was a desire to present on the international stage as modern, progressive states. In Kenya and Namibia, the agenda was nationalistic, unabashedly anticolonial and centered around peacebuilding. Women's groups prudently wound their issues into these agendas. They identified opportunities and synergies to present women's legal rights as a tool of political capital. Even in Namibia, where women were already seen as having earned a public platform, groups made sure to present gender rights as an issue of political concern.

Pilar Domingo of the Overseas Development Institute perhaps captures this best:

> [O]pportunities for women's influence are not single factors or moments of change that simply allowed [them] to mobilise and negotiate for a gender-progressive constitution. Rather, what emerged was a series of political openings that the women's movement took advantage of, which in turn created further political openings.[20]

A second point is that the women's groups lobbying for reform were not "pop up shops". They had evolved slowly and organically, usually over a period of decades. Their early work was often highly restricted and suffered many setbacks, but it paved the way for women to later turn out as protesters, lobbyists and political candidates.[21]

Finally, their winning strategy was built around broad and diverse support – strategic alliances with male politicians, key power holders in the private sector and, where it mattered, religious leaders. They also garnered the support of women outside the capitals and far removed from the political process.[22] In Morocco, women's groups had a long history in delivering civic education, while in Tunisia and Kenya they connected through community services. In short, these women's movements represent a masterclass in politically savvy.

The takeaways for development policy and programming are fascinating. To recap the dilemma, strong vested interests mean that progress in gender equality often requires a legal mandate, but the group with the power to command such change is often the one benefiting most directly from a gender unequal society. Occasionally, though, there will be circumstances where a change to the status quo becomes politically strategic to support, or too risky to avoid. These are the moments where the most impressive and sustained change processes take place.

Unfortunately, it doesn't appear that these circumstances can be brought to fruition. Neither policy advocacy nor women's empowerment programming seem able to generate the momentum or authenticity of concern needed to tip the scales. This is not to say that there is no role for development programming or policy support. A strong civil society – which often finds support from the international community – seems to be a prerequisite. Technical support offered by think tanks and feminist academics can likewise make important contributions.

The ones likely to receive this news the worst are those with responsibility for gender programming. It reminds me of a conference I attended in Washington where a World Bank project officer presented some compelling research highlighting a strong correlation between girls finishing secondary education and entering the workforce, and reductions in FGM. Her key point – that as a society reaches lower-middle income status, it naturally sheds a host of problems afflicting its members – was not well received. The annoyance emanating from the gender experts in the audience was palpable. No one wants to hear from an economist that the answer to the problem your group is charged with fixing is actually to hand responsibility and funding over to a rival sector.

Most difficult is the suggestion that change cannot always be manufactured. Maybe we can push it along a little and taper the worst violations, but for the big wins the moment has to be right. This implies a waiting game, during which a context needs to be monitored carefully and sound preparatory work undertaken with the idea that at some point in the future *something* will happen – a political disaster, a terror attack, or a king needing to demonstrate his liberalism. At this point, support needs to be provided – quickly and flexibly. Or perhaps not. As the Morocco example demonstrated, in some cases it is more strategic for the development community to stand back and to hold its breath. Victor Hugo was right; there is nothing more powerful than an idea whose time has come.

7.2 The climate change challenge: sceptics, economic losers and ideology

Before we begin, a short caveat is needed. I am not a climate expert, although I have gone to great lengths to get to know some outstanding thinkers in this field and understand their works. In this regard, the following sections condense a great deal of complex environmental and economic theory to home in on a few central arguments; I also endorse a range of entry points that I acknowledge to be contested. Finally, this discussion examines climate change through a specific development lens. Development and humanitarian actors are engaged on a range of extant issues – staple crops that are no longer viable, mass forced migration and the potential for water conflicts. The ideas posited in no way speak to such challenges, let alone offer to resolve them.

7.2.1 Climate change discontents and what they can tell us

Within the scientific community, climate change is both fact and a threat. In a 2015 meta-analysis of 69,406 peer reviewed scientific articles, only four rejected anthropogenic climate change.[23] And while we are all at threat of climate-related disasters, rising sea levels and loss in biodiversity, developing countries are the most exposed. The agriculture-dominated nature of their economies means that livelihoods and food insecurity will reach them first.[24]

Development actors (and probably most people reading this book) see the urgency in these challenges. This position is not held by everyone, however. Take climate sceptics. They believe that the climate debate is overblown – or even a hoax – and that we should place our faith in markets and technology to deliver solutions.[25] Some argue that the priority should be those living in poverty today, rather than the vulnerable of the future; they would like to see the funds currently dedicated to climate research rerouted into vaccine development or getting more girls into higher education.[26] Equally vocal is the deep green movement – those who repudiate technology and think we should all become part-time organic farmers. This group advocates that populations in developing countries be protected from industrialisation and globalisation and be allowed to retain their traditional way of life.[27] As we will see in Chapter 7, this is not at all what the poor want. They want cell phones, connectivity and toilets that flush.

There are, however, some valid points to be gleaned from these debates. Tackling climate change will most likely involve radical solutions, although retuning to a pre-industrial era is not the one of them. Quite the contrary, the development of poor countries is a key step in the climate fight. This is because as countries become wealthier, they become cleaner. Indeed, two of the worst pollutants – indoor cooking smoke and water contamination – "are afflictions of poor countries".[28] But the development process requires an enormous amount of energy. We should not forget that it was the same environmentally destructive period of Western industrialisation that also doubled life expectancy, slashed poverty, and emancipated women and children.[29] The upshot is that to win the battle against climate change, poor countries need to become wealthier. This will be a messy process that wealthier countries will need to offset.

There is an old saying that the stone age did not end because it ran out of stones. It is also true that most doomsday predictions – the kind peddled by the deep green movement – never came to fruition as they were solved by technological innovation. The population bomb never materialised. As countries got richer they stopped reproducing at high rates. The world also didn't run out of copper, nickel or zinc. As supply reduced, prices rose, incentivising people to innovate.[30] In practice, "societies have always abandoned a resource for better one long before the old one was exhausted".[31] It will likely be the same for energy. As set out in the July 2020 issue of *The Economist*, market forces are already operating to reduce carbon emissions as power stations switch from coal to natural gas.[32]

And it may well be that what saves us is yet to be invented. Meat cultured in-vitro, fertilizer derived from sewage, and undersea carbon-capturing organisms are among the many ideas being tinkered with by scientists today.[33] Real-world application depends, however, on continued and substantial investments in research and development. Even then, there are no guarantees. Given what is at stake, alongside innovation, a serious and workable decarbonisation agenda needs to be created.

7.2.2 *The politics of decarbonisation*

Let's start by placing some boundaries around what sustainable decarbonisation might look like. It will not lie in recycling and more efficient personal consumption choices – although no one can deny that a world where individuals think more prudently about waste wouldn't be a change for the better. Reform must be directed at gains that can be accrued at scale. The bulk of global greenhouse gasses – around 75 percent – come from heavy industry, buildings, transport and (ironically) the energy expended to produce energy.[34] How to bring this under control is a political problem as much as a technological one. Emissions have no natural owners, creating something akin to a free-rider problem. In this case, the resource getting overconsumed is clean air, and until users are forced to start paying for polluting it, they have no incentive to change their behaviour. The only solution is a universal intergovernmental agreement. We are not nearly there – "cap and trade" is too vulnerable to rent seeking, and "polluter pays" approaches are inequitable.

One challenge is that the solutions most likely to work will create losers across almost all economic groups. Rich countries will have to shoulder the costs of very poor countries limiting their emissions while they develop. Middle-income countries – who will host the majority of industrial production in the future – will need to bear some costs in terms of reduced profits. This is because the price of goods will need to increase to reflect the emissions embedded in their production and/or their use. If this can be achieved, the world will inevitably begin turning away from carbon, creating one final loser – energy exporting countries such as Russia and the Gulf states.

But these rentier economies were always going to have to diversify and indeed many are on their way. Today less than 1 percent of Dubai's GDP is derived from oil, down from more than 50 percent a few decades ago.[35]

Alongside a global emissions agreement, productivity needs to be decoupled from resources use – in layman's terms, doing more with less. Agriculture – which is hugely carbon producing – needs to become more calorific, all the while using less water and farmland. This will not be realised by organic farming (which is not ecologically sustainable as it requires vast land areas). Another part of the solution will be genetically modified (GM) crops engineered to be resistant to drought, flood and pests. The poor already dedicate a disproportionate amount of income to food, but moreover, as a warming climate compromises their ability to feed themselves they will be more dependent on volatile international markets and thus vulnerable to shocks.[36]

The other density-rich solution is nuclear energy, in the contexts to which it is suited. Nuclear energy production requires enormous amounts of water, so it's not an option for a country like Jordan which has none. It would also be unsuitable for countries that are prone to conflict and instability. But where conditions are right, it's very difficult to argue factually against the cost and environmental effectiveness of nuclear power. Unfortunately, nuclear energy (and GM food) production is shrinking in areas where it should be growing, not for any economic or safety reason, but because of politics.[37]

The stumbling block to the two things we need – an intergovernmental agreement on decarbonisation and a market transition to high-density food and energy products – is special interests. The industrial, anti-nuclear and agricultural lobbies are incredibly strong. As discussed in Chapter 3, one of the limits of democracy is that battles are frequently fought and won based not on the content of a shouting match, but on who yells the loudest.

7.2.3 Enter the development community

The development sector has rightly worked out that the political realm is the room where it happens, and that a few powerful countries hold most of the cards. Let's examine some of the main strategies. One entry point is advocacy. I would posit that encouraging the public to engage politicians on the climate emergency is probably not going garner the type of response needed. It may feel like the world is coming around to the seriousness of the climate situation, but this is being somewhat fed by the availability heuristic – the news feeds we (the demographic reading this book) watch, discussions we participate in, and "green" marketing we are exposed to. If we step back from this, the fact is that it is quite difficult for people to get worried about future events. Behavioural economists called it an un-situated risk – risks that we can't see or feel or "situate" within normal life experiences.[38] A principle called propinquity is also in play – this means that people closer to us (in distance, genetics and time) matter more, limiting our ability to be sufficiently responsive to the interests of future generations.[39] Even if we could feed better messages to politicians, would this be effective? As set out in Chapter 2, to the extent that voters are concerned about the climate, sacrifices don't come cheap. It's far preferable to appear green, but to push costs onto our successors.

In addition to encouraging individual stakeholders to shout about climate change, development actors are also weighing in on debates. By identifying the linkages between environmental degradation and humanitarian emergencies, crafting greener intervention strategies and promoting a diffusion of cleaner technologies, they are key participants in climate policy negotiations. The mistake here is the battle plan. They can shout as loud as they want about the science, including more elaborate modelling and scarier scenarios. They will be right, but it will not work, because views on climate change are driven largely by ideological positioning – they are a statement about a person or their group's identity. In other words, climate sceptics aren't suffering from a form of scientific illiteracy; they deny the evidence "not to express what they know but who they are".[40] Dan Kahan et al capture this concisely:

> The principal reason people disagree about climate change science is not that it has been communicated to them in forms they cannot understand. Rather, it is that positions on climate change convey values – communal concern versus individual self-reliance ... that divide them along cultural lines.[41]

Herein lies a key issue. It's not just that we lack a shared attention about our future (although we do), it's that these two viewpoints represent a clash in how we interpret the world and our place in it. The upshot – whichever way we look at it – is that the tools we are using are not working particularly well.

7.3 How change really happens

Let's take stock of where we are at. This chapter has argued that misdiagnosis of the problem plus weak tools are hampering the development sector's efforts to tackle two of the world's greatest challenges. In the case of gender relations, neither top-down nor bottom-up approaches have been particularly successful at overcoming the power dynamics at the heart of gender discrimination. Legal mandates for change – while they are by no means "screen solutions" – do seem to have impact in that they break down some of the political economy barriers that prevent women from participating in society under the same rules as men. What enables such advancements to be "downwards sticky", however, is rooted in the local – a defining event and other social forces that seem to be most potent when homegrown.

Climate change is a different story. Here, we are unable to broker a collective action solution because of a standoff in ideological positioning and the influence of overly powerful political lobbies. But is it possible that the answer is right in front of us, hidden in plain sight, in the experiences of an unlikely set of actors? In other words, should the climate community be looking to borrow some moves from the women's movements introduced earlier? Rather than an improved development strategy, better evidence or more resources, it might be that the area in which we need to operate more effectively is "playing politics".

Before we see how this stacks up against the evidence, let's examine how policymaking really works. When I was running the West Asia-North Africa Institute, I became very interested in how evidence impacted policy – after all, this is why most think tanks are created. It was my assumption that policymakers would be the principal consumers of the kind of research we were producing. The logic was fairly simple – policymakers need to deliver on the imperatives set by their constituencies and others, and evidence was the tool used this to make it happen. So why were we finding it so hard to get their attention?

It turns out that while policymakers being the principal consumers of evidence has inherent appeal, reality paints a different picture. Even within contexts of strong governance, there is little empirical support for the idea that policymakers base policy decisions on data, science or empirical evaluations. Enter Paul Cairney. He explains that this is because policymakers – irrespective of geography – are not problem solvers. What this group is doing can be best described as reacting to events with a view to balancing contesting sets of interests. In doing so, they operate under "bounded rationality" which means they have dynamic aims, limited information (and tools to process it) and unclear choices. They therefore use shortcuts, such as drawing from information sources they trust and adapting that information to the belief sets they already hold. When policy does get made, three dynamics are usually in play: public attention is directed onto a policy problem, a solution is available and policy makers are motivated to action the solution.[42] Even in this context, not all problems get solved; "policy makers lose interest when they run out of money, public attention shifts elsewhere or a 'good enough' solution is found".[43]

Cairney sets out three implications that are highly relevant to the current discussion. First, just because a problem exists does not mean that policymakers will act upon it. If the problem is not considered time sensitive, or is not a driver of public discontent, policymakers may be unenthusiastic about solving it.

Second, where there is motivation to act on a problem, the role played by evidence is problematic. Evidence also has to be available, and while the window for actioning a policy solution is usually weeks, a solid, empirically rigorous evidence-based one is generally a multi-year process.[44] Where it is available, it will only be one source of information taken into account when deciding on a course of action. Policymakers will also consider public opinion, opportunity cost, political feasibility and personal experience.[45] In fact, what a policymaker personally believes, coupled with their experiences, is usually the best predictor of the direction they will take. As a result, they have a tendency to reach out for and accept just enough evidence to get them over the line. Moreover, like all of us, they will subconsciously be on the lookout for evidence that supports what they want to do or what they believe.[46]

Finally, evidence of a problem is not the same thing as an effective solution, and problems can't be solved without them. If the proposed course of action is not popular, economically viable or requires behavioural change, there will be little motivation to use it – *even when this is the right thing to do*.[47]

A good example is tobacco. Even once the evidence on tobacco's health impacts was clear, action by policy makers was neither fast nor linear. This was largely because tobacco use was wound up with other imperatives like jobs, trade and the fact that people enjoyed it. It was highly unpopular to suggest that people should stop smoking.[48] This type of bottleneck also applies to climate change insofar as solutions involve both unpleasant behavioural change and multi-institutional cooperation.

Significant changes in policy do happen, however. And guess what, the same pattern we saw in the gender examples persist: an idea whose time has come, a defining event that creates a brief moment of opportunity and a movement that is ready to go, latches onto it and follows through.

For those thinking I have just declared a theory based on two examples, I haven't. It's even got a name. Punctuated Equilibrium Theory is a phenomenon where policymaking is stable for long periods, all the while ignoring evidence, followed by a burst of instability, where policymakers pay disproportionate attention to a body of evidence, usually because of a focusing event.[49]

There is no better example than Duncan Green's account of the 2015 Paris Climate Change Agreement. First, the context showed a world prepped and ready for a commitment. In the year leading up to the Paris talks, civil society action in the US and a smog crisis in China caused the world's two biggest emitters to reach an agreement over carbon. This showcased sentiments held around the world. In 2015, the Papal Encyclical issued a call to Catholics to embrace their environmental responsibilities. A strong private sector lobby including Ikea and Unilever all pledged their support for reducing emissions, pricing carbon and ending subsidies. All of this was made easier because the price of solar and other renewables had peaked and begun to fall dramatically.

Then there was a critical juncture (actually there were a few). Disastrous climatic events impacted the US, Australia and Russia, sending a message to the world that neither size nor wealth offered protection against Mother Nature pushed too far. Finally, just a few weeks before the summit was scheduled to begin, a coordinated group of attacks were perpetrated on the

Stade de France, the Bataclan theatre and a run of restaurants, killing 130 people from 17 countries. The effect was galvanising; attendees, observers and even provocateurs banded with their hosts, united against a common threat: the terror group ISIS.

This context allowed a group of leaders to act with unusual conviction. US President Obama was at the end of his term, and eager to cement his legacy, even if this meant using his executive powers. China's leadership realised that opportunity was knocking at the door. The growth of their economy coupled with their emissions levels meant that clever politicking could gain them entry to the club of global influencers. And then there were the "climate change vulnerables" – the lobby of poor countries that banded together in a collective effort to stand up and be heard.[50] Together, these enabling conditions allowed for an unprecedented agreement to limit the increase in global temperature this century to two degrees Celsius above pre-industrial levels.

7.4 New rules of the game: rethinking climate and gender strategies

With better insight into the world of policymaking, it is easier to see how these processes might be approached a little more strategically to support development outcomes.

7.4.1 Climate strategies

Let's start with climate. Most clear is that the development community needs to stop bemoaning politicians' unwillingness to use evidence by throwing more evidence at them. Instead, we need to set goals that reflect the context in which decisions are being made. It is neither pragmatic nor legitimate to expect policymaking around climate change to be based solely on evidence. In the best-case scenario, evidence will combine with public values, cost-effectiveness and other political imperatives.[51] It also must be accepted that evidence will not necessarily change policymakers' beliefs in an area like climate. This doesn't mean that change in policy will be impossible, but it does need to be approached differently.

First, the window for policy reform is both short and unpredictable and will generally happen around a focusing event. That event may even be disguised; the terrorist attacks in Casablanca and Paris proved critical to the gains made in gender and climate respectively.

During this moment, a space opens where policy makers can shift their beliefs, but only if they also have an enabling environment to act on evidence. This implies a strategy that combines a monitoring of the policy space with "ready to go" knowledge. Such evidence needs to be packaged in a format that responds to the way decision-makers think and internalise information. This means simple messaging, and tying research to the local and specific issues that the policymaker cares about or is trying to solve.[52] Examples include economic growth or migration, issues that have popular uptake like cost savings, or moral leadership – impelling a leader to make a decision that will land them on the kind side of history.

Effective packaging is also tactical. Remember the availability bias? Paul Cairney calls it What You See is What You Get, which is much catchier. Both terms mean that decisions are influenced by a person's processing fluency – in other words, a policymaker will pay more attention to something if they have existing knowledge or recall on the topic. It's a subconscious technique used to whittle down the choices they have, or the issues they need to act upon. Special interests and private-sector advocacy groups exploit heuristics all the time. They might weave their arguments into narratives they know the target policymaker endorses; they could reference anecdotes from people they know the policymaker trusts; or they make sure that their op-eds and interviews feature in the news feeds the policymaker tends to preference.[53] Whether you think that this is a bit over the top, or just plain weird, the fact is that it works. How else has the agricultural lobby been able to maintain tariff subsidies that make such little economic and environmental sense for so many decades? If you're wondering if this is something the development sector could ever do, let's borrow another example from Duncan Green. He recounts when, in the run up to the Copenhagen Climate Change Summit, the UK Foreign Office hired former Greenpeace activists to identify 100 elite best positioned to influence India's climate policy, and set out how they might be persuaded to act.[54] Green labels this disturbing and I see where he is coming from, but I also think it was kind of genius.

Even when evidence on a problem is packaged correctly, it will not be useful if it fails to set out viable solutions. Development agencies need to see their remit as including the development of different, workable-for-all policy options and an evaluation of their likely impacts and effectiveness.[55] Their expertise will prove vital. They can point out how and where cap-and-trade might have negative development or conflict externalities (e.g. the possibility that a nefarious government cashes in its carbon credits, even if this means damaging its economy).

Finally, development actors need to form alliances with stakeholders in related fields to generate a critical mass of interest and influence – scientists from agricultural and nuclear energy, business leaders and activists. These groups should also include lobbyists/advocacy coalitions – the ones whose job it is to examine the political feasibility of a solution. The aid community is not proficient at identifying the different ways that a policy problem might be interpreted, or the cross-implications of putting an idea into practice. Critical to alliance-building is the idea of "knowledge brokers" or "policy entrepreneurs" – persons within the policymaking system who understand the subsystems that feed evidence up to decision-makers, and use such insights to put evidence in front of the right people (who are not usually at the most senior levels) at the right moment.[56]

In short, to forge better policy outcomes a more complex, longer-term strategy needs to be adopted. What this strategy is currently lacking is not evidence; it's the stuff that goes around it – patience, groundwork, and an acknowledgement that this is as much a fight for the environment as it is a battle of world views.

7.4.2 Gender strategies

Might these same lessons feed back into how the development community approaches its work on gender? At 8 percent of ODA, the international community spends around USD50 billion in support of gender equality and women's empowerment each year.[57] This is not to say that these programs are unimportant or not impactful; enormous progress has been made in girls' education and expanding women's livelihoods opportunities. Protection work is also vital. Affirmative action quotas and constitutional bans on discrimination provide no immediate relief to the 6 million female victims of sexual exploitation, the 5 million children in forced marriages or the 4 million at risk of FGMC.[58]

At the same time, history's lessons speak clearly, so it makes sense that gender development strategies employ them. Women's movements in developing countries should be supported to understand and navigate the political realm in the same way as climate strategists. They need advanced skills in lobbying, building strategic alliances, and packaging messages. Academics and think tanks can play a role generating evidence on the linkages between gender and the topics they care most about, whether that be jobs, family cohesion or security. And civil society networks can be strengthened in particular ways. They need to reach a plurality of women, be inclusive of all socio-economic brackets, and set up in a way that guarantees long term sustainability.

Such a recalibration will have its share of dissenters. The UN agencies and NGOs with gender mandates appreciate the importance of women's political participation, but this sits among many other compelling issues such as violence against women, education and livelihoods. For reasons set out earlier, these agencies find it easier to identify funding for operational tasks with good optics and easily quantifiable targets. Indeed, a challenge in supporting such initiatives is that they are largely about preparedness – an expectation of a future event that women's groups *might* then tap into. These same pressures mean that the assistance on offer may not be what women's organisations need. As showcased in the Morocco example, central to the movement's success was how it separated itself from a liberal feminist agenda and that international supporters knew when to pull back and lie low. Development actors are getting better at identifying the situations where their logo does more harm than good. But the impetus to claim wins that can be fed back to line managers, headquarters and donors is still there.

For the INGOs whose main work is political participation, they too are spread thin. Gender competes with sexier topics such as elections, the youth bulge and corruption, and donors are equally reticent about strategies geared towards long-run, uncertain outcomes. As one staffer explained to me

> No one wants the gender file. Success is defined by the number of women holding office, which is a hard sell and takes forever. Even then it's not all that satisfying. The women who move forward in the political process are generally compromises. In some cases the ones selected are picked because they will cause the least amount of trouble.[59]

It is also worth noting that these organisations can come with baggage. The National Democratic Institute, despite being well resourced and professionally run, is American and broadly perceived as having a Western, paternalistic agenda. In many contexts, women's organisations make a strategic choice not to engage and thus shield themselves from accusations of foreign influence.

This leaves the development sub-sector, whose mandate is civil society strengthening. This group might have the best comparative advantage to offer support. This is not to suggest that the gender and political participation communities of practice should step back. Quite the opposite – experts in these fields need to step forward and contribute their voices. In doing so they can start to push back on the oft-cited criticism that the various fiefdoms that make up the development sector are not particularly good at working in a synchronistic and complementary manner.

7.5 What of awareness-raising and advocacy? Deploying people power where it counts

I want to return to awareness-raising and advocacy as a programming tool for behavioural and attitudinal change. At the beginning of the chapter, I gave this a pretty poor report card in terms of potential for success. Sensitising women (or men) about gender rights does little to improve their protection or their opportunities. Likewise, changed behaviours at the individual level cannot deliver the "at scale" response required to avert a climate crisis, and even if it was, it is complicated to motivate people to engage around a non-situated risk.

Many readers will be sceptical about this – they are thinking about recent climate protests, Greta Thunberg's UN address and the looks of distain cast when a shopper is made to purchase plastic because their reusable supermarket bags were left at home. I would encourage these readers to think about the bigger picture. Is this reflective of the world, or your space in it – the media you watch, the work you do and the people you associate with? There are more than seven billion people on the planet.

Many are living in poverty, have been displaced or are affected by conflict. Of those fortunate enough not to be included in this group, there is a significant number who reject climate change arguments. The Yale University–led survey "Climate Change in the American Mind" found that in 2017, only 58 percent of a nationally representative sample believe in human-induced climate change.[60] I would posit that we are the minority, so we should let go of that satisfied feeling that everyone is wising up and that world leaders are hearing our message. Think gender is any different? You'd be wrong again. The most recent Gender Social Norms Index indicates that 90 percent of people globally are biased against gender equality.[61] Perhaps most disturbing is how these attitudes pervade the genders; indeed some 86 percent of women showed some form of clear bias against gender equality in the areas of politics, economics, education, freedom from violence and reproductive autonomy.

So do attitudes matter? Of course they do. In fact it might be that for a change at the politico-legal level to work, society needs to be ready. To explain why I am going to invoke the research of Steven Pinker and his account of how rape laws evolved in the West.

Rape perhaps epitomises the brutality of gender inequality, and its legal codification throughout history demonstrates that the act knows no boundaries, whether by religion, geography or culture. Records of rape as a tool of war date back to 1200 BC. In medieval Europe fathers and husbands could sue rapists under the tort of theft; even today, laws exist that allow rape victims to be punished for adultery and rape perpetrators to escape punishment if they "repair" the damage through marriage. But in the West, commencing in the mid-1970s, crimes of rape started to plummet, and more rapidly and steeply when compared to other violent crimes such as murder. Pinker believes that a tipping point was Susan Brownmiller's 1975 bestseller *Against Our Will*. This book is best known for how it pushed social conventions of the time. By setting out how rape was overlooked by institutions, downplayed in the legal system and trivialised in popular culture, it did much to reroute social attitudes towards rape. Not long after, states began to criminalise different forms of sexual violence, police pursued allegations with far more vigour and technology breakthroughs (largely the use of DNA evidence) meant that conviction rates soared.

But change went beyond those most affected by rape; it reached the edges of social boundaries. The act became a red line – in jokes, film, video games and even pornography. These wins came relatively quickly and easily because – Pinker argues – society was *ready*. That women had joined the workforce and occupied other positions of influence forced society to re-examine what it meant for men to hold, wield and use power, including by raping women. With society's values becoming more feminist and humanist, there was no one with a vested interest in rape left to be won over. Apathy fell away and was replaced with indignation, not just for women, but for everyone.[62]

If we apply these insights to the examples of gender change discussed earlier, perhaps there are some parallels, for example, the Casablanca bombings, Muhammad Bouazizi's self-immolation, President Mwai Kibaki's re-election and Namibia's declaration of independence. These moments undoubtedly mattered, but they didn't happen in a vacuum. They worked as well as they did because society – or at least a large enough group within it – was ready. The takeaway: it's not that bottom-up awareness-raising and advocacy doesn't work; we just have to get far more strategic.

7.5.1 Ceding ground to popular media

First, practitioners should acknowledge that – just like with politicians – views and beliefs around climate are at least in part grounded in ideology. Attitudinal change is a complex, contested and non-linear process, so standard awareness-raising methodology is unlikely to do the trick. More innovative methods, however, are generally not within development practitioners' frame of reference. Steven Pinker goes on to argue that a key driver of more liberal and reason-based thinking is the technologies that have made ideas and people increasingly mobile: books, the facsimile, video, and of course the Internet. These tools of communication build an informed, insightful and empathic population, within which it is easier for biased reasoning and ignorance to be debunked.[63]

From a development perspective, the most potent vehicle for engaging people in critical reflection is almost entirely untapped. More than 500 million people – most of them between the ages of 16–25 – have watched at least one of the *Hunger Games* trilogy, *The Day After Tomorrow*, *Interstellar* or *Waterworld* – stories that are steeped in nuanced messages about resource exploitation, displacement and battles of right. Young people flocked to purchase, view and engage with these media without any external encouragement. This is not to pitch film and literature as entry points for fighting climate change. Indeed, surveys conducted to better understand how such films influenced different groups revealed only mildly positive outcomes.[64] However it does beg the question of whether, rather than trying to devise ways to instill environmental values in individuals, it may be more efficacious to work through the sources of influence they are naturally drawn to.

A further lesson is that when media deliberately target an issue, the approach must cater to the political underpinnings of climate change. Many experts believe that the documentary *An Inconvenient Truth* would have had stronger impact if it had not been so closely tied to the work of Al Gore.[65] Viewership mainly comprised individuals already committed to environmental protection, while scope for reaching those with more ambivalent views – the group most likely to influence social dynamics around climate change – was narrowed because of the film's democratic political packaging.

Extending this argument to gender is easier, perhaps because we have been making films, books and TV shows about the power of women for much longer. As a high-school student, I studied *Little Women* and poems by Virginia Woofe as required reading. Today, at least at my daughters' school, these have been replaced with *A Night Divided*, *The Diary of Anne Frank* and *The Help*, perhaps a reflection of Western society's most urgent struggles. But we still enjoyed Michelle Obama's *Becoming* and Cheryl Sandberg's *Lean In* – both best sellers, as well as the acclaimed films *Hidden Figures* (2016) and *Suffragate* (2015). So why do we see so much training of women in their Convention guaranteed rights, and so little translating and disseminating media that is both message-rich and entertaining? I will leave this for readers to ponder.

7.5.2 *Think like an advertiser*

To the extent that the development community continues to rely on sensitisation, advocacy and awareness raising, it may be time for them to lift their game. It may be an uncomfortable comparison, but these efforts are not unlike product advertising. Both are trying to create a consumer trend or "meme" – an epidemic of interest in a certain idea or product. Hijacking some of their tricks makes sense. A key one is not to assume that because a message is correct, informative and reaches its audience that it will have resonance. Here advertisers face the same problem as aid practitioners in terms of clutter. In the modern world, so many messages are received that it is impossible to process all of them. In response, advertisers invest enormous resources into piloting a product brand, making changes, and retesting, all to identify a message that will stick. They do this because it can be the smallest detail in presentation, relatability or convenience that makes the difference between a new product craze and a good product that never sold. Development actors are not resourced in the same way as big advertising agencies, making these kinds of projects what Corporate Social Responsibility was built for. Another tool is manipulating group size in ways that make an audience more receptive to new ideas. Tightly knit groups of seven or less are most likely to accept and internalise a new message, while groups of 150 or less are best situated to magnify its diffusion potential.[66] Practitioners designing awareness-raising and sensitisation activities need to understand this evidence so that they can push back against a donor or budget officer who would like to see beneficiaries packed like sardines in order to increase cost-effectiveness.

7.5.3 *Consumer superpower*

Engaging strategically and through diverse channels is important, but if we are intent on moulding people's beliefs and attitudes, the "bang for your buck" change will come not from targeting people in their capacity as voters and recyclers, but in their capacity as consumers. As discussed, the reforms that will limit climate change lie in the industrial sector, and changes in customer attitudes are essential for businesses to change. Indeed, the most impactful transformations in business practice have been profit driven. Energy and extraction companies increasingly see that it makes better business sense to run "clean" projects from the start, rather than bear the costs attached to a public relations scandal or the turnover of key senior staff. [67] Fairtrade and Marine Stewardship Council branding have shown equally good results. My children absolutely know the sustainable product labels. I'll buy them to show my 9-year-old how impressed I am with her smarts, but to avoid a fight with my teenagers. Any parent who has been involved one of these ethical standoff moments will agree that these companies are onto something special.

I have no doubt that in the near future someone will invest in a gender trademark – allowing companies to attest to specific standards, whether that be the percentage of women in leadership positions or equal pay. These products will be marketed in the West, but the winners will be the women engaged in manufacturing and production in the developing world. As these countries grow their economies, further gains will accrue. Poor women may have limited consumer choices now, but they are still responsible for the lion's share of household spending. This, coupled with the fact that they shop more ethically means that markets of the future will need to take the power of women's choices into account.

7.6 Development takeaways

This chapter has examined two development challenges where practitioners are fighting the right fight, but not making the desired gains because they are using the wrong tools. The antidote is a more sophisticated diagnosis – one which extends beyond the development problem itself to include the dynamics driving it, how power is distributed around it, and the broader rules of the game.

This is more complicated than gathering evidence on a problem and applying it remedially. While evidence will often provide clues on the way forward, there will be times where it can steer practitioners in the wrong direction. In the case of climate change, it is not lack of evidence that is the bottleneck, but the barriers preventing its uptake. At other times, evidence on the problem will not have a clear or easy relationship with the solution. The gains that accrue from more equal societies are indisputable, but this should not imply that the answer lies in a better appreciation of gender norms. Instead, it is overcoming the vested interests in maintaining a status quo that benefits men in terms of resources, decision-making and control.

What this means in practice is – wait, you guessed it – doing things that are counterintuitive or unpopular. Sometimes it will mean playing the long game. The pattern of social change being preceded by a latent or low-intensity call for action followed by a critical juncture is too recurrent – both between sectors and over time – to ignore. This is not to say that development programming geared towards reform is redundant; far from it. Investing in civil society and evidence in support of the desired change are critical enablers. But the most important thing seems to be an ability to react quickly and effectively at the right moment. Borrowing again from Duncan Greene, we must unwed ourselves from linear plans and replace them with a portfolio of ideas – multiple strategies that get modified iteratively as a situation evolves.[68]

Sometimes a win requires that we play politics. Development practitioners will not only need to become familiar with the opaque, diffuse and unpredictable workings of policy cycles and networks, but also start to see this as part of their job. This proposal may take some practitioners outside of their comfort zone. Simply put, there is something in the identity of development workers that makes it seem repugnant to immerse ourselves in the messiness of politics. Perhaps this is because we should be above all this. More likely, it just feels bad, because it shouldn't be like this. Governments *should* be able to come to an agreement on carbon output because this is the fair and responsible thing to do. They *should* likewise respond to pressure to advance gender equality if for no other reason than that these are embedded in the international human rights framework. Backing away from any approach that does not have human rights at its centre feels like selling out. Would abandoning the fight be a slippery slope that leads to a breakdown in the system as we know it? After all, who else will sound the international human rights call to arms if not the development community?

The counterargument is that while states should do the right thing around environmental protection, gender rights and countless other imperatives, the fact is that they often don't. The process by which new norms are set is not determined by global values. It is complex and involves power, compromise and opportunity. At the same time, development actors, environmentalists and civil society organisations are competing against a wide range of actors with clear agendas who are much more cognisant about how the policy process works. And at some point, if there is an alternate pathway, don't we just want to get it done?

Notes

1 C. Goldin and C. Rouse "Orchestrating Impartiality: The Impact of 'Blind' Auditions on Female Musicians" Working Paper 5903 National Bureau of Economic Research (1997).
2 D. Greene *How Change Happens*, Oxford University Press (2016) 62–65.
3 See generally, "The World Survey on the Role of Women in Development 2014: Gender Equality and Sustainable Development" UN-WOMEN United Nations (2014); E. Duflo "Women Empowerment and Economic Development" *Journal of Economic Literature* 50:4 (2012) 1051–1079; A. Mason and E. King "Engendering Development Through Gender Equality in Rights, Resources, and Voice" World Bank Group (2001); M. Doepke and M. Tertilt "Women's Liberation: What's in it for Men?" National Bureau of Economic Research

(2008); G. Psacharopoulos and Z. Tzannatos "Case studies on Women's Employment and Pay in Latin America" The World Bank Group (1992).

4 Z. Salime *Between Feminism and Islam: Human Rights and Sharia Law in Morocco*, University of Minnesota Press (2011) 33–34.

5 Under the *Mudawwana*, a woman was a minor under the guardianship of her father, husband or other male guardian. Marriage, employment and a passport required *wali* consent, the age of marriage for females was 15 (men could marry at 18), women could lose custody of their children if they remarried, and women could be divorced unilaterally and without judicial oversight.

6 Z. Salime *Between Feminism and Islam: Human Rights and Sharia Law in Morocco*, University of Minnesota Press (2011) 46–47.

7 L. Buskens "Recent Debates on Family Law Reform in Morocco: Islamic Law as Politics in an Emerging Public Sphere" *Islamic Law and Society* 10 (2003) 70–131.

8 Z. Mir-Hosseini "How the Door of Ijtihad Was Opened and Closed" *Washington and Lee Law Review* 64 (2007) 1499–1511.

9 Z. Salime *Between Feminism and Islam: Human Rights and Sharia Law in Morocco*, University of Minnesota Press (2011) 6–8, 14, 143–144, 126–128.

10 Z. Salime *Between Feminism and Islam: Human Rights and Sharia Law in Morocco*, University of Minnesota Press (2011) 23, 37, 44. See also D. Greene *How Change Happens*, Oxford University Press (2016) 59–60.

11 Z. Salime *Between Feminism and Islam: Human Rights and Sharia Law in Morocco*, University of Minnesota Press (2011) 129–131, 140–141.

12 Z. Salime *Between Feminism and Islam: Human Rights and Sharia Law in Morocco*, University of Minnesota Press (2011) 49–50, 86.

13 See generally, R. Dasgupta and G. Bangham *The New Constitution of Tunisia: Choices and Decisions*, The Wilberforce Society University of Cambridge (2012).

14 Article 27 (8) *Constitution of Kenya* (2010) provides for affirmative action where the State is required to take legislative and other measures to ensure that not more than two-thirds of the members of elective or appointive bodies are of the same gender.

15 J. Ubink "Stating the Customary an Innovative Approach to the Locally Legitimate Recording of Customary Law in Namibia" in J. Ubink (ed) *Customary Justice: Perspectives on Legal Empowerment*, International Development Law Organization (2011) 131–151.

16 H. Becker "'New Things after Independence': Gender and Traditional Authorities in Postcolonial Namibia" *Journal of Southern Africa Studies* 32:1 (2006) 47.

17 Article 10 *Constitution of the Republic of Namibia* (1990).

18 "Global Gender Gap Report" World Economic Forum (2020).

19 "Women in National Parliament" Inter-Parliamentary Union (data as at 1 February 2019).

20 P. Domingo and A. McCullough "Women and Power Shaping Kenya's 2010 Constitution" Overseas Development Institute (2016) 2.

21 L. Brand *Women, the State, and Political Liberalization: Middle Eastern and North African Experiences*, Columbia University Press New York (1998); N. Zoughlami "Quel Féminisme dans les Groupes-Femmes des Années 80 en Tunisie?" *Annuaire de l'Afrique du Nord* 28 (1999) 443–453.

22 M. Charrad and A. Zarrugh "The Arab Spring and Women's Rights in Tunisia" *E-International Relations* (2013) 1–6.

23 S. Pinker *Enlightenment Now: The Case for Reason, Science, Humanism and Progress*, Allen Lane (2018) 137–138.

24 P. Collier *The Plundered Planet*, Penguin Books (2011) xiv, 3, 173–174.

25 J. Sachs *The Price of Civilization: Economics and Ethics After the Fall*, Random House (2011) 36–37.

26 M. Hulme *Why We Disagree About Climate Change: Understanding Controversy, Inaction and Opportunity*, Cambridge University Press (2009) 265–266.
27 S. Pinker *Enlightenment Now: The Case for Reason, Science, Humanism and Progress*, Allen Lane (2018) 32, 122.
28 S. Pinker *Enlightenment Now: The Case for Reason, Science, Humanism and Progress*, Allen Lane (2018) 130–131.
29 S. Pinker *Enlightenment Now: The Case for Reason, Science, Humanism and Progress*, Allen Lane (2018) 123–124.
30 S. Pinker *Enlightenment Now: The Case for Reason, Science, Humanism and Progress*, Allen Lane (2018) 124–126.
31 S. Pinker *Enlightenment Now: The Case for Reason, Science, Humanism and Progress*, Allen Lane (2018) 127.
32 *The Economist*, July 2019, 14.
33 M. Hulme *Why We Disagree About Climate Change: Understanding Controversy, Inaction and Opportunity*, Cambridge University Press (2009) 315–316, S. Pinker *Enlightenment Now: The Case for Reason, Science, Humanism and Progress*, Allen Lane (2018) 128.
34 M. Hulme *Why We Disagree About Climate Change: Understanding Controversy, Inaction and Opportunity*, Cambridge University Press (2009) 263–264; S. Pinker *Enlightenment Now: The Case for Reason, Science, Humanism and Progress*, Allen Lane (2018) 140–141.
35 "From Fishing Village to Futuristic Metropolis: Dubai's Remarkable Transformation" World Economic Forum (2019).
36 P. Collier *The Plundered Planet*, Penguin Books (2011) 8; S. Pinker *Enlightenment Now: The Case for Reason, Science, Humanism and Progress*, Allen Lane (2018) 134–135.
37 S. Pinker *Enlightenment Now: The Case for Reason, Science, Humanism and Progress*, Allen Lane (2018) 146–147.
38 M. Hulme *Why We Disagree About Climate Change: Understanding Controversy, Inaction and Opportunity*, Cambridge University Press (2009) 139, 196–201.
39 P. Collier *The Plundered Planet*, Penguin Books (2011) 26.
40 S. Pinker *Enlightenment Now: The Case for Reason, Science, Humanism and Progress*, Allen Lane (2018) 357.
41 D. Kahan, M. Whittlin et al "The Tragedy of the Risk Perception Commons: Culture Conflict, Rationality Conflict, and Climate Change" Cultural Cognition Working Paper 89 (2011) 15.
42 P. Cairny *The Politics of Evidence-Based Policy Making*, Palgrave Pivot (2016) 5, 15, 25, 31–32, 87–88.
43 P. Cairny *The Politics of Evidence-Based Policy Making*, Palgrave Pivot (2016) 94.
44 P. Cairny *The Politics of Evidence-Based Policy Making*, Palgrave Pivot (2016) 7, 20–22, 53.
45 P. Cairny *The Politics of Evidence-Based Policy Making*, Palgrave Pivot (2016) 23, 42, 89, 120–122.
46 P. Cairny *The Politics of Evidence-Based Policy Making*, Palgrave Pivot (2016) 16–19, 25. At 87–88, Cairny cites a study of environmental policy which connected 18 percent of content to the theory and 9 percent to literature.
47 P. Cairny The *Politics of Evidence-Based Policy Making*, Palgrave Pivot (2016) 4, 108, 120.
48 P. Cairny *The Politics of Evidence-Based Policy Making*, Palgrave Pivot (2016) 67–68.
49 P. Cairny *The Politics of Evidence-Based Policy Making*, Palgrave Pivot (2016) 6–7, 31–32.
50 D. Greene *How Change Happens*, Oxford University Press (2016) 171–174.

51 P. Cairny *The Politics of Evidence-Based Policy Making*, Palgrave Pivot (2016) 61–63, 128–130.
52 P. Cairny *The Politics of Evidence-Based Policy Making*, Palgrave Pivot (2016) 60–61, 106.
53 P. Cairny *The Politics of Evidence-Based Policy Making*, Palgrave Pivot (2016) 26–27 34–35.
54 D. Greene *How Change Happens*, Oxford University Press (2016) 216.
55 P. Cairny *The Politics of Evidence-Based Policy Making*, Palgrave Pivot (2016) 90–95.
56 P. Cairny *The Politics of Evidence-Based Policy Making*, Palgrave Pivot (2016) 57–64, 77–78, 102–110, 129–130.
57 "Final ODA Data for 2018 What Does the Data Tell Us?" Development Initiatives (2020) <devinit.org/resources/final-oda-data-2018/#downloads>
58 "Global Estimates of Modern Slavery: Forced Labour and Forced Marriage" International Labour Organization (2017).
59 Interview date 11 April 2021, Geneva, notes on file with author.
60 A. Leiserowitz, E. Maiback, C. Roser-Renouf et al "Climate Change in the American Mind: May 2017" Yale University and George Mason University. Yale Program on Climate Change Communication (2017).
61 "Tackling Social Norms: A Game Changer for Gender Inequalities" UNDP (2020).
62 S. Pinker *The Better Angels of Our Nature: Why Violence Has Declined*, Penguin (2011) 399–414.
63 S. Pinker *The Better Angels of Our Nature: Why Violence has Declined*, Penguin (2011) 475–478.
64 M. Hulme *Why We Disagree About Climate Change: Understanding Controversy, Inaction and Opportunity*, Cambridge University Press (2009) 211–214; D. Greene *How Change Happens*, Oxford University Press (2016) 57.
65 M. Hulme *Why We Disagree About Climate Change: Understanding Controversy, Inaction and Opportunity*, Cambridge University Press (2009) 214.
66 M. Gladwell *The Tipping Point: How Little Things Can Make A Big Difference*, BackBay Books (2000) 93–99, 258–259.
67 J. Diamond *Collapse: How Societies Choose to Fail or Survive*, Penguin Books (2005) 467–468, 446–454, 484–485.
68 D. Greene *How Change Happens*, Oxford University Press (2016) 7–14.

8

DEVELOPMENT BEYOND THE DEVELOPMENT SECTOR

This last chapter tackles a perplexing question rarely uttered in development circles but regularly debated in donor offices, International Financial Institutions (IFIs) and university economics lectures. What if the solution to eliminating poverty lies outside the development sector – in globalisation, some parallel process, or an approach yet to be uncovered?

I've borne witness to quite a few of these discussions. Aid advocates generally point to the data that, since 1980, world poverty has been falling for the first time in history. Someone from the World Bank then chimes in, noting that this was half a century after the advent of modern aid and two decades before the Millennium Development Goals were launched, but incidentally around the same time as the Asian Tigers joined the global economy. Academics in the room usually criticise the methodologies behind these assertions and are laughed out of the room. And then someone – usually from a country on the receiving end of aid – asks, given the scarcity of data in support of any effective fast-track development process, do we not owe it to the 10 percent of humanity still living in extreme poverty to pay this question more than just lip service? There is an awkward silence because we are all humbled, and realise that of course, only one of these answers is correct.

In respect of this 10 percent of people globally, this chapter examines three processes: private donations to the poor, corporate sector giving, and profit-making that targets so-called suboptimal markets. We will learn at least three things. The development sector tends to make much ado about funding. Indeed, a lot of time and effort is spent preparing appeals and arranging pledges, and then grumbling that donors fail to make good. But if we consider remittances, *zakat*, corporate social responsibility and the R&D invested in poverty markets, it is quite clear that there is money around. Engaging these resources and the actors that control them is imbued with difficulty – practical and political. But their scale, especially in the context of the current geopolitical environment, means that they cannot be ignored. Sooner rather than later development actors will need to refocus their energies on how these funds might be leveraged to complement development strategies, and thus fight poverty more structurally.

    DOI: 10.4324/9781003376996-9

Another opportunity is to mobilise the investment capacity of big firms, guided by development sector knowledge, to craft win–win consumer-based solutions for the poor. Here the challenge will be to take down the walls dividing the for-profit and non-profit sectors. Ideological standoffs and turf boundaries are currently preventing development actors from identifying mutually beneficial partnerships and learning how to work at scale and under a financially sustainable framework.

A final peace that needs to be won is between development actors and IFIs. These latter entities claim no development expertise, but their mandate is such that their actions have enormous impacts on poverty, opportunity and wealth equality. Power differentials mean that only an evidence-based narrative that plays to their vested interests is likely to have traction. This may sound next to impossible, but read on, this chapter contains a few ideas.

8.1 Unlikely allies – harnessing the power of remittances and *zakat*

Remittances – the money sent from individuals accruing economic gains abroad to relatives in their countries of origin – total around USD580 billion annually.[1] Of this, some USD400 billion moves from developed to developing countries – making these transfers comparable to foreign direct investment and more than four times the global development aid budget.[2] Unsurprisingly, remittances constitute an important part of many developing economies, and a critical source of income for the most disadvantaged.[3] This is especially because remittances tend to be countercyclical relative to the recipient economy – like an informal type of insurance, they kick in or expand during a downturn in economic activity, natural disaster or conflict.

This has not escaped the attention of development economists, some of whom tout remittances as an under-tapped source of stimulus.[4] But whether remittances impact development or contribute to poverty reduction is complex to assess. Any measurement must take into account human capital loss (the opportunity forgone when a remitter applies labour to a different country's economy), and the reverse causality associated with remittances' countercyclical response to growth.[5] Moreover, while remittances do increase aggregate demand and indirect tax revenues, they must also be understood as unearned "rents", which cause exchange rate appreciation and lower export competitiveness.[6]

Empirical studies have yielded mixed results. The evidence is that remittances tend to fund basic material needs, as opposed to being used to diversify sources of income or support entrepreneurial endeavours.[7] At the same time, such basic needs include investment in education and health, which generally have high rates of socio-economic return. Overall though, even the studies that have linked remittances to increases in income and consumption, and decreases in poverty and inequality, have not been able to establish a clear and positive correlation with economic growth.[8]

Zakat is another facility that has piqued the interest of development scholars as having poverty-reduction potential. One of the five pillars of Islam, *zakat* requires that Muslims donate 2.5 percent of their wealth, above a specified amount, to one of eight purposes specified in the Qur'an.[9] The most frequent use of *zakat* is charitable donations to the poor. Again, the volume of these flows is enormous. It is estimated that USD200 billion to USD1 trillion is spent annually in *zakat* and voluntary charity across the Muslim world.[10] Even at the low end of this estimate, *zakat* sits among the 10 highest donors with respect to international development assistance.[11]

As an income distribution tool, *zakat* works a lot like remittances. It increases the poor's purchasing power, thus bolstering demand for goods and services.[12] The evidence that this carries over to stimulate growth, or reduce income inequality, however, is likewise thin. Few studies have been able to report reliable results and, of these, only marginal gains seem to be identifiable.[13]

The main difference lies in the potential for restructuring how these funds are administered. Unlike remittances, *zakat* is not a private transaction between family members. Instead, it is generally collected and distributed by governments or (increasingly) by dedicated agencies. This provides greater scope for channelling *zakat* for specific development aims. Moreover, because *zakat* is derived from domestically generated wealth, it does not operate like a rent in the same way as remittances, or indeed traditional forms of development assistance.

Such observations have sparked debate among scholars around whether, and if so, how, *zakat* might be harnessed for greater impact. Against those who argue that *zakat* giving must be strictly limited to the purposes referred to in the holy scriptures, other scholars interpret *zakat* as having a "transformational" mandate aimed at lifting the poor out of poverty to become *zakat*-givers (*muzaki*).[14] Moreover, this implies a much wider range of possibilities for *zakat* use, including supporting infrastructure projects, social cohesion or peace building.[15] A particularly novel idea is the establishment of a global or regional *zakat* fund that could receive contributions from states, organisations and individuals (channelled separately in accordance with scholarly doctrine) and allocate funds towards development projects.[16] Proponents argue that with a more evidence-based approach and transparent operating procedures, shortcomings around corruption, lack of accountability and subsequent noncompliance might be overcome.[17] Indeed, a 2006 study that surveyed 753 Malaysians found that 57 percent were dissatisfied with formal *zakat* institutions, and that this reduced their individual compliance.[18]

For development economists, this is exciting stuff. When used traditionally, both *zakat* and remittances operate as charity-giving models, with funds used to support short-term consumption needs (cash disbursements, housing support, food and non-food items etc.). This form of income support is not an effective means of promoting longer-term, sustainable and inclusive development. In fact, insofar as it facilitates a cycle of contributing to basic needs rather than providing tools to break free from it, it is more likely to entrench poverty traps than to close them.[19] To have development impact, financial flows must be seen as capital, and used as an investment tool to increase the productive potential of recipients through labour, knowledge, or production entitlements.[20] The University of Durham's Professor Habib Ahmad has put this to the test. He developed simulations to examine the impact of *zakat* on poverty in Bangladesh and found that the relationship only became significant when a certain percentage of collected funds was used for productive purposes.[21]

This suggests that the trick is to get recipients to save or invest their remittances or *zakat* receipts. Unfortunately, this is far easier said than done. Remittances work as well as they do in large part because they flow directly to the recipient, thus bypassing a government that has been unable to provide adequate access to livelihoods or investment opportunities.[22] There is also little empirical evidence to suggest that the poor do not use financial resources prudently and strategically. In other words, beneficiaries are unlikely to be "wasting" receipts on basic needs – they are exhausting them just getting by. So, while it might be more strategic to invest in entrepreneurial activity, it does not follow that opportunities will be available, nor answer the question of what a family will eat while that investment is bearing fruit.

Development practitioners might see this problem as having an obvious solution – augmenting the amounts received (for example through funds matching, or by reducing the costs of transferring money between countries) or providing better livelihoods and investment opportunities (such as micro-credit). This is actually quite sensible. The research suggests that when remittances rise unexpectedly, recipients do tend to save, fund capital investment or contribute towards income-generating activities.[23] Putting these ideas into practice, however, has not yielded a silver bullet result. In the case of remittances, the issue lies mainly with the benefactor. The size of transfers is determined more by what is needed to support basic needs than their disposable income. If the recipient starts to invest or save, or funds are matched, transfers tend to fall. The remitter's rationale is painfully legitimate. They know only too well the difficulty of establishing a profitable and secure livelihood in the country of origin. This is why they left in the first place. Moreover, if the endeavour fails, their commitment or responsibility to prevent their family from falling into poverty still exists. Perhaps if their commitment was broader or semi-permanent, they might be more interested in finding ways to disengage. Remittances, however, tend to bind only a single generation.[24] In short, remitters' lack of confidence in their home economy means that it's safer to stay the course and keep things simple.

The same cannot be said for *zakat*. In this case, the lack of personal connection linking benefactors and recipients has advantages. Because the goal is not poverty avoidance but discharging a religious obligation, benefactors are less tied to what their contribution supports, how, or through whom. This suggests that there is strong potential for engaging *zakat* agencies to move towards more effective strategies for collection, management and dissemination and from charity-based models to engagement models informed by poverty-reduction and development theory.[25]

Greater collaboration and coordination between *zakat* and development actors, however, is a lot to ask. This is a fairly bold statement, but one I am confident to make. At the West Asia-North Africa Institute, *zakat* reform was among our chairman's chief priorities. We had an excellent relationship with Jordan's Ministry of Islamic Affairs who had agreed to participate in a pilot program, and a budding academic partnership with the Faculty of Theology and Religion at the University of Oxford. Moreover, our chairman wasn't just anyone – it was His Royal Highness Prince Hassan bin Talal, a 42nd-generation direct descendant of the Prophet Mohammad. If anyone had the authority to endorse engagement in these messy issues, it was him. Unfortunately, this was not enough. Over a five-year period, my staff discussed the idea with countless donors, development agencies and philanthropic organisations. To cut a long story short, even for those who saw the logic, it was felt that the topic was too polarising and contentious. To an extent, this is understandable. Even in Islamic scholarship, whether the juridical sources are open to interpretation or not (*ijtihad*) is hugely controversial. Engagement can also be easily misinterpreted. During the Syrian refugee crisis, there was a short wave of interest in whether *zakat* funds could be used to support wayfarers (one of the eight categories set out in the Qur'an). Even though this interest came from local agencies and their argument – from an academic perspective – was sound, the story quickly became that Western-leaning humanitarian agencies were attempting to exploit a religious norm.

The disappointing irony is that when the driving issue is important enough, these challenges can be overcome. As examined in Chapter 6, the threats posed by violent extremist groups were more than enough for the development sector to engage – robustly and extensively – in religious counter-narratives, inculcating liberal norms and partnering with imams to lead anti–ISIS awareness raising. The conclusion is disquieting. It's not that we can't engage. More likely it's that the issue is just not important enough to overcome the messiness.

8.2 Angels of the deep

The development community has done a better job linking in with the private sector by way of its Corporate Social Responsibility (CSR) function. CSR emerged in the 1980s, gaining pace over the next two decades particularly in response to scandals linking major brands – including Nike, Gap, Disney and others – to sweatshops and child labour. Today, CSR is undertaken both reactively, and with proactive goals in mind. Programs can be a means of placating or reconciling an entity's operations with NGOs, consumer and shareholder concerns around environmental impact, working conditions and human rights. Alternatively, companies might engage in CSR to attract good press, expand into new consumer markets, create brand loyalty or draw in investors.

In the late 1990s, the idea that CSR could be leveraged as a project tool and/or source of financing was picked up by international organisations such as the World Bank as well as development cooperation agencies such as the UK's Department for International Development (DFID) and Germany's Federal Ministry for Economic Cooperation and Development (BMZ).[26] There should be no question as to why. Some company CSR programs rival entire UN agencies and INGOs in terms of budget. It was estimated that the combined CSR of Fortune 500 Companies in 2013 totalled around USD20 billion; Total, Shell and Exxon each spend well over USD100 million on community investments every year. Moreover, unlike remittances and *zakat* disbursements which already formed part of the poverty-response architecture, CSR commitments were perceived as more "up for grabs".

Early efforts to partner up with corporate interests had mixed results. Placating communities, creating goodwill and generating exposure, was often most easily achieved by building a school, health clinic, road or solid-waste treatment plant. Whether this corresponded with a beneficiary population's structural development needs was usually a matter of chance. Support also tended to last as long as the company's business interest. Over time this meant a lot of unstaffed schools, potholes and unmaintained equipment.[27] This gave the development community a lot to complain about, and with good reason. Efforts, however, to convince CSR decision-makers that partnering up could result in better outcomes largely fell on deaf ears. Companies saw development agencies as inefficient, bureaucratic and lacking in rigour – also perhaps for good reason. Moreover, to the extent that partnerships were formed, companies generally preferred to offer in-kind support in the form of goods, services or technical support, as opposed to funds.

A turning point was the 1999 World Economic Forum in Davos. Then–UN Secretary-General Kofi Annan called upon CEOs "to embrace, support and enact a set of core values in the areas of human rights, labour standards, and environmental practices".[28] With his characteristic eloquence, he painted a picture of a global market with a human face, shaped by a set of corporate trailblazers who had made a choice to lead and place responsibility and a long-term outlook at the fore.

In 2000, this vision was realised with the launch of the Global Compact – an initiative whereby CEOs committed to a new "business as usual" structured around ten core principles (subsequently expanded to include the undertaking of partnerships in support of UN goals). Today, the Compact counts more than 11,000 companies across 157 countries in its membership, taking its place alongside other important corporate governance programs such as the Global Reporting Initiative and the Extractive Industries Transparency Initiative. Perhaps more importantly, the Compact marked a transition in thinking, away from companies as development contributors and towards them effecting greater impact by carrying out business activities in a socially responsible manner, such as by upholding minimum standards around sustainability, decent wages and safe working conditions.[29]

It's quite difficult to assess how effective either approach has been. While there is significantly more published research on the impact of CSR vis-à-vis charity-giving approaches, such outcomes are principally examined through a lens of shareholder perception and profitability. In short, does CSR pay?[30] To find out whether and in what ways CSR contributes to development ends, the buy-in of CSR principals would need to be secured. How willingly corporations would expose themselves to external scrutiny is questionable. Companies have few obligations beyond complying with the law and maximising shareholder profits. As Milton Friedman famously wrote in 1970, the only social responsibility of business is to make profit. It follows that when they engage in development-type activities, this is to promote these underlying goals.

If readers are experiencing some déjà vu, it's not misplaced. Corporations engaged in CSR draw similarities with governments acting as donors. Think about it. Is engaging in CSR programming to appease shareholders, avoid criticism or attract investment all that different to donors providing aid as a means of realising foreign policy goals? It isn't really, so we should be able to apply some of the insights from Chapter 2. For example, it follows that while corporations ostensibly engage in development programming, because decision-makers are seeking a different reward, how impactful such programming is may not be a deep concern. We know how this story ends. When the outcome is not the most important driver of decision-making, bad programs get repeated, good ones are overlooked for scale up, and a culture of self-learning and innovation never materialises.

As in the case of donors, this doesn't necessarily mean that corporate actors are ill-suited to operating in this space or addressing development imperatives. We just need to better understand what they care about and look for those moments of synchronicity where interests align. Many of the scenarios and strategies discussed in previous chapters have carryover. Examples include educating shareholders to demand not just development engagement, but development impact; lobbying the public to exercise their power as consumers; and gathering evidence on emerging trends such as impact investment and how this might serve an organisation's broader goals. Wins can also accrue by capitalising on specific moments. While no one wants to be accused of taking advantage of an environmental disaster, historically these have been the precursors of significant normative change within extractive organisations. If environmental development experts are ready and empowered to step up during these moments of recalibration, then they have an opportunity to influence decision-making and nudge business-as-usual towards a better place.

One outstanding question is, within whose mandate does this responsibility fall? Development agencies are stretched as it is, and have their own efficiency and impact issues to work on. Moreover, this is a mighty task to take on. Working with players that have very different approaches and world views is a frustrating process, and one with no guaranteed wins. It does make sense, however, that someone assumes the role. Given the breadth of CSR assets, it is arguably more efficient to seek improvements or course corrections in a going concern than to generate an equivalent amount of "development value" from scratch. This is something for the development community to consider. We should also not ignore the role of practitioners within corporate entities and particularly those staffing CSR programs. In the case of small and medium companies, CSR tends to be delegated to staff with philanthropic side interests. Only in large and transnational corporations are posts generally filled by qualified and experienced practitioners. In either case, there is no reason they cannot champion these ideas in the same way that this book has encouraged workers inside development organisations to do.

8.3 Gain for good

If engaging with *zakat*, remittances or CSR made any reader uncomfortable, wait until you meet CK Prahalad. He is on board with the idea that the private sector has a key role to play in poverty reduction, but he thinks that the answer is re-pitching poverty as a market opportunity. As he explores in his book – *The Fortune at the Bottom of the Pyramid* – the poor may be poor, but the sheer size of the market they represent means that they are an opportunity to be harnessed. He goes as far as to predict that the world's 5 billion poor, and their USD13 trillion in purchasing power parity, will constitute the next round of global trade.[31]

Prahalad takes his readers on a deep dive into corporate thinking. He details how the corporate sector – largely through monopolistic practices and the power of its market access – plays a large role in maintaining poverty traps. Often referred to as the "poverty penalty", the poor pay disproportionately vis-à-vis the rich for services such as money lending, as well as for consumer goods which they tend to purchase in small units.[32] Energy is good example; the 1.8 billion poor who lack electricity not only spend more on ad hoc energy sources such as wood, propane lamps and batteries, but these sources are highly polluting and a lead cause of lethal and debilitating accidents.[33]

Prahalad argues that companies do not set out to exploit the poor. Exploiting the rich is far more efficient. The poverty penalty is simply a consequence of the modus operandi of big business. Companies design and make products for Western markets where they can reap the most profits.

But of course, they want to sell to a wider audience if they can. They are not going to start from scratch – that's just bad business. But to sell to the poor at a price they can afford, products need to be adapted, often by compromising on quality but also by repackaging.[34] Pantene, for example, was designed as a luxury shampoo for sale in the West, but to make it marketable to the poor, Proctor and Gamble discovered that it needed to be sold in single-use sachets. This indeed facilitated a huge market expansion; however, the costs borne by the poor are greater overall, not to mention the issue of plastic packaging waste.

The ugly side of adaptation pricing for poverty markets is that as long as companies are profiting, it's hard to get them to stop. Prahalad doesn't think that any CSR reform or wrangling for a more humanitarian outlook will get them there, and even if it did, it would not be the most efficient approach. Instead, he wants us to think like a CEO. For the poor to extricate themselves from poverty traps, they need to stop paying poverty penalties, which means that companies need to supply them with access to affordable, safe products that met their needs. The only way to develop such goods is if there is a profit to be had. And herein lies his point. There *are* profits to be made, if businesses would move beyond their biases, think more creatively and get to know the poor as consumers in their own right.

The evidence supports the idea that there are market opportunities in poor populations. Because they lack land title, the poor do not invest in their homes, but they are ready consumers of luxury items like television and electrical connectivity. They are also well informed. They are brand and value conscious and they are good at assessing price and quality. They read, scrutinise and discuss among themselves. Finally, the poor readily and rapidly accept advanced technology. In fact, having little prior exposure makes it easier for them to adapt. The rich have already done that part for them.[35]

Companies need to apply this knowledge to design products specifically catering for the exigencies of poor lifestyles at a price they can afford, and at a scale capable of retuning a profit. Critically, this will not happen if it is viewed as CSR or a "feel good" pet project. It is only viable and will attract the right kind of thinking and resource attention if it is grounded in good business sense.[36]

These insights *should* get firms – in multiple sectors – excited. Indeed, some are. Hewlett Packard initiated a venture fund to invest senior management thinking time in examining these types of opportunities.[37] Others are interested in these ideas from an environmental opportunity perspective. Given that resources such as water and energy are comparatively expensive for the poor, the solutions marketable to them tend to be more environmentally conscious. Examples abound, from hyper-absorbency diapers created for populations who can only afford to change their infants once or twice daily; to a special "waterproof" soap made specifically for people who wash their clothes in streams and cannot afford large losses of detergent product.[38] It doesn't take much imagination for a savvy business entrepreneur to see the links between such products and the changing nature of trade and consumer interests, and thus the potential for applying such innovations in advanced markets.

None of this will be easy. The innovation and thinking required to realise these opportunities is almost the opposite of that applicable to the traditional consumer market. Rather than adding a margin to the cost of manufacturing a product and then sending it to market, businesses would need to start their thinking with what poor people can afford, and then work backwards to discover how it might be produced. Assumptions around refrigeration and electricity supply, connectivity and consumer education would also need to be revisited. But the logic is thorough – the breadth of the market makes these seemingly impossible innovations around price performance market sound.

The only greater challenge might be to get development actors to buy into this thinking. In conducting research for this chapter, it became clear that for many in the sector, the idea that the poor should be viewed as a market to profit from is repugnant, irrespective of the scope for or likelihood of positive impact. Risk adversity also seemed to play a role. Out of around 250 interviews, 33 made a reference to Nestlé marketing powdered milk to mothers who could not afford to dilute it safely, and the global boycott that followed.[39] Given that the development community had zero to do with this tragic episode, and that it took place more than 40 years ago, that's a lot of connective thinking. But the perception around risk is probably not misplaced.[40] In 2002, UNICEF and the World Health Organization in India partnered with three private sector entities to combat diarrheal disease, which at the time was the lead cause of death in children. The idea was to empower children to become activists in changing norms around handwashing. Unilever subsidiary Hundistan Level Limited (HLL) developed an antibacterial soap (and made a healthy profit from it) while UNICEF-WHO did what they were good at and initiated an awareness-raising program in schools. The success of the project did not prevent a storm of criticism levelled at HLL for exploiting the poor, or the specialist UN agencies for siding with a "brand".[41]

If nothing else, Prahalad's work should demonstrate that there are ideas out there and that this type of thinking needs to be encouraged. To access these ideas, development actors need to be able to identify unexpected allies and revisit existing ways of thinking. The lesson from the Nestlé scandal and UNICEF's India experience is to learn from it, not to never go there again. In the same way that institutional norms need to evolve to allow difficult conversations around local ownership and gender, they also need to move beyond assumptions that someone making a profit precludes a good outcome.

Development actors also need to be proactive in seeking out these moments. Their experience means that they often know what beneficiary populations need and the price they can afford. How to deliver it is a question they can pass off to the private sector. When the most recent flood of refugees entered Uganda from the Democratic Republic of Congo, telecoms companies did not see them as a potential new market. Perceiving this group as transient, poor, lacking in identity documents and far from tech-savvy, they stayed away. All it took was for UNHCR to play the role of conduit. They shared data on refugee demographics, their needs and incomes, and the importance they attached to being able to communicate with relatives back home. A solution took only weeks to forge. Companies realised that this was an instant market that – if captured – might provide them with an opportunity to expand into new markets when refugees returned home. They also found a way to quickly recoup their investment in a cell phone tower and new retail outlets. Refugees couldn't afford smart phones, which is where companies generally make their profits. Instead, they sold them "transactional phones" costing around USD10, and accumulated revenues in smaller bites through the financial transactions and entertainment purchases that refugees used their phones to make.[42]

A slightly modified logic is increasingly applied to develop crops with higher calorific or nutritional content, vaccines for diseases that are endemic to poor countries, and building materials able to withstand extreme climate events. Such innovations fall almost exclusively within the ambit of large companies with advanced R&D facilities. Without help, however, demand and supply rarely align. These are risky and expensive processes, and developing countries represent too weak a market to make the investment financially viable. Foundations and agencies might get around this by committing to purchase at scale a viable fertiliser, seed or vaccine, or a supply of goods that meet pre-set requirements.

8.4 One final battle: overcoming divisions around globalisation

This chapter started with an uneasy proposition: what if the solution for development lies outside of the development sector? I don't think that this is the case, but it does probably lie in a combination of forces. The work being undertaken by the development sector needs to be understood as sitting alongside a broader set of processes that are also contributing to poverty reduction. Remittances and *zakat* provide both stimulus to sluggish economies and a lifeline to the most vulnerable, taking the worst edges off what would be a much larger poverty problem. Corporate interests and global trade are likewise playing an undeniable role in broadening access to essential goods and services, as well as the technological advancements that human development depends on.

None of these processes are working as efficiently as they could or should. Earlier chapters outlined various ways that development practice might become more impactful. This one has suggested that aligning with, leveraging and fine-tuning charitable aid flows, CSR and corporate engagement in poverty reduction are complementary. The sheer scale of the funds in play mean that even small improvements will yield enormous benefits. Programs to steer a portion of remittances into entrepreneurial activity or livelihoods investment, for example, might not be a silver bullet, but at flows of USD400 billion annually, wins on the most marginal of scale have the potential to lift millions out of poverty.

Over time, engaging in these types of interventions may become less of a choice. The crisis in confidence that the development sector is able to deliver solid outcomes, coupled with a geopolitical climate marked by populism and insularity, may leave squeezing more out of what already exists as the only option. The COVID-19 pandemic may prove to be a critical juncture. If – against this backdrop – the world enters a global recession, the money available for development and humanitarian programming may fall to an unprecedented low.

With this in mind, let us consider what would need to happen to facilitate a better aligning of development, charitable and corporate interests. Exploiting the opportunities that remittances, *zakat*, CSR and corporate partnerships represent is not the easiest of propositions. It doesn't sit neatly within any development institution's mandate, is risk imbued, and has unpredictable consequences. A particularly intractable challenge is that the development community is highly divided on how it feels about globalisation, the interests that make it up and its relationship with development processes. This has been fueled by, and fueled a general distrust of the corporate agenda and a sense that the for-profit and aid sectors have irreconcilable mandates.[43] The result is that the community is insufficiently aligned in terms of what they believe the problem to be, and because of this, they lack an action plan for what needs to change.

To be clear on where I stand in this debate, I believe that overall, globalisation has been a force for good, including to the developing world. It has enormously lowered the cost of goods and facilitated huge reductions in poverty. Advances in science and medicine have benefitted everyone.[44] But these gains on a global level should not discount that large groups have been disadvantaged through globalisation. Moreover, as a global public good, globalisation requires proper management, at the heart of which lies a fair and inclusive inter-country agreement. Forging such an agreement has been problematic as it requires the cooperation and leadership of rich and powerful states – the ones that benefit most from globalisation and have the most to lose.[45]

So why does it seem that the development sector is decidedly anti-globalisation? In fact, it probably isn't. This appearance is probably to do with a small number of highly vocal interests within the sector, plus some misunderstanding that led us to misidentify the real culprit. The latter needs to be resolved, as it is misdirecting our efforts and closing off opportunities. To clear things up, enter former World Bank chief economist Joseph Stiglitz. He encourages us to distinguish between two rounds of globalisation that have produced two affected groups – the discontents and the new discontents.

The first round occurred in the decades following the second world war and dealt such a serious blow to the prospects of poor populations in poor countries that they have never fully recovered. Today it is widely believed that the main culprit was the IMF–brokered Washington Consensus – a combination of policies around loan conditionality and market liberalization, and in particular the removal of trade barriers. In short, these countries' deficits in innovation, credit, education and policy meant that exposure to market forces didn't foster competitiveness and productivity – it destroyed them. But for the fact that Western governments benefitted so directly, it might be possible to believe that those brokering these policies made honest mistakes. Tariffs on manufactured goods made it impossible for developing states to diversify and locked them into exporting the raw materials and unprocessed primary commodities that the West needed. At the same time, Western states continued to subsidise their own agricultural industries, driving down the global price of the few products that poor countries could export.[46]

The next round of globalisation saw the Asian Tiger states (and now India and China) quietly join the global economy, dismantling trade barriers slowly and on their own terms and creating unprecedented reductions in poverty.[47] Now players in their own right, these economies started to compete for capital by cutting tax rates and easing regulations around labour and carbon emissions.[48] Rich companies complied by relocating their plant, and within a few decades Asia was able to boast cost-effectiveness over complex and high-end manufacturing bound for export to advanced economies.[49] But while Asia reaped the benefits of "manufacturer of choice" for the exports demanded by the West, wages in America and Europe began to fall, leading to widespread unemployment among low- and semi-skilled workers.[50]

In short, globalisation round two has created winners – the West's elite corporate interests and Asia's burgeoning new middle class, and losers – the very poor in developing countries and the lower-middle classes in America and some other Western states.[51] When these outcomes are combined, inequality and poverty *at a global level* have quite clearly decreased. This is because the gains made in countries like China and India have impacted so many. This story has been largely drowned out, however, by the angry voices of those in the West who paid the price for this achievement.

Against this backdrop, it is not unsurprising that blame has been pinned on profit-oriented multinational corporations. It's a clean and relatable explanation that fits with the scandals regularly reported in the media around sweat shops, oil spills and tax avoidance. The result has been a highly polarised contest between the globalisation and anti-globalisation lobbies.

Stiglitz argues that the intensity of this debate has created a smokescreen around the actual problem – the one that the development community should rally around. This problem is that the system for creating global trade rules is stacked to favor the interests of rich states, corporate entities and special interests. This has been possible because in the IFIs responsible for negotiating trade policy, decision-making power is based on funds contributions, not the sovereign equality of states.[52]

It's development actors that are in a position to remedy this situation. Rules that allow companies to exploit cheap labor, pollute and avoid tax, all the while leveraging their power to preclude local entities from joining the global economy, is a fundamental cap on human development, second perhaps only to gender discrimination. Insofar as this compromises the work of all development (and humanitarian) agencies, refocusing the debate on how to make globalisation fairer should be understood as a shared responsibility.

The sector should prioritise setting out how these cause and effect relationships might jeopardise global economic stability – the issues in which IFIs have a strong and vested interest. The logic scarcely needs spelling out. When rules exempt companies from paying the true cost of emitting carbon, specious subsidies make it unprofitable to produce crops in logical locations, and tariffs prevent the poor from building a competitive export market, this drives climate change, food insecurity and loss of livelihoods. The resulting poverty can beget displacement, irregular migration and sometimes civil conflict. Indeed, some argue that any hollowing out of the middle class is the biggest threat to global stability. Each of these externalities disproportionately impact the most vulnerable, exacerbating inequality, gender gaps, limits on freedom and other factors known to hamper economic growth.

Alongside more equitable trade rules, corporate interests need to contribute fairly to poverty alleviation, at minimum offsetting the extent to which they are profiting at the expense of development agendas. This is by no means unreasonable. In a globalised world, rich companies need to be seen as comparable to rich individuals and countries. Indeed, 13 transnational corporations rank in the world's top 100 economies in terms of turnover.[53] The institutions and countries leading on this could be held up as examples for the West to follow. Some of the most inspiring are found in unlikely places. In response to wealthy Muslims relying on conservative interpretations of the Sunna to avoid paying *zakat* on key income streams and assets, the Islamic Research Centre of Al-Azhar University issued a *fatwa* ruling that the Egyptian government is obliged pay 20 percent *zakat* (the traditional amount payable on mineral deposits) on its oil and gas sales.[54] Kuwait recently followed suit, imposing mandatory *zakat* on the net profits of local public and listed companies. In India, the Companies Act (2012) requires that companies over a specified net worth, turnover or profit appoint a CSR Committee of the Board of Directors consisting of three or members and at least one independent director.[55]

If this is not enough, might it be possible to harness and reroute the energy of globalisation's current discontents? This group is understandably angry.

For the past three decades, their incomes have remained stagnant while costs of living have grown; and because social protection has not changed to accommodate their situation, this group's exposure to poverty has increased at rates not seen since the Great Depression. Arguably, only one politician picked up on this, and it got him elected President of the United States. But like most of Donald Trump's campaign commitments, his promise to bring blue-collar jobs back to America was hollow. When manufacturing companies followed the money and moved production to Asia, an unstoppable process was created. These economies "learned by doing", and are now equally as competitive as their predecessors. The upshot is that manufacturing jobs will remain in Asia, at least until those countries too become so wealthy that it makes sense to relocate again. Any new jobs created in the West will be technology based and suited only to youthful and educated workers. So, if there is anything to be angry about, it is that some governments are content to continue with a false narrative instead of devising programs to help these workers retrain or otherwise lessen the blow of long-term unemployment. This is a critical juncture in the making. With better outreach, the angry unemployed, the pro- and anti-globalisation activists working at cross purposes, and the developing states that have lost out twice to globalisation could unite and send a clear message to their leaders that it is time for a version of globalisation that serves a greater good.[56]

The development community is arguably not set up to take on this fight. Generating the empirical data needed to craft and execute a well-coordinated reform agenda is not the kind of work that specialised agencies and INGOs are known for. It is too big of a job for UNCTAD (the UN Conference on Trade and Development) – which is not only a small agency, but also a fairly weak one in terms of field reach and influence. The same could be said for UNRISD (the UN Research Institute for Social Development) – the closest entity the system has to a think tank and an ideal clearing house for inter-institutional research. Indeed, from a strategic perspective, if there are two agencies that require better support in terms of funding and capacity, it is them.

This means that something will have to give. It may be that the sector reaches a crisis point which forces it to recalibrate in a stronger and more strategic manner. The only alternative is that the matter is taken on directly. With evidence setting out the relationships between unfair trade on the one hand and migration, pandemics and conflict on the other, rich countries might attach the same importance to equity in trade rules as it has to the threat posed by extremism, and with this provide a similar flow of resources, political commitment and willingness to engage with unlikely allies such as *zakat* organisations. Development agencies might start to work strategically with corporations, viewing them as more than just a funding opportunity and letting go of the idea that "doing well" and "doing good" are fundamentally irreconcilable. And instead of globalisation being a source of polarisation, its development potential could be seen as something to unite around. Whether or not this is realistic, one thing is clear – a united effort that extracts the most good out of all available processes is the best chance we can offer the 10 percent of the world's population living in extreme poverty.

Notes

1 "International Migration at All-Time High" World Bank Press Release (18 December 2015); "Migration and Remittances Factbook 2016" International Bank for Reconstruction and Development/The World Bank Group, Washington (2016).

2 P. Collier *Exodus: How Migration Is Changing Our World*, Oxford University Press (2013) 207–208.

3 J. Woetzel, A. Madgavkar et al "People on the Move: Global Migration's Impact and Opportunity" Mckinsey Global Institute (2016) 72–73. See further J. Sandefur "Migration and Development: Who Bears the Burden of Proof?" Oxfam Blog, 19 March 2014 <http://oxfamblogs.org/fp2p/migration-and-development-who-bears- the-burden-of-proof-justin-sandefur-replies-to-paul-collier-2>.

4 See generally D. Kapur "Remittances: The New Development Mantra" Paper prepared for the G-24 Technical Group Meeting (2003); D. Ratha "Workers' Remittances: An Important and Stable Source of External Development Finance". Global Development Finance, World Bank, Washington DC. (2003).

5 J.A. Frankel "Are Bilateral Remittances Countercyclical?" NBER Working Papers 15419, National Bureau of Economic Research Inc. (2009).

6 S. Mohapatra, G. Joseph and D. Ratha "Remittances and Natural Disasters: Ex-Post Response and Contribution to Ex-Ante Preparedness" Policy Research Working Paper Series 4972, The World Bank (2009) 162.

7 P. Collier *Exodus: How Migration Is Changing Our World*, Oxford University Press (2013) 210–213.

8 W.R. Buhnig "Compensating Countries of Origin for the Out-Migration of Their People" International Labour Office (1977).

9 *Zakat* is payable on wealth that meets two conditions: (i) this wealth exceeds the *nisab*, a minimum amount equivalent to approximately 3 oz. of gold that is in excess of what is necessary to meet one's basic needs and the needs of those whom one is legally obliged to support and (ii) this wealth has been in one's ownership for at least a year. Wealth includes all items of value, including cash, precious metals, jewelry, agricultural crops, livestock, commercial and vacation property, collectibles, savings and retirement funds, among other items. While there is extensive debate among jurists and within the different schools of Islam, the popularly accepted uses of *zakat* are: *Al-fuqara* (the poor), *al-masakin* (the needy), *al-'Amilina 'Alayha* (administrators of *zakat*), al-Mu'allafate-Qulubuhum (those who have embraced Islam), fir-Riqab (those in bondage/slaves), al-Gharimin (those in debt), *fi sabil Allah* (in the cause of Allah), and *ibnas-Sabil* (the wayfarer). See e.g. I. Mattson, "Zakat in America: The Evolving Role of Islamic Charity in Community Cohesion" Centre on Philanthropy (2010).

10 "A Faith-Based Aid Revolution in the Muslim World?" *The New Humanitarian* (2012); A.M. Saleem and J. Mahmood, "Understanding the Role of Zakat in Global Humanitarian Response" *Global Humanitarian Assistance* May 23, 2014, accessed January 2016 <http://www.globalhumanitarianassistance.org/understanding-role-zakat-humanitarian- response/>.

11 C. Stirk "An Act of Faith: Humanitarian Financing and Zakat" Briefing Paper, Development Initiatives (2015); "Global Humanitarian Assistance Report" Development Initiatives (2016).

12 F. Johari, M.A. Aziz, and A. Ali, "A Review on Literatures of Zakat Between 2003–2013" *Library Philosophy and Practice* (2014: 2), accessed July 28, 2016 <http://digitalcommons.unl.edu/cgi/viewcontent.cgi?article=3045&context=libphilprac>.

13 G. Jehle "Zakat and Inequality: Some Evidence from Pakistan" *Review of Income and Wealth* 40:2, (1994) 205–216.

14 J. Bremer "Zakat and Economic Justice: Emerging International Models and their Relevance for Egypt" Paper presented at the Third Annual Conference on Arab Philanthropy and Civic Engagement, 2–6 June 2013, Tunis, 56–67.

15 Within the Islamic scholarship, some argue that the eight categories of *zakat* recipients are more flexible; they argue that *fi sabil Allah* might cover refugees, internally displaced persons and persons affected by conflict, and also cover the building of public infrastructure, such as schools, or agricultural infrastructure, which would facilitate recipients developing their businesses.

16 A portion of the funds would be retained and re-invested according to *Shari'a* law, with a *waqf* governance structure overseeing the maintenance of such funds and outlining their proper use, allowing it to become independent and self-sustaining. See generally A. Minor "Zakat and Development Finance: Filling In the Gaps" blog Aiddata (2014) <http://aiddata.org/blog/zakat-and-development-finance-filling-in-the-gaps>; A. Minor "Faith in Finance: The Role of Zakat in International Development" Master's thesis (2014) copy on file with author; N. Shirazi and M.F. Bin Amin, "Poverty Elimination Through Potential Zakat Collection in the OIC-member Countries: Revisited" *The Pakistan Development Review* 48:4 (2009) 739–754.

17 S.N.S. Yusuf, N. 'Azam Mastuki and G. Din "Changes in Management Accounting Practices of Zakat Institution: Is it Successful?", *International Conference on Islamic Economics and Finance* (2012). Muhammad Firdaus et al "Economic Estimation and Determination of Zakat Potential in Indonesia" *Islamic Research and Training Institute* (2012): 2.

18 F. Johari, M.R. Ab Aziz and A.F. Mohd Ali "A Review on Literatures of Zakat Between 2003–2013" Library Philosophy and Practice (2014).

19 H. Ahmed "Zakah, Macroeconomic Policies, and Poverty Alleviation: Lessons From Simulations on Bangladesh" *Journal of Islamic Economics, Banking and Finance* (2004) 102; F. Johari, M.A. Aziz, and A. Ali "A Review on Literatures of Zakat Between 2003–2013" *Library Philosophy and Practice* (2014:2) 343. see further R. Lupin *Toxic Charity: How Churches and Charities Hurt Those They Help*, Harper Collins (2011).

20 A. Rahman Abdul Rahim "Pre-Requisites for Effective Integration of Zakah Into Mainstream Islamic Financial System in Malaysia" *Islamic Economic Studies* 14:1–2 (2007).

21 H. Ahmed, "Zakah, Macroeconomic Policies, and Poverty Alleviation: Lessons From Simulations on Bangladesh" Durham University (2004) 1–9.

22 D. Kapur "Remittances: The New Development Mantra" Paper prepared for the G-24 Technical Group Meeting (2003) 151–153.

23 P. Collier *Exodus: How Migration Is Changing Our World*, Oxford University Press (2013) 210.

24 P. Collier *Exodus: How Migration Is Changing Our World*, Oxford University Press (2013) 210–212, 223.

25 See generally L. Raimi, A. Patel and I. Adelopo "Corporate Social Responsibility, Waqf System and Zakat System as Faith-based Model for Poverty Reduction"

World Journal of Entrepreneurship, Management and Sustainable Development 10:3 (2014).

26 See, for example, chapter 4 "Harnessing Private Finance" in *Eliminating World Poverty: Making Globalisation Work for the Poor*, White Paper on International Development DFID London (2000). For a more recent summary of the DFID's position on CSR, see *DFID and Corporate Social Responsibility*, DFID London (2003).

27 See generally J.G. Frynas "Corporate Social Responsibility and International Development: Critical Assessment" *Corporate Governance* 16:4 (2008); J.G. Frynas "The False Developmental Promise of Corporate Social Responsibility: Evidence From Multinational Oil Companies" *International Affairs* 81:3 (2005); J.G. Frynas *Beyond Corporate Social Responsibility – Oil Multinationals and Social Challenges* Cambridge University Press (2009); M.J. Schölmerich "On the Impact of Corporate Social Responsibility on Poverty in Cambodia in the Light of Sen's Capability Approach" *Asian Journal of Business Ethics* 2 (2013) 1–33; R. Jenkins "Globalization, Corporate Social Responsibility and Poverty" *International Affairs* 81:3 (2005) 525–540.

28 "Secretary-General Proposes Global Compact on Human Rights, Labour, Environment, in Address to World Economic Forum in Davos" Press Release SG/SM/6881(1 February 1999).

29 J. Nelson "Leveraging the Development Impact of business in the Fight against Global Poverty" in L. Brainard (ed) *Transforming the Development Landscape– The Role of the Private Sector*, Brookings (2006) 41–54.

30 J. Margolis and J. Walsh "Misery Loves Companies: Rethinking Social Initiatives by Business" *Administrative Science Quarterly* 48 (2003) 268–305.

31 C.K. Prahalad *The Fortune at the Bottom of the Pyramid: Eradicating Poverty Through Profits*, Wharton School Publishing (2006) xv, 3–11, 21.

32 C.K. Prahalad *The Fortune at the Bottom of the Pyramid: Eradicating Poverty Through Profits*, Wharton School Publishing (2006) 11.

33 C.K. Prahalad *The Fortune at the Bottom of the Pyramid: Eradicating Poverty Through Profits*, Wharton School Publishing (2006) 137–139.

34 C.K. Prahalad *The Fortune at the Bottom of the Pyramid: Eradicating Poverty Through Profits*, Wharton School Publishing (2006) 16, 21–30.

35 C.K. Prahalad *The Fortune at the Bottom of the Pyramid: Eradicating Poverty Through Profits*, Wharton School Publishing (2006) 12–16.

36 C.K. Prahalad *The Fortune at the Bottom of the Pyramid: Eradicating Poverty Through Profits*, Wharton School Publishing (2006) 6–8, 16.

37 C.K. Prahalad *The Fortune at the Bottom of the Pyramid: Eradicating Poverty Through Profits*, Wharton School Publishing (2006) xvi.

38 C.K. Prahalad *The Fortune at the Bottom of the Pyramid: Eradicating Poverty Through Profits*, Wharton School Publishing (2006) 48–49, 57.

39 Notes on file with author.

40 The problems associated with the promotion of breast milk substitutes in developing countries by Nestlé arose to a significant extent because the company *did* target low-income consumers who were then unable to buy sufficient quantities of infant formula or used polluted water to dilute it. D. Greene *How Change Happens*, Oxford University Press (2016) 158–159.

41 C.K. Prahalad *The Fortune at the Bottom of the Pyramid: Eradicating Poverty Through Profits*, Wharton School Publishing (2006) 41, 235–243.

42 Interview dated 15 June 2019, Geneva, notes on file with author.

43 M.B. Steger and E.K. Wilson "Anti-Globalization or Alter-Globalization? Mapping the Political Ideology of the Global Justice Movement" *International Studies Quarterly* 56 (2012) 439–454.

44 J. Stiglitz *Globalization and its Discontents Revisited: Anti-Globalization in the Era of Trump*, Penguin Books (2017) xi, xv, 52.
45 J. Stiglitz *Globalization and its Discontents Revisited: Anti-Globalization in the Era of Trump*, Penguin Books (2017) xxxviii, 50, 55, 76; J. Sachs *The Price of Civilization: Economics and Ethics After the Fall*, Random House (2011) 96.
46 J. Stiglitz *Globalization and its Discontents Revisited: Anti-Globalization in the Era of Trump*, Penguin Books (2017) xii-xxvi, 59, 104–105, 142–156.
47 J. Stiglitz *Globalization and its Discontents Revisited: Anti-Globalization in the Era of Trump*, Penguin Books (2017) 118, 180–185.
48 J. Sachs *The Price of Civilization: Economics and Ethics After the Fall*, Random House (2011) 93–4, 99–100.
49 P. Collier *The Bottom Billion: Why the Poorest Countries Are Failing and What Can Be Done About It*, Oxford University Press (2007) 81–85; J. Stiglitz *Globalization and its Discontents Revisited: Anti-Globalization in the Era of Trump*, Penguin Books (2017) 56.
50 J. Sachs *The Price of Civilization: Economics and Ethics After the Fall*, Random House (2011) 15, 88–89; J. Stiglitz *Globalization and its Discontents Revisited: Anti-Globalization in the Era of Trump*, Penguin Books (2017) xvi–xvii, 46–47.
51 J. Stiglitz *Globalization and its Discontents Revisited: Anti-Globalization in the Era of Trump*, Penguin Books (2017) xiii–xiv, xxxviii; P. Collier *The Bottom Billion: Why the Poorest Countries Are Failing and What Can Be Done About It*, Oxford University Press (2007) 80; J. Sachs *The Price of Civilization: Economics and Ethics After the Fall*, Random House (2011) 97–98.
52 J. Stiglitz *Globalization and its Discontents Revisited: Anti-Globalization in the Era of Trump*, Penguin Books (2017) xxi, 77, 110, 158, P. Collier *The Bottom Billion: Why the Poorest Countries Are Failing and What Can Be Done About It*, Oxford University Press (2007) 159–160.
53 D. Greene *How Change Happens*, Oxford University Press (2016) 151–152.
54 H. Ahmed "Role of Zakah and Awqaf in Poverty Alleviation" Occasional Paper No. 8, Islamic Development Bank Group Islamic Research & Training Institute (2004) 42; see further M. Kahf "Zakah: Unresolved Issues in the Contemporary Fiqh" *Journal of Islamic Economics* 2:1 (1989) 1–22.
55 Section 135 of India's Companies Act (2012).
56 J. Stiglitz *Globalization and its Discontents Revisited: Anti-Globalization in the Era of Trump*, Penguin Books (2017) 4, 13.

9

CHARTING A PATHWAY
TOWARDS ENHANCED AID
EFFECTIVENESS

This book has attempted to explain why, in an era of artificial intelligence and big data, ten percent of the world's population is still battling extreme poverty. It was posited that myths around how the development sector works have prevented us from addressing the fact that aid provision is a highly political process. Donors, government recipients, implementing agencies and beneficiaries are connected through a web of complex relationships determined by incentives that do not always align, and sometimes work at cross-purposes. One outcome is that the systems set in place to ensure impact and efficiency do not work as robustly as they should. In the worst case, these dynamics operate to mask programmatic failure, prevent upwards learning and discourage innovation. This is not to say that development programming never creates impact, just that it does so in a sluggish way too much of the time. This outcome is not just disappointing; it lacks reason because all states have a large stake in development outcomes. Peace, stability and growth are good for everyone, irrespective of your nationality, gender or bank balance.

Although it has been posited by some, the answer is not a dismantling of the foreign aid system as we know it. The development sector and the architecture that encases it may be inefficient and unwieldy, but it is the single edifice working in pursuit of a global common good. It does, however, require wholesale reform.

Delivering on this will be harder than ever before. The past decade brought the developed world face to face with a set of unprecedented challenges. The threats posed by violent extremism have spread fear, reduced freedoms and exposed deep fissures in the social fabric. The world might technically be a safer place, but it doesn't feel safer. This week British Colombia saw temperatures of 49.6 degrees Celsius – what scientists described as a one-in-one-thousand-year event, unequivocally linked to the climate emergency.[1] And a global pandemic – which last year brought the world to a standstill – continues to yield death, economic losses and uncertainty.

These challenges are undeniably rooted in development deficits. The rise of ISIS cannot be disconnected from geopolitical rivalries, religious

DOI: 10.4324/9781003376996-10

discrimination and political marginalisation, not only in Muslim-majority states, but also in rich, Western democracies. Climate change has been accelerated by unfair trade rules and global wealth disparities, and while COVID-19 was arguably a scientific inevitability, its effects have laid bare the consequences of inequality, unchecked urbanisation and overconsumption.

That these are development problems requiring multilateral solutions doesn't mean that they will be addressed as such. This is because – and this is crucial – on the eve of this new fragility, states had already lost confidence in the development sector and were looking to alternatives.

Over the past decades, scandals, exposed inefficiencies and little proof of progress had sparked a growing debate around aid effectiveness and musings around the sector's raison d'etre. When former World Bank economist Dambisa Moyo declared that "there is no other sector, whether it is business or politics, where such proven failures are allowed to persist in the face of such stark and unassailable evidence", few disagreed.[2] Against growing skepticism around the efficacy of development programming, stakeholders began to act. Aid was merged into foreign policy portfolios, China entered the development space and donors increasingly diverted funds towards philanthropic institutions.

On the back of this, a reckoning that wealth and democracy cannot protect against global hazards is not likely to move us towards better development solutions. It is moving us further away. As traditional donor states turn inward and strive for greater self-reliance, priorities will be food security, guarding against unchecked migration, and replacing global supply lines with domestic ones. The upshot is that the environment in which the development sector needs to reestablish its value added is a tough one, marked by populist rhetoric and far less money. But perhaps this is the critical juncture needed. Crisis invokes reform.

(i) *The System We Need*

The previous chapters offered somewhat of a roadmap to navigate towards a more impactful and deliberate development space. The common thread linking these ideas was a more strategic approach that acknowledges the political economy of aid. This does not mean pushing back on vested interests, pretending they're not there, or exposing players for a lack of commitment. It means finding ways to operate alongside these realities by identifying pockets of opportunity, leveraging politics when it is strategic, and partnering with unlikely allies. Instead of expecting development assistance to be an all-encompassing solution, it should be seen as one tool among several.

Two main sets of entry points were discussed. A first idea concerns interest convergence – homing in and capitalising on situations where the interests of donors and recipient states align with development imperatives, fighting the fights we can win quickly, easily and completely. The second was to exploit system dynamics to enable interest convergence. In other words, finding ways to bind aid effectiveness to issues of importance for those with the power to make change. A strong case can be made here. The costs of conflict, instability and poverty far outweigh the costs of reform.

To pull this off, the aid sector would need to become something very different from what it is today.

Development practitioners would need to be the scientists of aid effectiveness, people who understand underdevelopment and mal-governance as complex *systems* problems. Agencies would need to adopt high standards of academic rigor, using systematic research methods, big data and multi-system analytics. Multidisciplinary thinking would sit at the fore as it is only by understanding the interconnectedness of development problems that goals can be matched with solutions. Neither the UN cluster system, the 2018 UN development system reforms, or the humanitarian-development-peace nexus have brought us close to this.

Beyond the development science, practitioners would need to bridge aid as a tool of statecraft and aid as a tool of poverty reduction as separate schools of inquiry. The reality is that donors will support issues and countries that reflect their broader interests, whether it be controlling unwanted migration, bolstering food security, promoting fairer rules for global trade or negotiating an intergovernmental agreement to control carbon emissions. Recipient states will likewise use aid and the relationships therein to achieve their goals, and these ends will range from altruistic to development compatible or extractive. Only by understanding these dynamics will it be possible to find areas of common interest and opportunities to present the case for development-geared outcomes. If nothing else, smokescreens that obscure the behaviour of stakeholders beget waste, and waste is not a luxury this sector can afford.

Finally, the development remit would need to be widened to include being an honest conversation broker. It is disappointing that peacekeeping works, but has been largely shelved because bad press has crowded out the evidence on its cost effectiveness as a cap on conflict recidivism. What is ridiculous is that this occurred outside of an informed and objective discussion. The development community needs to be able to stand between donors and recipient states as a neutral broker of fact, presenting evidence on implications, alternatives, and humanitarian customary norms. The decision may still be that peacekeeping is not worth the hassle, but the conversation needs to happen, and someone has to be the adult in the room.

Could the development sector become like this? It might sound unlikely, but change happens all the time. An example might be playing out in the Sahel right now.[3]

Since 2011, a small group of countries has captured the attention of almost all stakeholders. Burkina Faso, Cameroon, Chad, Mali and Niger face a toxic mix of conflict-induced displacement, violent extremism and protracted poverty, compounded by climate change and most recently the

COVID-19 pandemic. These crises risk enveloping other countries in the Sahel and spilling over to neighboring fragile states. In search of a more forward-looking, risk-sensitive plan, the UN Special Coordinator for Development locked onto the predictive analytics work being spearheaded by UNHCR. They started not with the current crisis, but an analysis of trends and future scenarios. They realised that by 2040, temperatures in the Sahel would not support livelihoods nor food security. This spoke to mass migration, first to the coast, but also possibly northwards. Other questions followed. Where would people buy their food, and would this inflate the cost of basic commodities? Assuming that trained workers would be the first to seek better options elsewhere, at what point would medical systems collapse? This list went on. Employing a technique they labelled "backcasting" they inched in reverse through the various scenarios to identify watershed moments. Data accuracy proved a stumbling block. The UN agencies just didn't have it, especially at the sub-societal level, so a partnership was forged with Upsala University. This is feeding into what they hope will be an open-source data set that all development players will contribute to, verify, improve and act upon.

Having a strategy grounded in hard data and predictive analytics provided the team with a strong basis to push back on dissenters. It especially allowed them to bypass what someone described as the "UNCT roadshow" – competing agency and INGO voices each advocating for their separate development mandates. In short, the data made it hard to argue that LGBTQI rights or democratic reform was equal to the imperatives of climate adaptation and sustainable livelihoods. The idea that agencies (and recipient governments) need to "make their case" against the evidence may be a step towards resolving a largely unspoken tension in development and humanitarian programming. While rights cannot be hierarchised, not every aim should be entitled to an identical piece of the pie. The approach might also provide better options for winning over extractive leaders. Backcasting allows them space to consider likely future scenarios and – able to better anticipate the international community's support – work towards an endgame that everyone can live with. As the team moves forward, they might even consider bringing in some additional stakeholder voices. Remember "skin in the game" – that people who have a vested interest in a likely outcome make far more rational decisions, less impacted by cognitive bias. It follows that if the goal is a strategy that will prevent the Sahel from failing, then the views of neighboring countries should be heard.

This is just one example, and it is far from clear how it will fare. No doubt there will be resistance, but for now the idea is getting traction, and attention. This is important. If it works, it may encourage players in similar situations to do things differently.

(ii) *The "Big Push"*

Although we should be inspired by the Sahel example, it is probably not enough to induce deep change in the system as a whole. While it is accepted that data and evidence need to play more of a role in planning and programming, moving towards new ways of working has been proven to be a slow and unhappy process.

A real time snapshot reveals a scattering of mixed-performing plans. UNRISD – the UN Research Institute for Social Development – is underfunded, disenfranchised and largely unknown. The same might be said for the United Nations University, despite its mandate being unquestionably sound. Some organisations have made exceptional efforts to integrate research into their operations. UNICEF's Inocenti Research Centre is a standout example. They hired strategically, allocated funds liberally and their research is credible. ICRC's Centre for Operational Research and Experience likewise boasts a growing reputation for knowledge production. Other agencies found it more strategic to outsource. UNHCR has joined forces with Upsala University while Mercycorps benefits from an ongoing research arrangement with Yale University. Still, progress is slow and mainstreaming evidence-based approaches into programmatic units is an uphill battle.

It may be that the kind of sea change needed can only be imposed. We learned this in Chapter 2. Evidence is not enough; it needs for a principal to say that it matters, and systems to integrate it into practice. The takeaway is that for any transition in working methods to take root, this message needs to come from the top, it needs to be unambiguous and it needs to be at scale. Donors would have to get behind this. Not all donors, but at least a likeminded group with collective power that they are willing to exercise. After all, the only reason that evidence is ignored is because principals permit it. Such a transition would be a bumpy and unpopular ride, riddled with animosity on the part of staff wedded to using their field experience as a barometer for gauging effectiveness. Any such angst should be taken as a sign that the process is moving in the right direction.

Leading this type of change at the agency level will be hard. Like in all periods of innovation, the benefits will not be immediate and some false starts are inevitable. At present there may be too many competing players – each ready to fill the void left by an agency trying to find its feet – for them to stay the course. There is also a leadership issue. Heads of agency are traditionally political appointments, usually positioning themselves for their next step up, and ultimately beholden to the donor hand that feeds them.

The "big push" could come from the current Secretary-General, or the next one if they chose to run on this platform. It would mean a huge investment in research capacity, tough conversations and follow through. The Secretariat hasn't been able to command that type of force yet, but history is not determinative. Another reason for the Secretary-General to lead is the "grown up in the room" argument. Standing between donors and recipient states, acting as a deal broker, drawing attention to impossibilities and compelling moral leadership is an unenviable job – donors can't play that role and agency leaders are just not that strong.

(iii) *Deciding to Do Better*

Of the reforms needed to promote more impactful human development, the lion's share concern development sector institutions, processes and norms. There is far less discussion about what the developed world needs to stop doing, or the extent to which "business as usual" is detracting from the progress being made. This may actually be the hardest battle; I would posit that the West is largely unaware how little legitimacy they have in the minds of recipient states, and has even less of a clue how important it is to win this back.

The idea that developing and conflict-affected states hold deep angst is not novel, and most would agree that such feelings are legitimate. Colonial empires plundered the assets of vulnerable countries. Some of these countries never recovered and remain poor. The undermining of national sovereignty epitomised in the Sykes-Picot Agreement largely explains the ongoing unrest in the Middle East. And the IMF–brokered Washington Consensus policies wrought such extensive destruction on fledging economies that many are still experiencing repercussions.

These mistakes cannot be undone, and being an apologist is not constructive. Yet it is frustrating that comparable acts continue. The prowess of the American, French and German arms trade *does* de-legitimise their work in Syria. The influence of Israeli special interests in US politics *is* inhibiting a peaceful solution for the Occupied Palestinian Territories. These dynamics probably will not change. But there are other things that can be done (or stop being done) quickly, quietly and cheaply.

At this moment of writing, European states are locked in a bureaucratic stalemate, having been unable to reach an agreement on reciprocal vaccine status recognition. This has compelled many of the vacation-hungry citizens who have already had and recovered from COVID-19 to opt in for a second shot. This is not because it is medically necessary, but because proof of their single vaccine dose may not be enough to get them to a beach on the Italian coast. If everyone was to take this route, *57 million doses* would be administered unnecessarily. Tell me that low-income countries – which have vaccinated only 1 percent of their total populations – shouldn't be angered by this.

Donor states should also consider what it might take to regain the trust of the countries they purport to fix. It was alluded to in past chapters, but front and centre should be respect, which costs nothing and would be well received. The return of improperly obtained artwork and artifacts, reforming educational curricula to more accurately reflect historical events, and other acts of restitution do much to bolster national identity as well as inter-country relations. Even easier – and perhaps even more impactful – would be to admit how many challenges are commonly shared. The rise of ISIS showcased that youth marginalisation, disempowerment and exclusion are not problems exclusive to autocracies. Scratching beneath the surface, from Hungary's controversial LGBTQ law to Donald Trump's tweets provoking an assault on the US Capitol, it is clear that the West is far from squeaky clean. There are important areas where the "norm-touters" are being overtaken. Despite how much the West talks about diversity in political participation, Rwanda, Cuba and Bolivia are the only countries that have managed to make women parliamentarians a majority.[4] Being more transparent about these struggles could be a powerful equaliser.

There is much in the legacies of poverty that cannot be changed. We cannot modify natural resource endowments, rewrite history or manufacture critical junctures. The way poverty reduction is conceptualised and how development agencies approach it can and must change.

This book has set out some ideas around how such a transition might begin. Poverty, fragility and conflict are too important to be treated as subjects of charity. To do so is paternalistic, short sighted and dangerous. Equally important is the idea that there will be no success in aid unless it is in the interest of both the beneficiary and the benefactor. Putting this into practice will require critical reflection, innovation and living with mistakes – all things that the humanitarian and development communities of practice are not good at. But if it can be pulled off, it will be the closest thing to a win–win deal that my generation of development actors has seen. It could be the current generation of development practitioners' legacy, but only if they decide to take it.

Notes

1 M. McGrath "Climate Change: US-Canada Heatwave 'virtually impossible' Without Warming" *BBC* <www.bbc.com/news/science-environment-57751918> (accessed 11 July 2021).
2 D. Moyo *Dead Aid: Why Aid is Not Working and How There is Another Way for Africa*, Allen Lane (2009) 47.
3 D. Passarlli, F. Denton and A. Day "Beyond Opportunism: The UN Development System's Response to the Triple Planetary Crisis" United Nations University (2021) 11.
4 "Women in National Parliament" Inter-Parliamentary Union (data as at 1 February 2019).

INDEX

Pages followed by n denotes notes.

For Product Safety Concerns and Information please contact our EU representative GPSR@taylorandfrancis.com
Taylor & Francis Verlag GmbH, Kaufingerstraße 24, 80331 München, Germany